THE COMPLETE *New York* GUIDE FOR SINGLES

# THE COMPLETE *New York*

# GUIDE FOR SINGLES

## AN INSIDER'S HANDBOOK TO ENTERTAINMENT, ESTABLISHMENTS, ACTIVITIES & SERVICES

## BY SUSAN CARTOUN

*Collier Books*   A Division of Macmillan Publishing Co., Inc.

NEW YORK

Macmillan Publishing Co., Inc.
866 Third Avenue, New York, N.Y. 10022
Collier Macmillan Canada, Inc.

Library of Congress Cataloging in Publication Data
Cartoun, Susan.
The complete New York guide for singles.
Includes index.
1. New York (N.Y.)—Description—1981-
—Guide-books.   2. Single people—New York
(N.Y.)   I. Title.
F128.18.C37   1983   917.47'10443'0880652   82-12856
ISBN 0-02-097360-8

10  9  8  7  6  5  4  3  2  1

Designed by Jack Meserole

Printed in the United States of America

To Pris, Donna, P. and D., James, Em, and Mike. And to New Yorkers—you're undeniably the warmest, funniest, most helpful people I know, with the wonderful capability to cut through the smog and get down to the actual nitty gritty.

# Contents

Chapter 2

# Organizations, Agencies, Clubs, and Services  *233*

Chapter 3

# Special Interest Index  *266*

*Contents*

THE COMPLETE *New York* GUIDE FOR SINGLES

# Introduction

## The New, Free Single

The Complete New York Guide for Singles *is based on one premise—there's no such thing as a typical single.* Each person is an individual with different needs. Every one of us is at a different point in our lives. We are eighteen-year-old classical music freaks and sixty-year-old disco lovers. We are widows and widowers who need support and counseling in addition to new social contacts. We are single people who would rather fill our lives with travel, new wave music, wine-and-cheese, brunch-and-the-*Times,* theater, church or temple, gourmet cooking or sports rather than a depressing search for Ms. or Mr. Right. And here in the New York area there's a club, lounge, rock concert, support group, disco, brawling bar, cozy nook, hillbilly hangout, roller rink, rap session, travel agent, sex club, or discreet dating service to fit everyone's need, whim, dream, age, and wallet. So if you're "not the singles type"— good. Because no one else is either.

*This book is a step toward freedom.* It is but one of many tools today's single person can use to experience life to the fullest. There's no need to stay home anymore for lack of a date. If there's a concert you've wanted to see, you go. That's all there is to it. Either you'll meet some new friends at that concert or you'll simply enjoy an evening of music. Either way, you can't lose!

The Complete New York Guide for Singles *is not just a listing of "singles bars."* Instead, it's a catalog of places where a single person can go and feel comfortable. Restaurants where you're not the only person at a table for one. Blues clubs where other blues lovers, some of whom are single, meet and listen and talk about the music. Nightclubs and cabarets where you can sit with groups of people you didn't know before. Piano bars where you can enjoy a drink without being hassled. And yes, some great social bars where you simply can't leave without five or ten phone numbers (which you may or may not throw out when you get home). The city is a veritable playground! You need no invitation. So why not go out and play?

## For the Newcomer to the Singles Scene: Some Troubleshooting in Advance

The trouble is, it's too easy to make up excuses to stay home. Many people become disappointed and lethargic when relationships just don't seem to work out. Others who are new to the city may not know, among seven million strangers, how to build a small circle of friends. Still others find themselves suddenly single after years of marriage and haven't had the experience of going out alone—perhaps not even to the movies.

So we just give up. Stay home. Forget about it. Who cares. With TV and therapy and self-help philosophies and fitness regimens and late hours at work, we've learned to develop many alternatives to friendships and commitments. We've found it easy at times to deny the basic human need for social contact, the need for an occasional dose of lights and laughter and shared feelings. Why not take a moment to see if any of the following "buts" sound familiar? It's not necessary to give up, if you can just get past a few blocks.

*"But the city is so huge—where do I begin?"* Find your groove, then find your place. If you're into tennis, look up "Sports and Fitness" in the Special Interest Index. If you like art, check out the listings under "Art." If you want to practice roller skating, look that up in the Special Interest Index and find one that suits your mood. If you're a widow, find that section. Anyone wanting to just get away from it all can look up "Travel" or even "Singles Bars." Remember, it's not necessary anymore to sit and wait for fate to choose your mate. Today we take control of our lives; we initiate events; we are accountable for what happens to us.

2 *Introduction*

*"But I'm into my solitude."* It's fulfilling to have "alone time" to "work on yourself," "regroup," and plan your strategy for the next five years. But after a while it becomes merely an escape. You can only plan for so long, and then the time comes to execute that plan.

*"But I'm afraid of the city."* We've spoken to many men and women who don't think twice about walking around at night, and many men and women who do. If you are afraid, there are still alternatives to the 11 P.M. TV news. Go to neighborhoods that you know. Take taxis. Or plan daytime activities like Happy Hours which are early and great for socializing. If you're still afraid of the city go to Westchester, Long Island, or the other boroughs. Go somewhere close to home. Just go!

*"But I'm shy. I can't start up a conversation."* If you're shy, perhaps you should go to a disco or a country-western room. The focus is on the activity rather than you, and you'll be less likely to feel conspicuous. These are perfect rooms for meeting people—all you have to do is say "Wanna dance?" A health or sports group, rap session, roller rink, or party club would also work well for you. But don't forget, you don't *have* to talk to people. Why not go out simply to enjoy your chosen activity?

*"But some of the nicer places seem intimidating."* The thing to remember is this—a truly sophisticated place is not snobby or intimidating. It's simply a lovely room with a courteous staff, and you'd be missing a lot if you passed it up.

*"But I don't want to leave my children home all the time. Besides, a babysitter is expensive."* For divorced parents there are organizations and all kinds of neighborhood and religious-sponsored groups to get you out of the house—with your kids. There are even discos with special parent-children programs! Or you can try a parent-child activity at a nearby roller rink. Look under "Single Parents" in the Special Interest Index.

*"But I'm just widowed and really have no interest in socializing."* The newly divorced or widowed individual will probably not want to go out right away. It is important to experience the pain of loss rather than party it up as a cover for real feelings. This period of grief may last for a long time—perhaps years. But when the

mourning time is over, it's important to let it go. Don't cling to it out of other fears—fear of the unknown out there, fear of rejection by new people, fear of being conspicuous. The only way to work through these fears is to face them. Make the outside world known to you. Get out, see who's there, learn how to handle them, test new methods of controlling your environment and defining your own lifestyle. You're not dependent on anyone else. There comes a point when you're not staying home out of grief anymore, but out of habit.

## Making This Book Work for You!

Whatever your motives, whatever your level of experience, you can get what you need from *The Complete New York Guide for Singles*. The book is organized to take you where you want to go.

- *Chapter 1 is set up according to location,* so you can plan to visit many places in one evening without becoming emotionally distraught over parking or transportation.
- Each restaurant and club listed in Chapter 1 tells you what the basic mood of the room is, what to wear, who else will be there, what financial setbacks to expect, what you can eat, what else there is to do, and any other quirks you need to know before you go.
- *Chapter 2 pinpoints the type of person each dating organization caters to,* and tells exactly how to join and what will happen to you. Some services were hesitant about quoting prices for publication, so we suggest that if it looks good, call. *Chapter 2 is also your resource for singles travel.* If you just have to get away, the agencies and organizations listed here will cater to your individual needs.
- *Use this all in conjunction with the Special Interest Index, which has all the listings in the entire book reorganized according to their particular niches in life.*

Use the chapters and Index to find places that suit your temperament. A woman who loves to wear a finely tailored suit and drink champagne cocktails would have a better time at Astor's in the St. Regis Sheraton than she would at the Village Vanguard, even if there were more men at the Vanguard. Her time is more effectively used by having an interesting conversation with another woman than by talking to forty men about their sun signs. By the same token, a guy who likes to don his Stetson and Fryes on weekends would meet more people who know the two-step at The Lone Star Café than he would at La Ronde in The Sheraton Centre.

The point is, you don't have to go to a place simply because it's mobbed with members of the opposite sex. Making just one friend, even of the same sex, can be more meaningful. And who knows? Maybe that one friend was planning a fantastic roof party in the Village, and you'll now be invited. *You can never go wrong if you surround yourself with the environment that makes you comfortable.*

## Strategic Planning

Psychologists say that the people who reach their goals are the ones with maps and plans and strategies. While you don't want to stifle your spontaneity, you still don't want to be wandering around the East Village at 3 A.M. in your tuxedo, looking for a Beethoven concert. A plan can't hurt.

WHICH STRATEGY IS FOR YOU?

*Wild:* If you've got the time, enjoy surprises, and can look forward to an evening of undetermined outcome, you're a candidate for the club, music, or bar scene ("clubbing" as the hard-core call it).

*Tame:* If, on the other hand, you need a quieter, more controlled environment in which to make friends, you might check out the community or religious organizations, the friendly neighborhood lounges, or even the professional party clubs.

*Efficient:* Perhaps you work long hard hours, or your job is simply exhausting. Worse yet, you're also taking courses at night school. You've got neither the time nor the patience to go out and take your chances. So a dating service may be the answer. You can meet people on a one-to-one basis who supposedly like the same movies, food, and hang-ups. And you'll avoid wasting time on people with whom you're outlandishly incompatible. (It's not guaranteed, but it's possible.)

*Mixed Bag (The "All of the Above" Theory):* We've found perhaps the most useful strategy is a scientifically designed mixture of all of the above. Take, for example, a man we know who is happily occupied every weekend and always on his way to important events after work. An investigation into his strategy reveals that he is not only a regular subscriber to one of the inexpensive computer dating services but also a regular at a favorite after-work bar. In addition, he's on the mailing list of two of New York's pay-at-the-door party clubs. For him, there's always something going on. And it's so easy to plan. Why not give the Mixed Bag Strategy a try?

*The Numbers Game:* Whether it's an impeccable introduction through your grandmother or a perfect match through a computer, you can never be assured of meeting a compatible mate. The best strategy for those who are looking for definite companionship is to meet as many people as you can. Join the clubs, go to the parties, the bars, the concerts, and don't stop. Don't give up. All it takes is for that one person to walk through the door. And if that's the night you decided to stay home to polish the toaster, you'll have missed out. A woman we know was meeting people through her dating club whom she just didn't like. She was about to give up on the whole thing, but instead decided to make one last phone call. It was the last name on her list—and they got along beautifully.

*The Plan "B" Theory:* Whatever strategy you choose, make sure you have an alternative. Never go out to find your fortune with just one option in your pocket. You'll be setting yourself up for failure. If your desire is to go see The Psychotic Frogs at a rock club, you must be prepared for the fact that it may be too crowded and you won't get in. So you go ahead to Plan "B," which may be to catch The Pencils at another club nearby. Your evening is successful, no matter what. Many people we know have Plans "C," "D," and even "E."

First let's say you don't want to make friends. You simply want to get out where there's life happening, have a drink, perhaps review a report from the office or write a poem and be left alone. As one of the new, free singles you don't have to feel pressured to meet people when you go out. Many of the places in this book are perfect for unwinding or enjoying an evening alone. If that's your mood for tonight, you'll have fewer chance encounters with well-meaning conversationalists if you sit at a cocktail table or booth rather than at the bar. Cabarets or even jazz clubs are good if you don't want to be bothered, because people don't talk during the performance.

## HOW NOT TO BE LEFT ALONE: BAR STRATEGY

There are basically two types of bars where conversation can be nurtured: (1) bars with a good 90 percent singles infiltration, at least on weekends (listed as "Singles Bars" in the Special Interest Index), and (2) the more soft-core lounges (listed as "Low-Key Places for Singles"—they're not necessarily singles bars—in the Special Interest Index) where it's a more rounded mixture of couples and singles.

If you feel like making a connection fast and with minimal effort, we need not tell you to go to a singles bar. You know already. A singles bar can also be fun if you simply want to socialize, learn first names, perhaps practice your "lines," and then go home. The mood is pure party. You can talk to anyone who strikes your fancy, and ignore anyone who doesn't.

Many people consider Friday the best singles night, with Saturday and Wednesday running a close second and third. Times vary. Friday in Manhattan, for instance, Happy Hour glasses are often raised at 5:30 and continue nonstop until 4 A.M. Friday elsewhere and Saturday everywhere, most of the action begins at 10:30 or 11 P.M. If you go too early and there's no one there, go get something to eat and come back. Unless you want a good seat right next to the piano player (in which case you must go early and wait it out), it's dreadful to be the only one in the place.

Happy Hours are excellent Monday through Friday pastimes

from 5:30 to about 8, with 7 being the height of the season. Many places have snacks or buffets and the mood is one of great camaraderie, even with strangers, since everyone has just come from the same place (work) and needs a drink.

*Soft-Core Bar Strategy:* In rooms with a mixture of couples, singles, and business people of undetermined marital statuses, head for the bar or cocktail area if you want to socialize. That's where the other singles will have gathered. The dining areas will be mostly couples.

Another soft-core possibility—brunch. Most places that serve food have easy, casual weekend brunches, often with live jazz, classical, or background music—and often with lower prices.

*Bar Strategy for Women:* Many woman don't need a strategy. They already know how to walk into a place alone, sit down confidently, order a drink casually, and perhaps start up a conversation. It's not a big deal. It's easy.

But there are others who simply have not had the practice— either they stay home, go out with other women friends, go on dates, or just go for dinner alone and then come back home. Many are divorced with children. Many are widows—young and older. Many live in Westchester or Long Island and are not aware of the clubs that are near them.

The point is, if we're talking to you, it's time to flex your social muscles and get out there and enjoy life. The hard-core singles bars, if they appeal to you, are easy. All you really have to do is walk in and stand there. That's it. The soft-core rooms, however, have the advantage of being quieter and less hysterical, allowing conversations to develop.

The problem to overcome in the soft-core room is the feeling of discomfort you may experience sitting there with nothing to do. Here are some things to do: Go specifically to hear a particular band. Go to hear a singer you like. Go to hear a new piano player who was just reviewed in the paper. This gives you the mental ammunition you need to sit there and not feel uncomfortable. You have a purpose. Perhaps a friend told you a particular bar has excellent photographs on the walls—go to see the photos, then sit down for a drink, and tell the bartender that you dabble in photog-

8                                                          *Introduction*

raphy yourself. (Bartenders are great people to practice your conversational arts on.) And of course you can always watch the bar television if they have one.

If you can't start a conversation but want to make friends, bring something along that will arouse the curiosity of the person sitting next to you. Start with the inevitable blank book, sit down, order a drink, and start writing in it. Someone will undoubtedly ask if you're writing a novel. That question is almost as tired as the blank book, but it does break the ice. Or bring a sketch pad—it's certainly gimmicky, but you can explain later that you don't usually go in for games.

If the bar itself is unbearably intimidating even with all these defenses, sit at a cocktail table. Just don't immerse yourself amid tables of couples.

And don't forget, Happy Hours are very good in the soft-core rooms because they are low on the Pretense-Necessity Scale: It's always OK to sit and have a well-earned drink after a hard day, without having to say you came to admire the chandelier.

*Bar Strategy for Men:* There are those men who have their strategy down so well it's no longer premeditated. It's natural. In that case you've been enjoying the city and all it has to offer, both culturally and socially. And you probably have some great phone numbers. Chapters 1 and 2 are packed with new ideas on where to bring your dates or where to increase your circle of friends.

On the other hand, maybe you've run out of numbers, or you're just not meeting the type of people you want. Since the singles ratio is reported to be almost two women to one man, you've got a huge thing going for you. You owe it to yourself to get out there and mingle.

First, our basic premise: Choose a place that suits your needs. If evening is the only time you have to exercise, why not work out at one of the coed fitness centers? If you live with a child, see what your community organizations are offering this weekend. If your passion is Monday night football, then you should go to a bar that shows the game on TV. One woman we know has a thing for men who like sports, so she goes to the lounges with sports TVs. The only word of caution here is that, in order to find this woman, you

MUST take you eyes off the screen periodically. Otherwise you won't see her. She'll be there, but she's not going to tap your shoulder to ask for the score.

Women's main complaint about New York men is that they don't walk over and smile and just say "hi." Believe it or not, many women, even today, still will not make the first overt move. Of course it's hard to know exactly how loud and long the "hi" should be. Too laid back, and that will be the beginning and end of the entire conversation. Too strong, and you may discover hidden karate talents she didn't look like she had. Why not catch her eye first, and see if she's interested. The same woman who wouldn't make the first move, *will* make eye contact if she's curious—and that's really the best way to gauge the situation. Then you can get up and walk over to her in confidence. A sincere "How's it going?" or "Can I join you?" can open the door to vast new worlds.

## DATING SERVICES

There are certain things everyone should know before deciding which dating service to employ. First of all, you must decide what you want from your matchmaker. If you just want to party for the summer, or boogie for the winter, there are many inexpensive computer services to check out. On the other hand, you may be ready to settle down and all you really need is Ms./Mr. Compatible to settle down with. In that case, you may prefer one of the more personal (though often more expensive) services. Remember, though, no one can guarantee to find you a mate. Human beings remain as surprisingly uncategorizable as they are uncomputerizable.

Fees range from $1.00 to $1000.00 and up, depending on what kind of approach you take. You can fill out a mail-order form and receive a computer printout of phone numbers; you can have yourself videotaped for prospective dates to see; you can go in person to the agency for anything from a ten-minute screening to a two-hour in-depth interview. It all depends on how involved you want to get.

Oddly enough, prices are not necessarily indicative of the matches you'll get. We've had good and bad dates through both the cheap and the expensive agencies. And method is not indicative either—we've had good times and awful times through both the computer and the personalized agencies. The best ways, then, to choose your organization, are these:

1. Check through Chapter 2. If it looks like your type of group, call them up, interview them on the phone if possible, or see them in person. Don't make an impulsive commitment.
2. If it's expensive, ask to be invited to a function as a guest, if applicable, before signing up. Ask for references.
3. Check out five or six agencies in this way before parting with the interior of your wallet. Or try some of the organizations that don't require a membership fee. You'll get a better feel for what the singles industry has to offer.
4. We have checked every agency in Chapter 2 with the Better Business Bureau. But you may wish to call the BBB yourself for any late breaking information. The Manhattan BBB has a useful "Subject Report" on "Dating, Matrimonial and Social Referral Services" that you should ask for.
5. Ask your friends or acquaintances which agencies they especially liked.
6. Don't be afraid to ask ahead of time EXACTLY what your cost covers. Get it in writing, either in the form of a brochure, a letter, or a contract. Some services guarantee a minimum number of personal introductions. Others give you a list of phone numbers. Some organize and sponsor a number of parties per month, all of which you're entitled to if you've paid your fee.

As a safety precaution, we do advise people to choose a public place during the day for meeting someone new on a one-to-one basis. Don't let anyone pick you up at home until they've passed your most objective, scrutinizingly detailed inspection.

## Everyone's Invited!

*Out-of-Towners.* Welcome! We hope *The Complete New York Guide for Singles* will add color and excitement to your business trip or vacation. For openers you might want to locate some mellow piano bars near your hotel. Or after the show you may choose a theater district cabaret for a nightcap. There's no doubt that any piano player you hear will do the tune "New York, New York" at least once during the night. Heed the lyrics: You're in "the city that never sleeps!" Why not map out an all-night social tour for yourself of Greenwich Village and Soho—or up and down First and Second avenues—or both! The book lists all closing times so you can plan your evening with precision. And after your favorite places are putting up the bar stools, go back to the book and find a late-night nightclub.

*Native New Yorkers.* We know you've never climbed the Statue of Liberty, but there's really no excuse to miss out on the nightlife. You have the advantage of knowing the city, knowing the public transportation, knowing what parts of the city have the most parking spaces, knowing your favorite neighborhoods. You can take advantage of all the information you have at your fingertips.

*There are clubs, lounges, and organizations that cater to any kind of crowd you'd feel good with*—older crowds, artist crowds, executive and professional crowds, the swing set, the jet set, or the neighborhood jeans set. There are singles groups sponsoring everything from camping to concerts to singing workshops to wine-tasting classes.

*So no matter what you want—a fun evening, a full calendar, or marriage—it's right here in the New York area.* Be assured, however, that very little will happen to you while sliding quarters into the dryer in the basement. You must let the laundry go this weekend, and take a chance. The first move is up to you. The rest is easy—as easy as saying "hi."

# For Your Safety:

1. Don't go to unfamiliar neighborhoods at night.
2. Call before you go. Every listing in *The Complete New York Guide for Singles* has been verified either in person or by phone. BUT. Clubs come and go, prices change, credit card requirements change, new policies bring in different crowds. We can assume no responsibility for any clubs or organizations listed. The final judgment is up to you.
3. With travel groups, be sure to (a) get references, (b) avoid those that give high pressure sales pitches, and (c) get travel information and receipts in writing.

We're counting on you to be intelligent and use your own discretion. Don't get involved in anything you can't handle. There are over 500 listings in this book—if a place or group doesn't feel right, find someplace else that better suits your personality!

# Chapter 1

# *Places to Go*

---

## ABBREVIATIONS

| | |
|---|---|
| AVERAGE DRINK | Average Mixed Drink Price |
| COVER OR MINIMUM | Average Cover or Minimum |
| AE | American Express |
| CB | Carte Blanche |
| DC | Diners' Club |
| MC | MasterCard |
| V | Visa |

## Upper East Side

EAST OF FIFTH AVENUE AND NORTH OF 59TH STREET

**Adam's Apple**                                    *Restaurant/Disco*
1117 First Avenue (at 61st St.)
(212) 371-8651

No, you're not walking into a lush jungle. Yes, there are plants all over the place, but there are lots of singles, too—especially at the horseshoe bar on the first floor. Suspended above the bar, amid more plants, is a small dance floor. Second floor dancing and dining area is mainly for couples. So stay downstairs and enjoy the fun. The mood is elegant and sociable.

|  |  |
|---|---|
| AVERAGE DRINK | $2.00 |
| COVER OR MINIMUM | $7.00 |
| PLASTIC | AE, MC, V |
| CROWD | In their 20s, 30s, and 40s; celebrities show up from time to time |
| DRESS | Some in suits and sports jackets, others more casual |
| OPEN | Seven days, from 11:30 A.M. to 4 A.M. |
| FOOD | Lunch, supper, late supper, Sunday brunch; dinner entrées range from $4.25 to $14.00 |

**Barrymore's** *Café*
1431 York Avenue (between 75th and 76th Sts.)
(212) 650-1033

This small, intimate café attracts some singles, though it is not primarily a meeting place.

| | |
|---|---|
| AVERAGE DRINK | $2.00 |
| COVER OR MINIMUM | None |
| PLASTIC | None |
| CROWD | Neighborhood people from 20 to 64 |
| DRESS | Casual |
| OPEN | Seven days, from 8 A.M. to 4 A.M. |
| FOOD | None |

**Bartholomew's** *Café/Restaurant*
1501 York Avenue (between 79th and 80th Sts.)
(212) 737-8383

The mood here is casual and cozy, with wood and stone decor and a bar area with tables that hold forty to fifty couples and singles. The bar itself holds thirteen, with live piano (and occasionally singing) in the background Tuesday through Saturday from 8 P.M.

| | |
|---|---|
| AVERAGE DRINK | $2.25 |
| COVER OR MINIMUM | None |
| PLASTIC | AE, CB, DC, MC, V |
| CROWD | Neighborhood, family, and others from 20 to 50 at the bar |
| DRESS | Casual |
| OPEN | Seven days, noon to 2 A.M. |
| FOOD | Continental; lunch and dinner, with dinner priced from about $7.00 to $12.00 |
| SPECIALS | Prices are cheaper till 6 P.M. |

**Beach Café**                                    *Bar/Restaurant*
1326 Second Avenue (at 70th St.)
(212) 988-7299

A medium-sized but intimate singles watering hole, with "no live entertainment, but live people," says the bartender/manager.

| | |
|---|---|
| AVERAGE DRINK | $2.00 |
| COVER OR MINIMUM | None |
| PLASTIC | None |
| CROWD | Doctors, executives, people in the arts; age range 21 to 45 |
| DRESS | Jackets worn but not required |
| OPEN | Seven days, 11:30 A.M. to 4 A.M. |
| FOOD | Lunch, dinner, late supper; American cuisine; brunch on Saturday and Sunday; expect to pay from $3.50 to $10.75 at dinnertime |

**Boodles**                                    *Restaurant/Café*
1478 First Avenue (at 77th St.)
(212) 628-0900

Gathering spot for many singles, with live music one night (call to find out when) and simply socializing the rest of the week. The atmosphere is airy, attractive, and tastefully done.

| | |
|---|---|
| AVERAGE DRINK | $2.25 |
| COVER OR MINIMUM | None |
| PLASTIC | AE, MC, V |
| CROWD | All kinds of people, mostly in their 30s |
| DRESS | Proper attire |
| OPEN | Seven days, from 11 A.M. to 2 A.M. |
| FOOD | Continental menu; dinner prices run from $3.95 to $11.95 |

**Cachaca**                                                  *Nightclub*
403 E. 62nd Street (between York and First Aves.)
(212) 688-8501

It's large enough for dancing, and intimate enough to cozy up on one of the many couches. The flavor is Brazilian, with carnival music, live Brazilian pop music after 11 P.M., and even some disco between sets. Friday night is when a fair number of singles go. Many couples, too.

| | |
|---|---|
| AVERAGE DRINK | $4.00 to $5.00 |
| COVER OR MINIMUM | No minimum at the bar; $12.00 at tables includes three drinks |
| PLASTIC | AE, CB, DC, MC, V |
| CROWD | Professional and older people, many Europeans and tourists; ages go from 25 on up |
| DRESS | Anything goes |
| OPEN | Tuesday through Sunday, 8 P.M. to 4 A.M.; closed Monday |
| FOOD | Brazilian/French/Continental menu |

**Carnaby Street**                                          *Rock Pub*
1189 First Avenue (between 64th and 65th Sts.)
(212) 535-6423

Wear comfortable shoes, because it's dancing, all dancing. Live d.j. spins nightly. Holds up to 300 people on weekends.

| | |
|---|---|
| AVERAGE DRINK | $3.00 |
| COVER OR MINIMUM | $3.00 after 10 P.M. on weekends |
| PLASTIC | None |
| CROWD | Party crowds between 18 and 30 |
| DRESS | Anything goes |
| OPEN | Seven nights, 7 P.M. to 4 A.M. |
| FOOD | None |
| SPECIALS | Happy Hour from 7 to 10 P.M. |

**Copacabana**                                    *Disco*
10 E. 60th Street (between Fifth and Madison Aves.)
(212) PL 5-6010

The singles that go to Copacabana are there on Friday and Saturday for the disco. It's a big place with live d.j., usually a live show,
and the whole sound/lighting bit.

| | |
|---|---|
| AVERAGE DRINK | $2.75 to $4.00 |
| COVER OR MINIMUM | $10.00 |
| PLASTIC | AE, CB, DC, MC, V |
| CROWD | Over 21; all types of people including celebrities |
| DRESS | Fashionable disco attire, from designer jeans on up |
| OPEN | Friday and Saturday disco from 10:30 P.M. to 5 A.M. |
| FOOD | None |

**Court Street**                          *Restaurant/Disco*
1544 Second Avenue (near 80th St.)
(212) 650-9326

The singles congregate at the bar and the disco. It's a cozy and
intimate neighborhood place with a d.j. spinning records.

| | |
|---|---|
| AVERAGE DRINK | $2.00 |
| COVER OR MINIMUM | Friday and Saturday $5.00 at the door |
| PLASTIC | AE, CB, DC, MC, V |
| CROWD | An early 20s rock crowd on weekends, older and more sophisticated during the week |
| DRESS | Casual or disco |
| OPEN | The dancing goes on from 9 P.M. on Friday and Saturday, and from 10 Sunday through Thursday, but Court Street is open for food and drinks from 4 P.M. to 2 A.M. Monday and Tuesday, 4 P.M. to 4 A.M. Wednesday, Thursday, and Friday, and from noon to 4 A.M. Saturday and Sunday |

FOOD American; $4.95 to $10.95 for dinner
SPECIALS Happy Hour 4 to 6 P.M. daily

## Cronie's                                          *Restaurant/Bar*
1695 Second Avenue (between 87th and 88th Sts.)
(212) 860-1919

The bar seats twelve plus standing. On weekends it's about half singles, half couples.

| | |
|---|---|
| AVERAGE DRINK | $2.00 |
| COVER OR MINIMUM | None |
| PLASTIC | AE, CB, DC, MC, V |
| CROWD | 25 to 40, executives and professionals |
| DRESS | Most men wear jackets |
| OPEN | Seven days, from 11:30 A.M. to 4 A.M. |
| FOOD | Continental |

## Demarchelier                                      *Restaurant/Bar*
808 Lexington Avenue (between 62nd and 63rd Sts.)
(212) 223-0047

Many singles frequent this "in" spot with its softly lit dark-wood bar and friendly crowd.

| | |
|---|---|
| AVERAGE DRINK | $2.75 to $3.00 |
| COVER OR MINIMUM | None |
| PLASTIC | AE, CB, DC, MC, V |
| CROWD | Models, celebrities, professionals; age range 25 to 40 |
| DRESS | Casual but chic |
| OPEN | Monday through Saturday, noon to midnight-ish |
| FOOD | French bistro; a la carte dinner entrées run from $10.50 to $15.75 |

**D.L. Sutton's** *Disco*
1584 York Avenue (between 83rd and 84th Sts.)
(212) 879-5299

A medium-sized casual disco with two bars and plenty of tables. The atmosphere is relaxed, with live music on Wednesday and a d.j. spinning discs from Thursday through Sunday. Some singles, some couples.

| | |
|---|---|
| AVERAGE DRINK | $2.50 |
| COVER OR MINIMUM | Varies |
| PLASTIC | None |
| CROWD | All types of people in the 25 to 35 age group |
| DRESS | Fashionable disco attire and designer jeans |
| OPEN | Wednesday through Sunday from 8:30 P.M. to 4 A.M. |
| FOOD | None |

**Drake's Drum** *Pub/Restaurant*
1629 Second Avenue (between 84th and 85th Sts.)
(212) 988-2826

A cozy, intimate pub with a forty-foot bar and sawdust on the floor. The bartender describes it as a "hangout place" with a jukebox and lots of socializing.

| | |
|---|---|
| AVERAGE DRINK | $1.75 |
| COVER OR MINIMUM | None |
| PLASTIC | AE, MC, V |
| CROWD | All types of people in the 25 to 35 age range |
| DRESS | Casual |
| OPEN | Seven days, 11:30 A.M. to 4 A.M. |
| FOOD | Burgers to steaks, $2.25 to $7.95 |

**Eric** *Bar/Restaurant/Music Room*
1700 Second Avenue (at 88th St.)
(212) 534-8500

Live music nightly with everything from rock to jazz—that's in the back room with a stage and tables, seating about seventy. In the front is a dining room and the bar. The mood is relaxed and very casual, and has been for twelve years. Many singles.

| | |
|---|---|
| AVERAGE DRINK | $2.75 |
| COVER OR MINIMUM | $3.00 to $6.00 |
| PLASTIC | AE, MC, V |
| CROWD | A wide array of people in the 25 to 35 age range, plus some spillover from nearby Elaine's |
| DRESS | Clean |
| OPEN | Seven days, noon to 4 A.M. |
| FOOD | American food served from noon to 3:30 A.M., with dinner ranging from $5.00 to $11.00 |

**Finnegan's Wake** *Pub/Restaurant*
First Avenue and 73rd Street
(212) 737-3664

The room is usually packed wall-to-wall and floor-to-ceiling with people—mostly singles—so the old English pub decor with wood paneling is hard to see. Get there early for a good seat. No reservations.

| | |
|---|---|
| AVERAGE DRINK | $2.00 to $2.75 |
| COVER OR MINIMUM | None |
| PLASTIC | None |
| CROWD | Actors, literary people, nurses, interns, business people, and a small sprinkling of neighborhood regulars; all ages |
| DRESS | Neat and casual |
| OPEN | Seven days, 11 A.M. to 4 A.M. |

| FOOD | Irish/English/Pub/American/Slightly Continental; lunch and dinner both served, with dinner prices ranging from $5.25 to $8.95 |
|---|---|

## Flanagan's                                     *Restaurant/Bar*
1215 First Avenue (between 65th and 66th Sts.)
(212) 472-0300

The bar is forty-five feet long—how can you go wrong? Live guitar/ vocal music nightly provides atmosphere and a lot of fun.

| AVERAGE DRINK | $1.75 |
|---|---|
| COVER OR MINIMUM | $7.50 on Thursday, Friday, and Saturday |
| PLASTIC | AE, CB, DC, MC, V |
| CROWD | Professional people of all types in their 20s and 30s |
| DRESS | Jackets preferred, jeans not allowed; many people wear business suits |
| OPEN | Seven days, 11 A.M. to 4 A.M. |
| FOOD | Fish, steaks, hamburgers; dinner prices range from $4.50 to $11.95 |

## George Martin                                 *Restaurant/Bar*
1420 Third Avenue (between 80th and 81st Sts.)
(212) 988-4500

George Martin is often so crowded that it's hard to see the beautiful natural wood bar and the sleek, contemporary, almost Scandinavian-type decor. The evening crowd is an ultra-friendly group of single people, both at the bar and in the dining area.

| AVERAGE DRINK | $3.50 |
|---|---|
| COVER OR MINIMUM | None |
| PLASTIC | AE |
| CROWD | Sophisticated business people, 25 to 45 |
| DRESS | Jackets and ties required |
| OPEN | Seven days, noon to 4 A.M. |

| | |
|---|---|
| FOOD | American/Continental; $13.95 prix-fixe dinner until 7:30 P.M.; regular menu entrée prices go from about $9.75 to $19.75 |
| SPECIALS | Happy Hour from 5 to 7 P.M. weekdays with hors d'oeuvres |

**Gleason's**                    *"Friendly Neighborhood Tavern"*
1414 York Avenue (at 75th St.)
(212) 535-8702

Socializing goes on at the thirty-five-foot bar, and while many people already know each other, the day bartender promises that they "don't bite strangers." The atmosphere is very easygoing.

| | |
|---|---|
| AVERAGE DRINK | $2.00 |
| COVER OR MINIMUM | None |
| PLASTIC | AE |
| CROWD | Locals, from 18 to 25 |
| DRESS | Casual |
| OPEN | Seven days, from 11 A.M. to 4 A.M. |
| FOOD | Continental menu, with dinner prices ranging from $2.75 to $11.95 |

**Grass**                                    *Restaurant/Bar*
1445 First Avenue (at 75th St.)
(212) 737-3328

Enjoy piano/vocal four or five nights. Call to find out when.

| | |
|---|---|
| AVERAGE DRINK | $2.75 |
| COVER OR MINIMUM | None |
| PLASTIC | AE, CB, DC, MC, V |
| CROWD | All types, all ages |
| DRESS | Casual |
| OPEN | Seven nights, from 10:30 P.M. to 3 A.M. |
| FOOD | Varied menu, with dinner ranging from $5.95 to $13.95 |

**The Greenery**                                    *Restaurant/Bar*
1340 First Avenue (at 72nd St.)
(212) 570-0060

The fifty-foot bar is quiet and relaxed. Couples and singles.

| | |
|---|---|
| AVERAGE DRINK | $2.75 |
| COVER OR MINIMUM | None |
| PLASTIC | AE, CB, DC, MC, V |
| CROWD | All types, most in their 20s |
| DRESS | Most men wear jackets |
| OPEN | Seven days, from 11:30 A.M. to 4 A.M. |
| FOOD | Continental menu, with dinner ranging from about $5.00 to $13.00 |

**Harper**                                          *Restaurant/Bar*
Third Avenue (between 74th and 75th Sts.)
(212) 472-8636

A dark-wood bar area in front seats many couples and singles, with separate dining area in the back. Not a singles dominated room, it's a good place for sophisticated socializing.

| | |
|---|---|
| AVERAGE DRINK | $2.00 to $2.75 |
| COVER OR MINIMUM | None at the bar |
| PLASTIC | None |
| CROWD | Business people, all ages |
| DRESS | Neat; some casual, some jackets and ties |
| OPEN | Seven days, 11:45 A.M. to 1:30 A.M. |
| FOOD | American/Continental, lunch and dinner; average dinner, $9.00 |

**Herlihy's**                              *Restaurant/Bar/Piano Bar*
1479 First Avenue (at 77th St.)
(212) 535-9448

A very active place with a lot going on at all times! Upstairs there's a restaurant till 11 P.M. Then on Wednesday through Saturday it turns into a lively piano bar with many guest celebrities dropping in to do a few tunes. Downstairs is a great old drinking bar in true turn-of-the-century saloon atmosphere. The bar itself is the original mahogany and oak, with brass and glass ornamentation.

| | |
|---|---|
| AVERAGE DRINK | $2.00 |
| COVER OR MINIMUM | None |
| PLASTIC | AE |
| CROWD | Athletes, theatrical people, soap opera actors and executives; average age range, 20s and 30s |
| DRESS | Jackets preferred in summer; proper attire at all times |
| OPEN | Seven days, from 4 P.M. to 4 A.M. |
| FOOD | American/Continental menu; prices run from $9.95 to $14.95 |
| SPECIALS | Afternoon Delight from 4 to 8 P.M.; free buffet |

**Hoexter's Market**                    *Restaurant/Bar/Disco at Midnight*
1442 Third Avenue (at 82nd St.)
(212) 472-9322

The decor is simple but elegant, with lots of singles.

| | |
|---|---|
| AVERAGE DRINK | $2.75 to $3.00 |
| COVER OR MINIMUM | None |
| PLASTIC | AE, CB, DC, MC, V |
| CROWD | Sophisticated, from age 25 |
| DRESS | Jackets required; no jeans |
| OPEN | Seven nights; bar and restaurant open at 6 P.M.; disco begins at midnight |
| FOOD | Continental dinners till about midnight; a la carte entrée prices run from $10.50 to $18.00 |

**Holbrook's**                                    *Restaurant/Bar*
1313 Third Avenue (near 75th St.)
(212) 734-2050

It's worth a stop here to see the hand-carved, etched window panes
and original silk screens from the 1920s. The gas lamps, pink decor,
and taped 1920's music give the room a delightful atmosphere.
Singles have been known to walk many blocks just to savor the
Amalua Almond from the menu of special ice cream drinks.

| | |
|---|---|
| AVERAGE DRINK | $3.00 |
| COVER OR MINIMUM | None |
| PLASTIC | AE, MC, V |
| CROWD | Lawyers, jet-setters, executives; all ages |
| DRESS | Coat and tie preferred but not required |
| OPEN | Seven days, noon to 2 A.M. Sunday through Thursday, and till 4 A.M. Friday and Saturday |
| FOOD | Continental/Northern Italian till midnight; a la carte dinner entrées from $8.95 to about $16.95 |
| SPECIALS | Happy Hour from 4:30 to 6:30 P.M. Monday through Friday |

**Home**                          *Restaurant/Bar/Music Room*
1748 Second Avenue (at 91st St.)
(212) 427-3106

Nicely decorated antique shop atmosphere, with brick walls and
interesting old items hanging on them. Enjoy jazz or rock nightly
from 10 or 11 P.M. and dancing on Friday and Saturday.

| | |
|---|---|
| AVERAGE DRINK | $2.00 to $2.50 |
| COVER OR MINIMUM | $2.00 during the music |
| PLASTIC | MC, V |
| CROWD | All types of people from 25 to 30 and older |

| DRESS | From suits to jeans |
|---|---|
| OPEN | Seven days, noon to 4 A.M. |
| FOOD | Lunch, dinner till midnight; the most expensive item is $5.95 |
| SPECIALS | Drinks half-priced during the day |

## Hudson Bay Inn                                          *Restaurant/Bar*
1454 Second Avenue (at 76th St.)
(212) 861-5683

Thirteen years in business has made this a well-established place in the neighborhood. It's cozy and casual with lots of character.

| AVERAGE DRINK | $2.50 |
|---|---|
| COVER OR MINIMUM | None |
| PLASTIC | AE, CB, DC, MC, V |
| CROWD | Neighborhood |
| DRESS | Casual |
| OPEN | Seven days; Monday through Friday 4 P.M. to 4 A.M.; Saturday and Sunday noon to 4 A.M. |
| FOOD | Pub fare from $3.50 to $14.95 |
| SPECIALS | Happy Hour Monday through Friday, 5 to 7 P.M.; Monday is "Spaghetti Night" at the bar—free spaghetti and salad with a drink from 7:30 to 10 P.M.; also at the bar on Monday you can wolf down a dozen mussels for $1.00 |

## The Ice Studio                                          *Ice Skating*
1034 Lexington Avenue (at 73rd St.)
(212) 535-0304

Some singles, some couples—but the adults start skating at around 6 P.M. and go all day Saturday and Sunday. It's a studio, not a full-sized rink, so you must call ahead for reservations. Very cozy—and only twenty to twenty-five people can skate at a time.

| | |
|---|---|
| AVERAGE DRINK | Hot chocolate, reasonably priced |
| COVER OR MINIMUM | $4.50, skate rental about $2.00 |
| PLASTIC | None |
| CROWD | Neighborhood and business people of all ages |
| DRESS | Casual |
| OPEN | Seven days, from 9:30 A.M. to 8 P.M. and till 10 P.M. on Tuesday, Thursday, and Friday |

## Ichabod's                                                 *Restaurant/Bar*
1481 Second Avenue (at 77th St.)
(212) 861-3600

A dark, Casablanca atmosphere with lots of plants and a gorgeous bar. Crowded on weekends with plenty of socializing.

| | |
|---|---|
| AVERAGE DRINK | $2.50 |
| COVER OR MINIMUM | None |
| PLASTIC | AE, CB, DC, MC, V |
| CROWD | Sophisticated, young business people in the 25 to 45 age range |
| DRESS | Proper attire |
| OPEN | Seven days, from 11:30 A.M. to 4 A.M. |
| FOOD | Fish, meat, chicken, salads; dinner ranges from $3.50 to $10.95 or $11.95 |

## Janus                                                         *Restaurant*
1461 First Avenue (at 76th St.)
(212) 879-7676

This warm and sophisticated room is not really a social center, but if you're alone and want to eat fine Italian food without feeling conspicuous, here's the place.

| | |
|---|---|
| AVERAGE DRINK | $2.50 |
| COVER OR MINIMUM | None |
| PLASTIC | AE, CB, DC, MC, V |
| CROWD | Executives, working people, ages 20 to 60 |

Jackets preferred
OPEN Monday through Saturday 5 P.M. to
11:30 P.M.
FOOD Full dinner menu with average prices
checking in at $7.95 to $9.95

## Jewel Restaurant
*Restaurant/Bar*
1279 First Avenue (at 69th St.)
(212) 737-3735

The singles that go to Jewel will be at the bar on Wednesday,
Thursday, Friday, and late Saturday, although the bar is small.
There's an outside café and a restaurant with live piano/vocal
nightly.

AVERAGE DRINK $2.25 to $3.50
COVER OR MINIMUM None on Monday, Tuesday, or Wednesday;
$3.00 music charge Thursday, Friday, and
Saturday if you're not eating
PLASTIC AE, DC, MC, V
CROWD Neighborhood and professional people from
25 up
DRESS Casual
OPEN Monday through Saturday, 4 P.M. to closing
FOOD American/Continental menu with prices from
about $7.00 to $12.00

## J.G. Melon
*Restaurant/Saloon*
1291 Third Avenue (at 74th St.)
(212) 744-0585

A big, comfortable, often-crowded place with lots of singles and
pictures of melons all over the walls.

AVERAGE DRINK $2.25 to $2.75
COVER OR MINIMUM None
PLASTIC None
CROWD All types of people, all ages
DRESS Casual

| | |
|---|---|
| OPEN | Seven days, noon to 4 A.M. |
| FOOD | Saloon food (hamburgers, steak, chile) from $2.25 to $12.00 |

## J.P.'s                                                    *Restaurant/Nightclub*
1471 First Avenue (at 77th St.)
(212) 288-1022

Tiffany lamps and a wooden bar make the atmosphere warm and friendly. Listen to soft rock groups nightly and enjoy the ambience.

| | |
|---|---|
| AVERAGE DRINK | $2.50 |
| COVER OR MINIMUM | $2.00 |
| PLASTIC | AE, DC, MC, V |
| CROWD | All types, mostly in the late 20s |
| DRESS | Casual |
| OPEN | Seven nights from 9 P.M. to 4 A.M.; may open earlier in the warm months |
| FOOD | Steak, burgers, soup; you can eat here for about $5.00 |

## The Mad Hatter                                              *Restaurant/Bar*
Second Avenue (between 77th and 78th Sts.)
(212) 628-4917

A great place to get involved! It's comfortable but not too fancy, with sawdust on the floor, Tiffany lamps, a cozy pub mood, and interesting hats hanging all over. There are many activities, such as movies during ski season. Management is presently considering mud wrestling contests.

| | |
|---|---|
| AVERAGE DRINK | $1.75 to $3.50 |
| COVER OR MINIMUM | None |
| PLASTIC | AE, MC, V; "just no gas credit cards," says the bartender |
| CROWD | Neighborhood people during the day, and many sports people at night; age range is 20 to 35 |
| DRESS | No T-shirts with rolled up sleeves |

OPEN Seven days, noon to 4 A.M.

FOOD Dinner entrées run from $4.00 to $6.00; lunch and Sunday brunch also available

## Magique                                        *Nightclub*
1160 First Avenue (at 61st St.)
(212) 935-6060

"Do whatever you want but just be chic about it," advises Laura the club photographer. There's lots of dancing and conversation, with a d.j., laser shows, and slide shows. It's more of an "in," avant garde event than a singles meeting spot, but with all the different types there the lonely single may feel the least out of place.

| | |
|---|---|
| AVERAGE DRINK | $3.00 |
| COVER OR MINIMUM | $12.00 to $15.00 |
| PLASTIC | None |
| CROWD | Celebrities, models, and other "pretty people" in the 25 to 35 age range |
| DRESS | Trendy, punky apparel or high fashion |
| OPEN | Tuesday through Sunday; opens at 10:30 or 11 P.M. and goes until 4 A.M.; the action starts around midnight |
| FOOD | None |

## Martell's                           *Restaurant/Bar/Sidewalk Café*
1469 Third Avenue (at 83rd St.)
(212) 861-6110

Considered the oldest bar in Yorkville. Couples and singles enjoy the two fireplaces and the antique decor. Gaslights, old-time records, an old-fashioned jukebox and large bar make for a pleasant, laidback evening.

| | |
|---|---|
| AVERAGE DRINK | $2.50 |
| COVER OR MINIMUM | None |
| PLASTIC | AE, CB, DC, MC, V |
| CROWD | Professionals and neighborhood people in the late 20s and 30s |

| | |
|---|---|
| DRESS | Casual |
| OPEN | Seven days, noon to 3 A.M. |
| FOOD | American/Continental—large or small meals; a big dinner goes for $10.00 to $25.00 |

## Maxwell's Plum                                 *Restaurant/Bar*
First Avenue (at 64th St.)
(212) 628-2100

The ultimate in the East Side singles experience. Lots of fun, laughs, lines, and no meaningful relationships. Turn-of-the-century decor, tastefully done. A favorite pastime is to look at the limousines out front and the people at the bar and try to guess who goes with which.

| | |
|---|---|
| AVERAGE DRINK | $2.75 to $3.50 |
| COVER OR MINIMUM | None at the bar |
| PLASTIC | AE, CB, DC, MC, V, but not at the bar |
| CROWD | Executives, professionals, and other affluent people aged 24 to 50 |
| DRESS | Most men wear jackets and ties (or turtlenecks) though it's not required |
| OPEN | Seven days, noon to 2 A.M. |
| FOOD | Large restaurant, Continental menu till 1 A.M.; an average a la carte entrée is $13.00 |

## Molly Maguire's II                              *Restaurant/Bar*
1031 Third Avenue (at 61st St.)
(212) 759-4770

Copper and brick decor, friendly atmosphere, lots of unmarried people.

| | |
|---|---|
| AVERAGE DRINK | $1.75 to $2.00 |
| COVER OR MINIMUM | None |
| PLASTIC | AE, CB, DC, MC, V |
| CROWD | Professionals in their 30s |
| DRESS | Stylish |

| OPEN | Seven days, noon to 4 A.M. |
|---|---|
| FOOD | Dinner goes from $4.50 to $11.95; lunch served also |

## Mr. O's Pub                                                    *Pub*
Second Avenue (between 76th and 77th Sts.)
(212) 650-0655

This is the definitive small neighborhood bar, where regulars (singles and couples, and not *all* regulars) go to relax, chat, or kill time. The wood paneling with mirrors, a fan on the ceiling, and pictures of celebrities on the walls provide atmosphere for the seventy-person-capacity room. And for a good time on Tuesday night, you're invited to join the dart tournament.

| AVERAGE DRINK | $1.75 |
|---|---|
| COVER OR MINIMUM | None, except for private parties |
| PLASTIC | None |
| CROWD | Neighborhood folk and others in their 20s and 30s |
| DRESS | Informal |
| OPEN | Seven days, 10 A.M. to 4 A.M.; closed occasionally for private parties |
| FOOD | None |

## Nicola's                                              *Restaurant/Bar*
146 E. 84th Street (between Third and Lexington Aves.)
(212) 249-9850

An intimate, sophisticated drawing room atmosphere with dark wood and book jackets on the wall. The cozy bar area is where the many singles will be discussing their latest books, movies, or court cases.

| AVERAGE DRINK | $3.00 |
|---|---|
| COVER OR MINIMUM | None |
| PLASTIC | None |

36

CROWD    Sophisticated—editors, models, lawyers, writers; "people who can afford to pay cash," explains Nick the owner; all ages

DRESS    Classically fashionable

OPEN    Seven nights, 5:30 P.M. to midnight

FOOD    Northern Italian cuisine, with dinner about $10.00 or $12.00

## 92nd Street Y       *Total Environment*
1395 Lexington Avenue (at 92nd St.)
(212) 427-6000
For singles' programs ask for Liz Mintzer on extension 179.
Box Office: (212) 427-4410 or call Chargit at (212) 944-9300

There's something to suit every mood. Here's a partial rundown:

- Health Club—pool, two gyms, track, yoga, calisthenics, aerobics, organized and impromptu games.
- Special singles' events such as lectures, discussion groups, "summer camp," and classes in theater, music, wine tasting, dining, and general fun.
- Folk dancing—Wednesday: Israeli folk dancing; Saturday: International folk dancing; $2.50 to $3.00.
- Poetry readings Monday nights from September to June.
- Theater events from September to June.
- Concerts

COSTS    Call for information

PLASTIC    MC, V; the box office also accepts personal checks

OPEN    Closes Friday at 4 P.M. and reopens Saturday at 6 P.M.

## Oren and Aretsky       *Bar/Restaurant*
1497 Third Avenue (between 84th and 85th Sts.)
(212) 734-8822

A haven for sports fans and players with many singles at the bar and lots of socializing. The light walls with brass fixtures give the room a casually sophisticated atmosphere. Study up on your scores.

| | |
|---|---|
| AVERAGE DRINK | $3.00 |
| COVER OR MINIMUM | None |
| PLASTIC | AE |
| CROWD | Sports players and Ford Agency models—this makes for stiff competition all the way around; age range, 20s and 30s |
| DRESS | Casual |
| OPEN | Seven days, 4 P.M. to 4 A.M. |
| FOOD | American/Continental menu for dinner, which averages $12.00 or $13.00 |

**Profiles**                                    *Restaurant/Bar with Dancing*
323 E. 79th Street (between First and Second Aves.)
(212) 249-5412

An equal mixture of couples and singles dance up a storm from about midnight.

| | |
|---|---|
| AVERAGE DRINK | $2.75 |
| COVER OR MINIMUM | None |
| PLASTIC | AE, CB |
| CROWD | Young neighborhood people from 20 to 40 |
| DRESS | Jackets preferred but casual OK; no old dungarees or sneakers |
| OPEN | Monday through Saturday 5 P.M. to 4 A.M.; Sunday noon to 4 A.M. |
| FOOD | American/Continental menu with dinner prices ranging from $6.50 to $11.95; Sunday brunch available noon to 6 P.M. |
| SPECIALS | Reduced drink prices 5 to 9 P.M. |

**The Racing Club**                                    *Restaurant/Lounge*
206 E. 67th Street (between Second and Third Aves.)
(212) 650-1675

Intimate atmosphere with brick, wood, and pictures of racing scenes on the walls. A good mixed crowd listens to the live jazz piano Wednesday, Friday, and Saturday.

| AVERAGE DRINK | $2.50 |
|---|---|
| COVER OR MINIMUM | None |
| PLASTIC | AE, DC |
| CROWD | All kinds, all ages |
| DRESS | From casual to jackets and ties |
| OPEN | Monday through Saturday, noon to midnight; closed Sunday |
| FOOD | Continental/Italian; a la carte dinner entrées range from $4.00 to $16.00 |

## Rascals                                       *Restaurant/Bar*
1286 First Avenue (at 69th St.)
(212) 734-2862

If you miss the country but can't get out of the city, go to Rascals. The Vermonty feeling—with natural wood, barrels of peanuts, hanging plants, and windows—will make you breathe deeply again. Lots of other earthy singles, too. Live Top 40 music Tuesday through Saturday.

| AVERAGE DRINK | $1.75 to $2.25 |
|---|---|
| COVER OR MINIMUM | Varies |
| PLASTIC | None |
| CROWD | Neighborhood people and professionals |
| DRESS | Casual |
| OPEN | Seven days, 11:30 A.M. to 4 A.M. |
| FOOD | Lunch, dinner till 2 (till 3 on Friday); sandwiches, burgers, salads |

## Rathbone's                                    *Restaurant/Bar*
1702 Second Avenue (at 88th St.)
(212) 369-7361

A large, friendly place with lots of flowers, sawdust on the floor, and paintings on the wall. Singles and couples.

| AVERAGE DRINK | $1.75 to $2.00 |
|---|---|
| COVER OR MINIMUM | None |
| PLASTIC | AE, MC, V |

| | |
|---|---|
| CROWD | Executives, tourists, and neighborhood people from 22 to 40 |
| DRESS | No tank tops |
| OPEN | Seven days, 4 P.M. to 4 A.M. |
| FOOD | American menu with dinner prices from $3.35 to $7.00 |

## The Ravelled Sleave                                    *Bar/Restaurant*
1387 Third Avenue (at 79th St.)
(212) 628-8814

A romantic, English-style mood with dark wood and handsome brick walls. Live piano at dinner and Sunday brunch. Fireplace in winter. Mixed couples and singles.

| | |
|---|---|
| AVERAGE DRINK | $2.25 |
| COVER OR MINIMUM | Dining room minimum is $10.00 |
| PLASTIC | AE, CB, DC, MC, V |
| CROWD | Brokers, bankers, neighborhood people from the late 20s to 40 |
| DRESS | Most wear jackets and ties but a shirt with collar is OK |
| OPEN | Seven days, 4 P.M. to 2, 3, or 4 A.M. |
| FOOD | Continental menu offered from 5:30 P.M. to 11 or 12:30 A.M., with entrées ranging from $7.00 to $18.00 |
| SPECIALS | Weekday Happy Hour 5 to 7 P.M. |

## The Red Blazer                                          *Bar/Restaurant*
1571 Second Avenue (between 81st and 82nd Sts.)
(212) 535-0487 or 650-1868

Casual friendly atmosphere, lots of easy socializing.

| | |
|---|---|
| AVERAGE DRINK | $2.25 |
| COVER OR MINIMUM | None |
| PLASTIC | AE |
| CROWD | Neighborhood people and professionals; 25 to 35 |

|       |                                              |
| ----- | -------------------------------------------- |
| DRESS | Casual                                        |
| OPEN  | Seven days, 4 P.M. to 4 A.M.                  |
| FOOD  | Seafood and other American fare; average prices—$6.95 to $7.95 |

## The Red Blazer Too                    *Bar/Restaurant*
Third Avenue (at 88th St.)
(212) 876-0440

Dark, friendly pub with fireplace and live entertainment. Call to find out who's playing.

|                    |                                              |
| ------------------ | -------------------------------------------- |
| AVERAGE DRINK      | $2.25                                         |
| COVER OR MINIMUM   | None                                          |
| PLASTIC            | AE                                            |
| CROWD              | All kinds, plus a neighborhood crowd; 20s to late 30s |
| DRESS              | Casual                                        |
| OPEN               | Seven days, noon to 4 A.M.                    |
| FOOD               | American; average dinner prices—$7.95 to $9.00 |

## Ridings                               *Bar/Restaurant*
1683 First Avenue (between 87th and 88th Sts.)
(212) 348-0670

An intimate, friendly room done in dark wood. The bar seats fifty singles and couples. Guitar/vocal five or six nights.

|                    |                                              |
| ------------------ | -------------------------------------------- |
| AVERAGE DRINK      | $1.75                                         |
| COVER OR MINIMUM   | None                                          |
| PLASTIC            | MC, V                                         |
| CROWD              | Neighborhood people of all ages               |
| DRESS              | Casual                                        |
| OPEN               | Seven days, noon to 4 A.M.                    |
| FOOD               | Seafood, steak, omelets; average dinner runs from $5.50 to $6.50 |

**Rupperts**                                    *Piano Bar/Restaurant*
1662 Third Avenue (at 93rd St.)
(212) 831-1900

An elegant three-level pub with a thirty-five-foot bar, high windows
and ceilings, butcher block tables, fresh flowers, and linen napkins.
Tuesday through Saturday enjoy a mellow jazz sound from 8 P.M.
till closing. Classical music Sunday and Monday.

| | |
|---|---|
| AVERAGE DRINK | $2.35 |
| COVER OR MINIMUM | $7.00 at tables during some peak hours |
| PLASTIC | AE, DC, MC, V |
| CROWD | Neighborhood people of all ages |
| DRESS | Casual |
| OPEN | Seven days, noon to 4 A.M. |
| FOOD | American/Continental till 12:30 A.M. weeknights, 2:30 A.M. weekends; dinner entrées range from $5.00 to $33.00, with the average being $8.00 |

**The Salty Dog**                              *Restaurant/Bar/Disco*
Second Avenue (between 82nd and 83rd Sts.)
(212) 879-3777

A friendly mixture of couples and singles (from fifty to seventy of
them at the bar alone) and disco from 10 P.M. nightly except Sunday, can only mean a good time. Seafaring atmosphere with fish-
nets and anchors, and a live d.j. Friday and Saturday.

| | |
|---|---|
| AVERAGE DRINK | $2.00 to $2.50 |
| COVER OR MINIMUM | None; the weekend disco has a three drink minimum |
| PLASTIC | AE, V |
| CROWD | Business and neighborhood people; age span is 25 to 40 |
| DRESS | Casual but neat |

| | |
|---|---|
| OPEN | Monday through Saturday from 5:30 P.M.; closed Sunday; dancing till 4 A.M. weekends, slightly earlier closing weeknights |
| FOOD | Hamburger to steak, $4.50 to $10.00 |

## September's                                    *Restaurant/Bar*
1442 First Avenue (at 75th St.)
(212) 861-4670

Friendly, open café with Tiffany lamps. Live bands Wednesday through Saturday play country-rock, Top 40, and requests. Many many singles.

| | |
|---|---|
| AVERAGE DRINK | $2.25 |
| COVER OR MINIMUM | $3.50 cover on weekends plus $1.00 minimum |
| PLASTIC | AE |
| CROWD | Executives and neighborhood people from 21 to 45 |
| DRESS | Casual |
| OPEN | Seven days, 11 A.M. to 4 A.M. |
| FOOD | Barbecue burgers to sirloin, $3.25 to $10.50 |
| SPECIALS | Happy Hour 5 to 7 P.M., Monday through Friday |

## Sign of the Dove                        *Cocktail Lounge/Restaurant*
1110 Third Avenue (at 65th St.)
(212) 861-8080

An elegant, large, light-colored room with a very open, airy feeling. Big doors in the cocktail lounge are opened in spring and summer to let the fresh breezes in. Romantic for couples, but delightfully comfortable for singles, too.

| | |
|---|---|
| AVERAGE DRINK | $4.25 |
| COVER OR MINIMUM | None |

| PLASTIC | AE, CB, DC, MC, V |
| CROWD | "Beautiful People," the bar crowd is mainly over 30 |
| DRESS | Jackets required in dining room, preferred in cocktail lounge |
| OPEN | Seven days; lounge hours—Tuesday through Saturday noon to 2 A.M.; Sunday, noon to 1 A.M.; Monday 4 P.M. to 1 A.M. |
| FOOD | Continental menu; dinner prices range from $15.00 to $30.00 |

**The Studio**                                    *Dance Instruction and Parties*
227 E. 85th Street (between Second and Third Aves.)
(212) 794-9095

The great thing about New York is that there are always new concepts popping up. This one is mainly a dance instruction studio, but most of the clientele is single—so they've set up a d.j., a light show, and a cash bar, and they sponsor parties as well! Wednesday from 8 P.M. to midnight is a good singles night. Owner Bill Davies is a former U.S. Dance Champion.

| AVERAGE DRINK | $1.75 |
| COVER OR MINIMUM | $3.00, $5.00, $10.00 |
| PLASTIC | None |
| CROWD | Varied, mainly in their 20s, 30s, and 40s |
| DRESS | Neat and casual |
| OPEN | Call for schedule |
| FOOD | There's a Chinese restaurant downstairs; you can bring the food up to The Studio and eat it at their tables |

**T.G.I. Friday's**                                    *Restaurant/Bar*
1152 First Avenue (at 63rd St.)
(212) 832-8512

Antique stained glass adds to the cozy atmosphere. Singles and couples. Very friendly.

| | |
|---|---|
| AVERAGE DRINK | $2.25 |
| COVER OR MINIMUM | None |
| PLASTIC | AE, CB, DC, MC, V |
| CROWD | All types of people from 20 to about 35 |
| DRESS | Casual |
| OPEN | Seven days; from lunch till 2 A.M. during the week and till 4 A.M. Friday and Saturday |
| FOOD | American; burgers to steaks, $4.25 to $13.00 |

**Uzies**                                                    *Restaurant*
1444 Third Avenue (at 82nd St.)
(212) 744-8020

Many couples and some singles enjoy the elegant atmosphere.

| | |
|---|---|
| AVERAGE DRINK | $3.00 |
| COVER OR MINIMUM | None |
| PLASTIC | AE, CB, DC, MC, V |
| CROWD | Glamorous people from the late 20s up |
| DRESS | Jackets required |
| OPEN | Monday through Friday from 6 P.M. to about 2 A.M.; Saturday and Sunday, noon to about 2 A.M. |
| FOOD | Northern Italian; dinner ranges from $10.00 for pasta to $30.00 for steak; weekend brunches available also, till 4 P.M. |

**Wednesday's**                                       *Restaurant/Disco*
210 E. 86th Street (between Second and Third Aves.)
(212) 535-8500

Looks like a French village street with lamp posts and a wine and cheese shop. Half singles, half couples, and an eighty-foot bar. You can't go wrong with an eighty-foot bar. Disco nightly at 9 P.M. with a d.j. and recorded music. Saturday is "Nostalgia at Midnight."

| | |
|---|---|
| AVERAGE DRINK | $2.50 |
| COVER OR MINIMUM | $5.00 |
| PLASTIC | AE, CB, DC, MC, V |

| | |
|---|---|
| CROWD | Mixed bag; ages 18 to 30ish with Friday being a little younger and Saturday a little older |
| DRESS | Neat and casual |
| OPEN | Six nights, Tuesday through Sunday, 6 P.M. to 4 A.M.; Saturday 8 P.M. to 4 A.M. |
| FOOD | American menu, with dinner served Wednesday through Saturday only; $4.00 to $11.00 |

## Who's On First                                         *Pub*
1205 First Avenue (at 65th St.)
(212) 737-2772

A brass rail, wooden ceiling and brick floor-type place with an easy, casual ambience. Mostly singles, some couples.

| | |
|---|---|
| AVERAGE DRINK | $2.25 to $2.50 |
| COVER OR MINIMUM | None |
| PLASTIC | AE |
| CROWD | Neighborhood people, junior executives, and others; from 23 to 35 |
| DRESS | Casual but neat |
| OPEN | Seven days from 4 P.M.; closes around 1 A.M. Sunday through Thursday; bar stools go up around 2 A.M. Friday and Saturday |
| FOOD | American/Pub menu, from $4.50 to $9.95 |
| SPECIALS | Happy Hour Monday through Friday from 5 to 7 P.M. with free hors d'oeuvres |

## The Wicked Wolf                                  *Restaurant/Bar*
1623 Second Avenue (between 84th and 85th Sts.)
(212) 744-7446

Despite its name, it's not all singles. But it is a very busy, friendly place with Tiffany lamps, and a thirty-foot oak bar.

| | |
|---|---|
| AVERAGE DRINK | $2.00 |
| COVER OR MINIMUM | None |

| | |
|---|---|
| PLASTIC | AE, DC, MC, V |
| CROWD | All types, from 25 to 60 |
| DRESS | Casual, with some suits |
| OPEN | Seven days, 11:30 A.M. to 4 A.M. |
| FOOD | Steaks, chops, fish; dinner prices range from $3.75 to $10.50 |

**Willie's**                                                        *Restaurant/Bar*
1426 Third Avenue (at 81st St.)
(212) 650-9754

Small, cozy, friendly place with some couples, some singles, and no hassles.

| | |
|---|---|
| AVERAGE DRINK | $2.00 |
| COVER OR MINIMUM | None |
| PLASTIC | None |
| CROWD | All kinds, ages 25 to 35 |
| DRESS | Casual |
| OPEN | Seven days, noon to 4 A.M. |
| FOOD | American menu, with dinner going from $2.95 to $9.95 |

**Wilson's**                                                        *Restaurant/Bar*
1444 First Avenue (at 75th St.)
(212) 861-0320

A warm and comfortable atmosphere with a big bar, and many singles on weekends.

| | |
|---|---|
| AVERAGE DRINK | $1.50 to $3.00 |
| COVER OR MINIMUM | None |
| PLASTIC | AE, CB |
| CROWD | Many athletes (Rangers and Jets!), and professional people; ages 20s and 30s |
| DRESS | Proper dress required |
| OPEN | Seven days, 11:30 A.M. to 4 A.M. |
| FOOD | American menu, with dinner averaging $7.95 to $11.95 |

**Augie's**                                                      *Bistro*
2751 Broadway (off 106th St.)
(212) 864-8707

Live music most nights—folk, rock, some jazz—and plenty of single
people. Friday night there is more listening and less talking, but the
rest of the week is for heavy socializing. Half restaurant, half bar.

|  |  |
|---|---|
| AVERAGE DRINK | $1.75 |
| COVER OR MINIMUM | None |
| PLASTIC | DC |
| CROWD | Writers, actors, painters, and Columbia University students; ages 18 to 35 |
| DRESS | Casual |
| OPEN | Seven nights, from 5 P.M. to 4 A.M. |
| FOOD | Late supper goes for about $4.50 to $8.00 |

**Café Central**                                           *Restaurant/Bar*
320 Amsterdam Avenue (at 75th St.)
(212) 724-9187

Soft lighting, a rich, shiny, dark-wood bar and posters on the wall
give the room an intimate, European atmosphere. The paper tablecloths and crayons, window plants, and vast abundance of singles
make it a comfortable, fun place to be.

|  |  |
|---|---|
| AVERAGE DRINK | $2.50 |
| COVER OR MINIMUM | Varies |
| PLASTIC | AE, CB, DC, MC, V |
| CROWD | Casually sociable, with celebrities and people from all professions; "the stars come in and no one runs over for autographs," explains the manager |
| DRESS | Casual but fashionable |

| | |
|---|---|
| OPEN | Seven days, noon to 4 A.M. |
| FOOD | Lunch and dinner, with a Continental/French menu; dinner prices range from $4.95 for a salad to $14.95 for a steak |

## The Cellar                                    *Restaurant/Nightclub*
70 W. 95th Street (between Central Park West and
Columbus Ave.)
(212) 866-1200

English pub decor. Live jazz and contemporary music on Thursday,
Friday, and Saturday.

| | |
|---|---|
| AVERAGE DRINK | $2.00 |
| COVER OR MINIMUM | $4.00 on Thursday, $5.00 on Friday and Saturday |
| PLASTIC | AE, DC, MC, V |
| CROWD | Varied, some celebrities; ages range from 22 to 40 |
| DRESS | Casual but neat |
| OPEN | Seven nights, from 4 P.M. to 4 A.M. |
| FOOD | Dinner from 6 P.M.; Continental; $2.25 to $12.95 |
| SPECIALS | Complimentary hors d'oeuvres with cocktails from 4 to 6 P.M. |

## Chip's Pub                                         *Bar/Restaurant*
150 Columbus Avenue (between 66th and 67th Sts.,
near Lincoln Center)
(212) 874-8415

A warm and cozy room with an enclosed garden and two dining
areas. The bar seats fifteen to twenty. It's not a singles meeting
place, but you really should go just to meet some of the interesting
regulars.

| | |
|---|---|
| AVERAGE DRINK | $2.25 |
| COVER OR MINIMUM | None |
| PLASTIC | None |

| | |
|---|---|
| CROWD | Celebrities from ABC-TV, professionals, executives, Lincoln Center musicians, film people (bring your 8 × 10 glossies); all ages |
| DRESS | Casual |
| OPEN | Seven days, from 10:30 A.M. to 2 A.M. |
| FOOD | Italian menu, with dinner prices ranging from $5.95 to $12.95 |

## The Conservatory                             *Lounge/Bar/Restaurant*

61st Street and Central Park West (in the Mayflower Hotel)
(212) 581-0896

The bar/lounge area is about 65 percent singles. Strike up a conversation with someone, or enjoy the live harp or piano/vocal music alone. (Music six nights.)

| | |
|---|---|
| AVERAGE DRINK | $2.95 |
| COVER OR MINIMUM | $7.00 |
| PLASTIC | AE, CB, DC, MC, V |
| CROWD | From 25 to 55; theater people, professionals, some celebrities |
| DRESS | Jackets are worn but not required |
| OPEN | Seven days, 11 A.M. to 2 A.M. |
| FOOD | Continental and American—restaurant hours differ from lounge hours, so call if you plan to eat; a la carte entrées range from $12.50 to $19.00 |

## The Cotton Club                                        *Nightclub*

West Side Highway (at 125th St.)
(212) 663-7980

Visit the famous Cotton Club and enjoy top name jazz, pop, and rock acts four nights a week. Some couples, some singles. Call first to see who's playing.

| | |
|---|---|
| AVERAGE DRINK | $3.50 |
| COVER OR MINIMUM | Show charge is $10.00 |
| PLASTIC | AE, CB, DC, MC, V |

| | |
|---|---|
| CROWD | All types, all ages |
| DRESS | Jackets required, tie optional; no jeans |
| OPEN | Thursday through Sunday, 9 P.M. to 4 A.M. |
| FOOD | American |
| SPECIALS | Group rates for private parties |

## Hurrah                                        *Disco*
36 W. 62nd Street (off Broadway)
(212) 541-4909

Dance to established rock and new wave bands, with a d.j. and video shows during breaks. Medium-sized room, holds about 600 people.

| | |
|---|---|
| AVERAGE DRINK | $2.50 |
| COVER OR MINIMUM | $8.00 on weekends, $6.00 during the week |
| PLASTIC | None |
| CROWD | Record industry people and other professionals of all kinds, age 18 and up |
| DRESS | Anything |
| OPEN | Wednesday through Saturday, 10 P.M. to 4 A.M. |
| FOOD | None |

## Jason's Park Royal                            *Cabaret*
23 W. 73rd Street (between Columbus Ave. and Central Park West)
(212) 874-8091

Many singles go to Jason's to hear the nightly live entertainment. The bar in this Mediterranean style room seats twenty-five, and the whole place holds about 100. Located in the Park Royal Hotel.

| | |
|---|---|
| AVERAGE DRINK | $2.50 at showtime, other times $1.50 |
| COVER OR MINIMUM | At showtime, $3.00 cover and two drink minimum |
| PLASTIC | AE, CB, DC, MC, V |
| CROWD | All types of people, all ages |
| DRESS | Anything |

| OPEN | Seven days, noon to 4 A.M. |
| FOOD | Continental; lunch, dinner, Sunday brunch; a dinner might cost you $8.95 |
| SPECIALS | Happy Hour 5 to 7 P.M., Monday through Friday, with hot hors d'oeuvres |

## Marvin Gardens                                       *Bar/Restaurant*
2247 Broadway (between 81st and 82nd Sts.)
(212) 799-0578

Big friendly bar and casual atmosphere. Many singles.

| AVERAGE DRINK | $2.25 |
| COVER OR MINIMUM | None |
| PLASTIC | AE, MC, V |
| CROWD | A nice, Upper West Side bar crowd; actors, doctors, working people; late 20s, early 30s |
| DRESS | Casual |
| OPEN | Seven days, 10 A.M. to 3 A.M. |
| FOOD | American menu; pasta and salad for dinner start at $5.00, steak for $14.00 |

## Mikell's                           *Bar/Restaurant/Sidewalk Café*
760 Columbus Avenue (at 97th St.)
(212) 864-8832

A rustic, intimate club with a glass enclosed sidewalk café and music nightly. Rhythm and blues, some jazz, and a fair share of singles.

| AVERAGE DRINK | $2.25 |
| COVER OR MINIMUM | $3.00 to $6.00 |
| PLASTIC | AE, CB, DC, MC, V |
| CROWD | Students and professionals from 21 to 50 |
| DRESS | From jeans to suits and ties |
| OPEN | Monday through Saturday, 4 P.M. to 4 A.M. |
| FOOD | Steak, chops; $6.00 to $9.00 |
| SPECIALS | Happy Hour 4 to 8 P.M. |

**Nanny Rose**                                      *Restaurant/Bar*
301 Columbus Avenue (at 74th St.)
(212) 787-3801

Socializing takes place at or near the small but effective fifteen-foot
bar, with Friday and Saturday being the best nights for singles. At
the tables are paper and Crayola crayons for drawing pictures
which Damian, the manager, tends to frame and hang on the walls.
Nanny Rose has a wood-burning fireplace and an elegant but comfortable mood.

| | |
|---|---|
| AVERAGE DRINK | $2.50 and up |
| COVER OR MINIMUM | None |
| PLASTIC | AE, CB, DC, MC, V |
| CROWD | Eclectic—all types, all ages, some celebrities |
| DRESS | Proper attire |
| OPEN | Monday through Thursday noon to 2 A.M.; Friday noon to 3 A.M.; Saturday and Sunday 11:30 A.M. to 3 A.M. |
| FOOD | Lunch, dinner, weekend brunch; a la carte dinner entrées range from $4.50 to $9.95 |

**O'Neals' Baloon**                                 *Restaurant/Pub*
48 W. 63rd Street (at Columbus Ave.)
(212) 399-2353

Walking in here after work is like entering a big, casual room full of
buddies. Everyone's friendly. There's a big bar area in the front and
a separate dining area. Many singles.

| | |
|---|---|
| AVERAGE DRINK | $2.50 to $2.75 |
| COVER OR MINIMUM | None |
| PLASTIC | AE, CB, DC, MC, V |
| CROWD | TV people, Lincoln Center people, musicians, artists, and others who work in the area; all ages |
| DRESS | Casual |
| OPEN | Sunday through Friday, 11:30 A.M. to midnight; Saturday 11 A.M. to midnight |

FOOD  American menu with dinner entrées going
from about $4.25 to $12.95

**Palsson's**                                    *Restaurant/Cabaret*
158 W. 72nd Street (between Columbus Ave. and Broadway)
(212) 362-2590

The twenty-two-foot downstairs bar is a popular nightspot. Upstairs you can enjoy all types of music, including some top name singers.

| | |
|---|---|
| AVERAGE DRINK | $2.50 |
| COVER OR MINIMUM | $4.00 with a $5.00 minimum |
| PLASTIC | AE, CB, DC, MC, V |
| CROWD | Theater and entertainment people in their 30s |
| DRESS | Casual |
| OPEN | The downstairs bar is open from 4 P.M. to 4 A.M.; upstairs 8 P.M. to 4 A.M. |
| FOOD | Continental menu from 5 P.M. to 4 A.M.; an average dinner is $9.00 |

**Piano Bar**                          *Piano Bar/Spontaneous Showcase*
Broadway and 68th St.
(212) 787-2501

A classic New York theater-oriented nightclub without the formality of a cabaret. Local talent gets up to entertain.

| | |
|---|---|
| AVERAGE DRINK | $2.50 |
| COVER OR MINIMUM | None |
| PLASTIC | AE, DC, MC, V |
| CROWD | Broadway actors, theatergoers, and a West Side neighborhood crowd |
| DRESS | Casual |
| OPEN | Seven nights, 9 P.M. to 2 A.M. |
| FOOD | Pub-style light dinners; $7.49 to $11.50 |

**Rollerrock**                                          *Disco/Roller*
3330 Broadway (between 134th and 135th Sts.)
(212) 926-1136

Known for their sound system and good wooden floor. Singles,
couples, families.

| | |
|---|---|
| AVERAGE DRINK | No alcohol |
| COVER OR MINIMUM | $5.00 plus $1.00 for skates |
| PLASTIC | None |
| CROWD | Neighborhood people and good skaters from all over |
| DRESS | Comfortable |
| OPEN | Call for times; closed Monday |
| FOOD | None |
| SPECIALS | Sunday is Two-For-One—call for details and other specials |

**Rúelles**                                          *Restaurant/Bar*
Columbus Avenue (at 75th St.)
(212) 799-5100

The excitement of the single life can be thoroughly explored in this
huge, plush two-story room. Forget about the homey coziness or
the casual friendliness of many New York bars—this one is pure
flash, pure drama. All the time. The octagonal bar, smack dab in
the center of the ground floor, is the focal point of the room with an
enormous crystal chandelier and many singles. A brass railing sepa-
rates the bar from the dining area and it's a good thing, too—the
bar often gets so crowded that latecomers must wait on line outside. Upstairs is more dining and another, smaller bar. The whole
room has that "contemporary plush" look that only track lighting,
gilt framed mirrors, old pictures of nudes on the walls, and slow-
spinning ceiling fans can provide.

| | |
|---|---|
| AVERAGE DRINK | $2.75 |

| | |
|---|---|
| COVER OR MINIMUM | $8.00 per person at the tables; if it gets crowded on weekends there may be a $10.00 door fee after 10 P.M. (If that happens, don't worry—it includes two drinks) |
| PLASTIC | AE, CB, DC, MC, V |
| CROWD | People from all over, celebrities, bankers, nurses, everyone; all ages |
| DRESS | Fashionable, chic; many jackets, many designer jeans |
| OPEN | Seven days, 11 A.M. to 2 A.M. |
| FOOD | American/Continental/nouvelle cuisine; lunch and dinner; average a la carte dinner entrée is $13.00 |

### Shelter                                         *New York Bar*
2180 Broadway (at 77th St.)
(212) 362-4360

Cozy art deco atmosphere with a big fifty-foot bar and an intimate dining area in the back. Friendly staff, many singles, and lots of socializing.

| | |
|---|---|
| AVERAGE DRINK | $2.25 |
| COVER OR MINIMUM | None |
| PLASTIC | AE, DC, MC, V |
| CROWD | Neighborhood people from 22 to 35 |
| DRESS | Casual |
| OPEN | Seven days from 11:30 A.M. to 4 A.M. |
| FOOD | Dine in a glass enclosed outdoor café; New York menu; sliced steak is $6.95 at dinner, and shell steak is $10.95 |
| SPECIALS | Free special drinks at lunch |

### Sweetwaters                       *Cabaret/Restaurant/Bar*
170 Amsterdam Avenue (behind Lincoln Center)
(212) 873-4100

The bar seats fifty, the café thirty, and the dining room 150 with about 30 percent singles, 70 percent couples. Music nightly—a variety of styles—begins at 11 P.M. during the week and at midnight on weekends.

|  |  |
|---|---|
| AVERAGE DRINK | $2.75 |
| COVER OR MINIMUM | No cover at the bar; $7.00 minimum in the restaurant; $7.00 entertainment charge |
| PLASTIC | AE, CB, DC, MC, V |
| CROWD | Professional people and business men and women; most singles are in their mid 20s |
| DRESS | Jackets preferred but not required; must be proper |
| OPEN | Seven days: Monday through Friday noon to 4 A.M.; weekends 11:30 to 4 A.M. |
| FOOD | Italian/Continental; brunch on weekends with live music; a la carte dinner entrées range from $8.00 to $15.00 |

**Teacher's and Teacher's Too**                    *Restaurant/Bar*
2249 Broadway (between 80th and 81st Sts.)
(212) 787-3500
2271 Broadway (between 81st and 82nd Sts.)
(212) 362-4900

Did you have a crush on your eighth grade math teacher? Come to Teacher's to relive those days—and develop a crush on a math teacher your own age! The many singles can be found at the bar, and the "schoolhouse decor" (blackboards for menus and schoolhouse lamps) is a great conversation starter. Talking in class may have been grounds for detention back then, but now it's a whole different carton of crayons. With the soft lighting and informal mood, you'd be happy to stay after school. And your mother won't even get mad! Isn't grown-up life wonderful?

|  |  |
|---|---|
| AVERAGE DRINK | $2.25 and up |
| COVER OR MINIMUM | None |
| PLASTIC | AE, CB, DC, MC, V |
| CROWD | Neighborhood people and others; ages 21 to 68 |

|       | DRESS | Informal |
| OPEN | Sunday through Thursday 11 A.M. to 1 A.M.; Friday and Saturday 11 A.M. to 2 A.M. |
| FOOD | Continental with Thai specialties; lunch and dinner served, with a la carte dinner entrées ranging from $4.95 to $11.95 |

### Ticker's                                    *Restaurant/Bar*
320 Columbus Avenue (at 75th St.)
(212) 799-4073

A cozy, polished, romantic atmosphere with a small bar and some singles. Live jazz Friday and Saturday from 10:30 P.M.

| | |
|---|---|
| AVERAGE DRINK | $2.00 |
| COVER OR MINIMUM | None |
| PLASTIC | AE, DC, MC, V |
| CROWD | All types, from 25 up |
| DRESS | Casual |
| OPEN | Friday and Saturday 11:30 A.M. to 3 A.M.; Sunday through Thursday 11:30 A.M. to midnight |
| FOOD | Fish, meat; average dinner ranges from $7.95 to $13.95 |

### Trax                                        *Rock Club*
100 W. 72nd Street (at Columbus Ave.)
(212) 799-1448

Live music, big name bands, video, and d.j. Call or check the paper for schedules. Singles, couples, and dancing.

| | |
|---|---|
| AVERAGE DRINK | $2.50 |
| COVER OR MINIMUM | Varies with the group |
| PLASTIC | AE, DC, MC, V |
| CROWD | Rock and roll lovers in their mid to late 20s |
| DRESS | Casual |
| OPEN | Monday through Saturday 9 P.M. to 4 A.M.; closed Sunday |
| FOOD | None |

**The West End Café**                    *Restaurant/Bar/Jazz Room*
2911 Broadway (at W. 114th St., near Columbia University)
(212) 666-8750

Sit at the 120-foot bar with a large number of other single people,
and enjoy the nightly jazz.

| | |
|---|---|
| AVERAGE DRINK | $2.00 |
| COVER OR MINIMUM | None |
| PLASTIC | AE, MC, V |
| CROWD | Students, some faculty |
| DRESS | Casual |
| OPEN | Seven days, 9 A.M. to 4 A.M. |
| FOOD | 80¢ for a slice of pizza, $5.95 for New York steak |
| SPECIALS | Happy Hour 5 to 8 P.M., Monday through Friday; Monday is "Beer Night," Wednesday is "Rum Night," and Thursday is "Tequila Night"—Cheers! |

---

## Midtown East

FROM 34TH TO 59TH STREETS, EAST OF FIFTH AVENUE

---

**Applause**                              *Restaurant/Club*
40th Street and Lexington Avenue
(212) 687-7267

Couples and singles enjoy the live piano/vocal from Wednesday
through Saturday, and the nightly entertainment by the singing
waitpeople. A small, Broadway-oriented room with colored stage
lighting, Broadway posters, and a cozy bar which seats fifteen plus
standing.

| | |
|---|---|
| AVERAGE DRINK | $2.00 |
| COVER OR MINIMUM | $5.00 at tables on Saturdays |
| PLASTIC | AE, DC, MC, V |
| CROWD | All ages, all types |

|      |      |
|------|------|
| DRESS | Casual, though many men wear jackets |
| OPEN | 11:30 A.M. till 1 A.M. during the week, till 2 A.M. Friday and Saturday; closed Sunday |
| FOOD | American and Continental menu till 11 P.M.; dinner prices range from $4.75 to $12.95 |

**Astor's**                                *Cocktail Lounge with Dancing*
(at the St. Regis Sheraton)
2 E. 55th Street (at Fifth Ave.)
(212) 753-4500 X 369

Sophisticated turn-of-the-century bar with a nice, no-hassle atmosphere. Chic but comfortable. Happy Hour with piano is from 5:30 to 8:30 P.M. Live dance music from 9 P.M. to 1 A.M. Tuesday, Wednesday and Thursday and till 2 A.M. on Friday and Saturday. Mostly couples at night.

|      |      |
|------|------|
| AVERAGE DRINK | $3.50 |
| COVER OR MINIMUM | None |
| PLASTIC | AE, CB, DC, MC, V |
| CROWD | Big after-work cocktail crowd with many people from the fashionable Fifth Avenue area; ages 20 to 40 |
| DRESS | Proper attire |
| OPEN | Tuesday, Wednesday, Thursday from 5 P.M. to 1 A.M.; Friday from 5 P.M. to 2 A.M.; Saturday 6 P.M. to 2 A.M.; closed Sunday and Monday |
| FOOD | Menu available in the evenings |
| SPECIALS | Happy Hour 5 to 7 P.M. |

**Billymunk**                                          *Restaurant/Bar*
302 E. 45th Street (near Second Ave.)
(212) 697-2470

The bar in this old-style pub may have up to 70 percent singles at times, but it's not a meat market atmosphere. There are many couples, and lots of good eating. Bar seats twenty, restaurant seats 300.

| | |
|---|---|
| AVERAGE DRINK | $2.00 |
| COVER OR MINIMUM | None |
| PLASTIC | AE, CB, DC, MC, V |
| CROWD | Big after-work crowd from 3-M and other big companies nearby; ages 19 to 45 |
| DRESS | Neat and casual |
| OPEN | Monday through Friday 11 A.M. to 4 A.M. |
| FOOD | American/Continental, with dinner prices ranging from $4.00 to $12.75 |
| SPECIALS | Free hors d'oeuvres with drinks after work |

## The Blueprint                              *Restaurant/Bar*
Park Avenue (at 40th St.)
(212) 684-4500

A large, sunken four-sided bar surrounded by leather booths provides a relaxed but sophisticated backdrop for the many singles
who gather here after work. A live dance band entertains nightly
from 6:30 to 11:30, making cocktail hour an easy time to meet new
people. The dining area, in another room, is mainly couples.

| | |
|---|---|
| AVERAGE DRINK | $3.00 |
| COVER OR MINIMUM | None |
| PLASTIC | AE, CB, DC, MC, V |
| CROWD | Business people, aged 35 to 65 |
| DRESS | Casual, but many men wear jackets |
| OPEN | Monday through Friday from lunchtime on; closed weekends |
| FOOD | Italian/American; an average dinner is about $10.00 or $11.00 |
| SPECIALS | Hot hors d'oeuvres at cocktail time |

## The Cattleman                              *Piano Bar/Restaurant*
5 E. 45th Street (between Madison and Fifth Aves.)
(212) MO 1-1200

A real saloon, done up in turn-of-the-century grand hotel style. The
friendly atmosphere is quite conducive to spontaneous conversation, especially at the bar. Lots and lots of singles.

| | |
|---|---|
| AVERAGE DRINK | $2.75 |
| COVER OR MINIMUM | None |
| PLASTIC | AE, DC, MC, V |
| CROWD | Professionals from 28 up |
| DRESS | Jackets worn but not required |
| OPEN | The bar opens daily at 5 P.M. and closes at 11 P.M. Monday through Friday and at 11:30 P.M. on Saturday |
| FOOD | Steak-style meals; dinner ranges from $10.00 to $20.00; lunch available |
| SPECIALS | Complimentary deli counter, free shrimp, and Texas barbecue; call for details |

**Central Parc**                                        *Restaurant/Bar*
Second Avenue (at 54th St.)
(212) 838-6360

The perfect place to go if you're on the town all by yourself. The room is comfortable and homey with that "wood and plants" look, and the crowd is casually sociable. The bar is medium-sized and friendly, with lots of standing room. When hunger strikes you can sit in the glass enclosed sidewalk café and watch people walk by. Many singles, some couples, and no hassles.

| | |
|---|---|
| AVERAGE DRINK | $2.00 |
| COVER OR MINIMUM | $1.50 at the tables |
| PLASTIC | AE, MC, V |
| CROWD | Young professionals, advertising and magazine people; age range 25 to 55 |
| DRESS | Informal, but many men wear jackets |
| OPEN | Seven days, noon to 4 A.M. |
| FOOD | American/Continental, lunch and dinner; weekend brunch available from noon to 5 P.M.; average dinner price is $8.95 |

**Charlie Brown**                                          *Bar/Restaurant*
45th Street in the Pan Am Building (between Lexington and
Vanderbilt Aves.)
(212) 661-2520

An English pub-type room that's jammed after work with singles,
couples, and executives trying to cool out after a hard day. Lots of
socializing.

| | |
|---|---|
| AVERAGE DRINK | $2.50 |
| COVER OR MINIMUM | None |
| PLASTIC | AE, CB, DC, MC, V |
| CROWD | Commuters, executives, secretaries, advertising people in the 25 to 55 age range |
| DRESS | Neat, casual |
| OPEN | Monday through Friday, 11:30 A.M. to midnight |
| FOOD | Restaurant with full menu; dinner prices range from $10.95 to $15.95 |

**Dustins**                                                *Bar/Restaurant*
988 Second Avenue (between 52nd and 53rd Sts.)
(212) 759-9055

Dustins has a large bar which gets loud and lively at times and is
always friendly. Many couples, but a fair share of singles too.

| | |
|---|---|
| AVERAGE DRINK | $2.50 |
| COVER OR MINIMUM | None at the bar |
| PLASTIC | AE, CB, DC, MC, V |
| CROWD | An after-work crowd, from 25 to 40 |
| DRESS | Many suits, but not required |
| OPEN | Seven days, noon to 2, 3, or 4 A.M. |
| FOOD | Seafood; dinners range from $6.95 to $10.00 |
| SPECIALS | Homemade potato chips at the bar, plus free hors d'oeuvres from 5:30 to 7 P.M., Monday through Friday |

**Ferdi's Sidewalk Café**                               *Restaurant/Bar*
765 First Avenue (between 43rd and 44th Sts., at the UN Plaza)
(212) 661-4160

Ferdi's cuts through all nationalities, age groups, and marital
statuses. The twenty-two-foot bar is for everyone, not primarily
singles.

| | |
|---|---|
| AVERAGE DRINK | $2.40 |
| COVER OR MINIMUM | None |
| PLASTIC | AE, CB, DC, V |
| CROWD | United Nations people |
| DRESS | Casual, though the after-work people wear jackets and ties |
| OPEN | Monday through Friday, 11:30 A.M. to 11 P.M. |
| FOOD | Italian/American/Continental; a la carte dinner served till 7 P.M., with entrées ranging from $4.25 to $8.50 |

**Freddy's**                                   *Restaurant/Bar/Cabaret*
308 E. 49th Street (between First and Second Aves.)
(212) 888-1633

More show-oriented than singles-oriented. Single people feel comfortable in groups at tables. Two shows nightly, usually singers or
comedians.

| | |
|---|---|
| AVERAGE DRINK | $2.50 |
| COVER OR MINIMUM | $6.00 with a two drink minimum |
| PLASTIC | AE, DC, MC, V |
| CROWD | Mixed, including theater people in their 20s and 30s |
| DRESS | Casual |
| OPEN | Seven nights, from 6 P.M. to 2 A.M. |
| FOOD | Dinner till midnight; a la carte dinner entrées on their Northern Italian menu range from $8.95 to $14.95 |

**Goose and Gherkin**                                    *Restaurant/Lounge*
251 E. 50th Street (between Second and Third Aves.)
(212) 371-4636

The bar seats seventeen plus tables, but the owner stresses that this
is not a pickup place. However. In the evening at cocktail hour,
singles are made to feel comfortable—the bartenders are happy to
introduce people, and the owner herself will try to introduce single
ladies to single gentlemen and make them feel at home.

| | |
|---|---|
| AVERAGE DRINK | $2.50 |
| COVER OR MINIMUM | Varies |
| PLASTIC | AE, MC |
| CROWD | Professional people from 23 to 40 |
| DRESS | Casual |
| OPEN | Seven days, from lunch to 3 or 4 A.M. |
| FOOD | American with Continental touches; dinner ranges from $5.00 to $14.50 |

**Hobeau's**                                              *Restaurant/Bar*
963 First Avenue (at 53rd St.)
(212) 421-2888

The sea shanty atmosphere and nautical decor provide a fun backdrop for the nightly socializing at the bar. Lots of singles after
8 P.M.

| | |
|---|---|
| AVERAGE DRINK | $1.75 |
| COVER OR MINIMUM | None |
| PLASTIC | AE, DC, MC, V |
| CROWD | Neighborhood professionals in their 20s, 30s, and 40s |
| DRESS | Anything |
| OPEN | Seven days, 11:30 A.M. to 4 A.M. |
| FOOD | Fish, of course, plus steaks and hamburgers; dinner is $4.25 to $7.95 |
| SPECIALS | After midnight all drinks are $1.25 |

**J.B. Tipton**                                              *Restaurant/Bar*
932 Second Avenue (between 49th and 50th Sts.)
(212) 759-7800

A large, two-level room with a fifty-five-foot drinking bar on the
first floor and a brick and brass atmosphere. About 60 percent
singles.

|                    |                                                    |
| ------------------ | -------------------------------------------------- |
| AVERAGE DRINK      | $2.75                                              |
| COVER OR MINIMUM   | None                                               |
| PLASTIC            | AE, CB, MC, V                                      |
| CROWD              | Professionals, business people from 30 up          |
| DRESS              | Jackets                                            |
| OPEN               | Seven days, 11:30 A.M. to midnight                 |
| FOOD               | Continental menu, with dinner entrées ranging from $8.50 to $14.95 |

**The King Cole Room**                               *Restaurant/Nightclub*
(at the St. Regis Sheraton)
2 E. 55th Street (at Fifth Ave.)
(212) 872-6140

Elegant room with three tiers, a gorgeous, massive chandelier, and
a Maxfield Parrish mural and paintings decorating the walls. Musical revues nightly featuring Broadway talent—weeknights at
9:30 P.M., Friday and Saturday at 9:30 and 11:30. Singles would do
best at the business lunch—it's mostly couples at night. Call for
reservations.

|                    |                                                    |
| ------------------ | -------------------------------------------------- |
| AVERAGE DRINK      | $5.00                                              |
| COVER OR MINIMUM   | No minimum; entertainment charge $7.50 to $12.50   |
| PLASTIC            | AE, CB, DC, MC, V                                  |
| CROWD              | Professionals and executives from 30 to 50         |
| DRESS              | Jacket and tie required                            |
| OPEN               | Monday through Thursday, 7 A.M. to 11-ish; Friday and Saturday 7 A.M. to midnight-ish; Sunday noon till 11 or 12 |

| | |
|---|---|
| FOOD | Continental; breakfast, lunch, dinner, late supper, weekend brunch; an average dinner might be $40.00; times vary, so call first |

**Kitty Hawk**                                                   *Bar/Restaurant*
565 Third Avenue (near 37th St.)
(212) 661-7406

A warm and friendly room with quiet, casual conversation. Sit at the large bar in the front, stand by the big window looking out onto Third Avenue, or enjoy the dining room in the back. The many singles that come here are very sociable.

| | |
|---|---|
| AVERAGE DRINK | $2.10 |
| COVER OR MINIMUM | None |
| PLASTIC | AE, CB, DC, MC, V |
| CROWD | Neighborhood people, young professionals |
| DRESS | Casual |
| OPEN | Seven days, 11:30 A.M. to closing |
| FOOD | Dinner entrées run about $7.95; lunch and brunch also available; American menu |

**Michael Phillips**                                             *Restaurant/Bar*
994 First Avenue (between 54th and 55th Sts.)
(212) 888-0018

A fresh, light, breezy mood is further enhanced when the large paneled front doors are opened in spring and summer. The big thirty-foot bar was hand-carved in St. Louis in 1879, and the piano/vocal on Thursday, Friday, and Saturday adds the finishing elegant touch. Mostly couples in the dining room, singles and couples at the bar.

| | |
|---|---|
| AVERAGE DRINK | $3.00 at night; the bartender pours only top brands |
| COVER OR MINIMUM | Two drink minimum at tables during slow hours, no drinking at tables during peak hours |

| PLASTIC | AE, CB, DC, MC, V |
|---|---|
| CROWD | The early evening brings in an older Sutton Place crowd, and later they are joined by the young professional set |
| DRESS | Jackets preferred |
| OPEN | Seven days, noon to whenever |
| FOOD | Continental leaning toward nouvelle cuisine; a la carte dinner entrées run from $10.00 to $16.50 |

**Mimi's**                                              *Restaurant/Piano Bar*
984 Second Avenue (at 52nd St.)
(212) 688-4692

If you're going alone, be sure to get there early enough to get a seat at the piano bar next to Jackson—the magic man who can play any tune in any key. All you do is ask for the mike, start singing, and Jackson will be right with you from 9:30 P.M. nightly. The mood is casual elegance, with Tiffany lamps, stained glass, and a glass-enclosed sidewalk café. Singles, couples. But very social.

| AVERAGE DRINK | $3.00 |
|---|---|
| COVER OR MINIMUM | None |
| PLASTIC | AE, CB, DC, MC, V |
| CROWD | Professionals and business people in the 30 to 50 age group; some good singers, too |
| DRESS | Casual to elegant |
| OPEN | Seven days, noon to 4 A.M. |
| FOOD | Italian menu with dinner entrées from $7.25 to $10.95 |

**Monkey Bar**                                              *Lounge*
60 E. 54th Street (in the Elysee Hotel between
Madison and Park Aves.)
(212) 753-1066

A pianist sets the cozy, intimate mood Monday through Friday from 5:30 to 7:30, and there's continuous entertainment from

9:30 P.M. to 3 A.M. Reservations are required. Many couples, some singles.

| | |
|---|---|
| AVERAGE DRINK | $4.50 at showtime |
| COVER OR MINIMUM | $5.00 at showtime, with a $7.50 minimum |
| PLASTIC | AE, CB, DC, MC, V |
| CROWD | Mostly travelers, business people and tourists from 25 up |
| DRESS | Jackets required |
| OPEN | Monday through Saturday from 5:30 |
| FOOD | Hors d'oeuvres with cocktails |

**O'Lunney's**                                   *Country-Western Club*
915 Second Avenue (between 48th and 49th Sts.)
(212) 751-5470

Country music nightly and a good time. Couples and singles feel equally at home.

| | |
|---|---|
| AVERAGE DRINK | $2.50 to $3.50 |
| COVER OR MINIMUM | None at the bar; $3.00 cover and $3.00 minimum at tables |
| PLASTIC | AE, DC, MC, V |
| CROWD | Very mixed, from 19 on up |
| DRESS | Casual |
| OPEN | Monday through Friday from noon; Saturday and Sunday from 7:30 or 8 P.M. |
| FOOD | American and country; dinner entrées range from $3.50 to $10.95 |

**Onde's**                                                *Supperclub*
160 E. 48th Street (between Lexington and Third Aves.)
(212) 752-0200

Elegant intimacy, with candlelight and suede walls. The singles that enjoy the piano bar/cocktail lounge after work find an easy, non-hassled atmosphere. Evenings it's mainly couples, with a dance band later on.

| | |
|---|---|
| AVERAGE DRINK | $2.75 |
| COVER OR MINIMUM | None |
| PLASTIC | AE, CB, DC, MC, V |
| CROWD | Executives, office people; in general, a sophisticated after-work crowd |
| DRESS | Jackets required |
| OPEN | Monday through Saturday 11 A.M. to 2 A.M. |
| FOOD | Italian/Continental; a la carte dinner entrées go from $10.75 up |

## P. J. Clarke's                                      *Restaurant/Bar*
915 Third Avenue (near 55th St.)
(212) PL 9-1650

It looks like your typical turn-of-the-century Irish pub. But it's very single, very sociable, and gets very crowded. Go there to party, to get some exciting new phone numbers, or to leave the office far, far behind. Don't go there to write in your diary or slowly unwind. The total capacity is about 200, divided among two rooms—a dining room and a separate bar.

| | |
|---|---|
| AVERAGE DRINK | $2.50 |
| COVER OR MINIMUM | $3.00 minimum per person in the back room |
| PLASTIC | None |
| CROWD | Artists, actors, advertising people from 18 to 80 |
| DRESS | From three-piece suits to designer jeans |
| OPEN | Seven days, 11 A.M. to 4 A.M. |
| FOOD | American food, lunch and dinner; an a la carte dinner might run you $15.00 |

## Paparazzi                                      *Restaurant/Bar*
964 Second Avenue (near 51st St.)
(212) 759-7676

Large bar area, a fair share of singles, and a casual, sociable atmosphere. Drop by for a drink, to unwind, or to chat with some interesting new people.

| | |
|---|---|
| AVERAGE DRINK | $2.00 |
| COVER OR MINIMUM | None |
| PLASTIC | CB, DC, MC, V |
| CROWD | All types, mainly 20 to 35 |
| DRESS | Neat and casual |
| OPEN | Seven days, 11:30 A.M. to 2 A.M. |
| FOOD | Italian; an average dinner is $6.95 to $7.95 |
| SPECIALS | Happy Hour daily from 4 to 7 P.M. |

## Parnell's Tavern                                         *Pub*

350 E. 53rd Street (between First and Second Aves.)
(212) 355-9706

It's about 50/50 couples to singles, with socializing, eating, and drinking in equal measure. Small and cozy, with pub/antique decor, Parnell's has a refreshingly friendly atmosphere.

| | |
|---|---|
| AVERAGE DRINK | $2.00 |
| COVER OR MINIMUM | None |
| PLASTIC | AE, MC, V |
| CROWD | Mixed bag, 20 to 80 |
| DRESS | Casual |
| OPEN | Seven days, 10 A.M. to 4 A.M. |
| FOOD | American food, lunch and dinner; average dinner price, $5.95 |

## Peartree's                                         *Restaurant/Bar*

1 Mitchell Place, on First Avenue (at 49th St.)
(212) 832-8558

A crisp, smart room with that late 1940's art deco look and interesting photographs on the walls. The crowd is sophisticated but sociable in a laidback way. There are many singles at the bar, and it's easy to start up a low-key conversation about politics, the economy, or other noteworthy news. (A short elevator ride away is "Top of the Tower." Though it is mainly couples, you might want to zip up there after 5 P.M. just to see the view. At twenty-six stories up, the scenery can be quite impressive.)

| | |
|---|---|
| AVERAGE DRINK | $2.50 |
| COVER OR MINIMUM | None |
| PLASTIC | AE, CB, DC |
| CROWD | International UN crowd, brokers, network sports people, and the Beekman and Sutton Place regulars; ages 28 to 45 |
| DRESS | Jackets preferred; jeans are out of place |
| OPEN | Seven days, noon to 4 A.M. |
| FOOD | Nouvelle American; dinners range from $8.00 to $14.00 |
| SPECIALS | "No gimmicks," says the manager with pride |

**Rumm's Tavern**                                    *Restaurant/Bar*
152 E. 46th Street (between Third and Lexington Aves.)
(212) 599-2021

Spanking new, with white wood, knotty pine, and large crowds of singles and couples. Sing-along piano Monday through Friday evenings.

| | |
|---|---|
| AVERAGE DRINK | $2.00 |
| COVER OR MINIMUM | None |
| PLASTIC | AE, CB, DC, MC, V |
| CROWD | Oil industry people, advertising, radio and TV executives, and other professionals from 25 to 35 |
| DRESS | Neat but casual |
| OPEN | Monday through Friday from lunch to 3 A.M. |
| FOOD | American menu; dinner ranges from $2.50 to $13.00 |

**St. Regis Lounge**                                 *Cocktail Lounge*
(at the St. Regis Sheraton)
2 E. 55th Street (at Fifth Ave.)
(212) 753-4500

Small and elegant with a private, drawing room atmosphere. Singles fit in better at cocktail time. Mostly couples at night.

72                                                   *Places to Go*

| | |
|---|---|
| AVERAGE DRINK | $4.00 to $4.75 |
| COVER OR MINIMUM | None |
| PLASTIC | AE, CB, DC, MC, V |
| CROWD | Professionals and executives from 30 to 50; many travelers |
| DRESS | Jackets preferred |
| OPEN | Monday through Saturday 11 A.M. to 2 A.M.; Sunday noon to 1 A.M. |
| FOOD | Luncheon Monday through Friday noon to 2:30 P.M.; $10.00 to $20.00 |

**Singles**                                            *Restaurant/Bar*
951 First Avenue (between 52nd and 53rd Sts.)
(212) 486-9832

Small and intimate, many singles, some couples. Dancing on weekends at midnight to recorded music with a d.j.

| | |
|---|---|
| AVERAGE DRINK | $1.75 |
| COVER OR MINIMUM | None |
| PLASTIC | AE, CB, MC, V |
| CROWD | All kinds of people from 25 to 35 |
| DRESS | Casual |
| OPEN | Seven days, 11 A.M. to 4 A.M. |
| FOOD | Seafood and other American dishes; sole is $7.95, filet mignon $11.95 |
| SPECIALS | Two-for-one daily from 11 A.M. to 7 P.M. |

**Starbuck's**                      *Restaurant/Disco and Then Some*
151 E. 45th Street (between Third and Lexington Aves.)
(212) 697-5544

Each of the four floors holds different surprises! You may ask some nice stranger to hold your beer while you go down the slide from the fourth to the third floor, or you may prefer the safety of exploring any number of their bars or dance areas. In your wanderings through this huge place with its campy decor (paintings of trucks, bales of hay, a pool table and more), you can usually stumble across live country-western or disco music on the first and third floors

(Wednesday through Saturday). And you can always stumble across other singles!

| | |
|---|---|
| AVERAGE DRINK | $3.00 |
| COVER OR MINIMUM | $5.00 |
| PLASTIC | AE, DC |
| CROWD | All types of people from 23 to 45 |
| DRESS | Neat and casual; some slacks with collared shirts, some business suits |
| OPEN | Monday through Saturday, noon to 4 A.M.; closed Sunday |
| FOOD | American/Continental, with dinner running you from $6.95 to $12.00 |

## Suspenders                                    *Pub/Bar*
700 Second Avenue (at 38th St.)
(212) 684-9410

Cute, cozy room with lots of wood. Many singles, lots of socializing, but not hard-hitting.

| | |
|---|---|
| AVERAGE DRINK | $1.50 to $2.00 |
| COVER OR MINIMUM | None |
| PLASTIC | None |
| CROWD | Neighborhood people, nurses, students, secretaries, firemen, policemen, business people; 20s to mid 40s |
| DRESS | Casual |
| OPEN | Seven days, 11 A.M. to 4 A.M. |
| FOOD | American—burgers to steaks; dinner from $2.25 to $9.95 |
| SPECIALS | Happy Hour Monday through Thursday, 5 to 7 P.M. |

## Top of the Tower

See Peartree's, page 71.

**Wylie's** *Restaurant/Bar*
891 First Avenue (at 50th St.)
(212) 751-0700

Lots of casual, old wood gives this pub a homey, laidback atmosphere. The bar seats about twenty singles and couples, and is
separate from the dining area.

| | |
|---|---|
| AVERAGE DRINK | $2.50 |
| COVER OR MINIMUM | None |
| PLASTIC | AE, CB, DC, MC, V |
| CROWD | Business people of all ages |
| DRESS | Casual |
| OPEN | Seven days, 10:30 A.M. to 1 A.M. |
| FOOD | American barbeque dinners go from $9.95; lunch available, too |

---

## Midtown West

FROM 34TH TO 59TH STREETS, WEST OF FIFTH AVENUE

---

**The Algonquin lounges** *Lounges in the Famous Hotel*
59 W. 44th Street (between Fifth Ave. and Ave. of the Americas)
(212) 840-6800

If you've been in business for seventy-five years, you must be doing
something right. The Algonquin is an exciting, busy, bustling place
with complimentary hors d'oeuvres at cocktail time and a piano
bar. Choose from "The Lounge" with its cocktail tables (mainly
groups rather than people alone), or the tiny, cozy "Blue Room."
While these are not pickup bars, many singles feel comfortable in
the warm, friendly atmosphere.

| | |
|---|---|
| AVERAGE DRINK | $2.75 |
| COVER OR MINIMUM | $1.00 |
| PLASTIC | AE, CB, DC, MC, V |
| CROWD | Highly sophisticated; all ages |
| DRESS | Jacket and tie; tie not required on Sunday |

<table>
<tr><td>OPEN</td><td>Seven days, with at least one room open at 7:30 A.M.; closing time, 12:30 A.M.; check for possible variances from room to room</td></tr>
<tr><td>FOOD</td><td>Menus available in the nearby "Oak Room," with a la carte dinner entrées starting at $15.50, and in the "Rose Room" (adjoining "The Lounge") from $20.00</td></tr>
</table>

## Barbizon Plaza Library                                   *Lounge/Disco*
106 Central Park South (tell the cab driver 59th St. and
Ave. of the Americas)
(212) 247-7000 and ask for the Library

A chic, sophisticated lounge with a small dance floor, large bar, and lots of nice singles. A live d.j. spins disco, rock and roll, and new wave music but you're still able to talk. Friendly atmosphere.

<table>
<tr><td>AVERAGE DRINK</td><td>$3.75</td></tr>
<tr><td>COVER OR MINIMUM</td><td>$10.00 on Saturday which includes two drinks</td></tr>
<tr><td>PLASTIC</td><td>AE</td></tr>
<tr><td>CROWD</td><td>The age span is from 25 to 50ish; there are regulars, and some out-of-towners</td></tr>
<tr><td>DRESS</td><td>No denims of any kind; gentlemen must wear jackets</td></tr>
<tr><td>OPEN</td><td>Seven nights: Monday through Friday 4:30 P.M. to 3 A.M.; Saturday and Sunday 9 P.M. to 3 A.M.</td></tr>
<tr><td>FOOD</td><td>None</td></tr>
</table>

## Bond International Casino                          *Concerts/Dancing*
1526 Broadway (at 45th St.)
(212) 944-5880

If you love a party, here's your place. It holds 4000 people and they all either listen or dance to the live music. Rock, pop, new wave, and disco, with art deco surroundings.

| | |
|---|---|
| AVERAGE DRINK | $3.50 |
| COVER OR MINIMUM | From $6.00 to $15.00 |
| PLASTIC | None |
| CROWD | Professionals and others from 18 to 25 |
| DRESS | Some jeans, some more dressed up |
| OPEN | Wednesday through Saturday, sometimes Sunday; call for times |
| FOOD | None |

**Café Un Deux Trois**                                    *Restaurant/Bar*
123 W. 44th Street (between Broadway and
Ave. of the Americas)
(212) 354-4148

If you've ever spent time in Paris' Montmartre cafés, you'll feel right at home here. Done up in the brasserie style of the 1920's, there are mosaics on the floor, murals on the walls, and old style café tables with wood chairs. The big bar has a brass rail at the bottom for your feet, and many many singles. The mood is low-keyed but sophisticated.

| | |
|---|---|
| AVERAGE DRINK | $3.00 to $3.50 |
| COVER OR MINIMUM | None |
| PLASTIC | AE, MC, V |
| CROWD | Actors, celebrities, Broadway people, models; all ages |
| DRESS | Casual |
| OPEN | Monday through Friday noon to 4:30 P.M. and 5:30 P.M. to 1 A.M.; Saturday noon to 1 A.M.; Sunday noon to midnight |
| FOOD | French with some Moroccan touches; lunch and dinner; average dinner might run you $14.00 to $18.00 including dessert and coffee |

**Caffé Fontana**                    *Continental Caffé/Piano Bar*
(at the Sheraton Centre Hotel)
Seventh Avenue (at 52nd St.)
(212) 581-1000

A cheery, open atmosphere with lots of green plants, a waterfall,
and a great view of Seventh Avenue. Piano bar with entertainment
nightly from 5 P.M. to 1 A.M. Couples and singles.

| | |
|---|---|
| AVERAGE DRINK | $3.50 and up |
| COVER OR MINIMUM | None |
| PLASTIC | AE, CB, DC, MC, V |
| CROWD | All types, all ages |
| DRESS | Neat |
| OPEN | Seven days, from 7 A.M. to 1:30 A.M.; bar from 10 A.M. |
| FOOD | Hot and cold delicacies and exotic coffees and teas; buffet luncheon is $10.75 |

**The Callback**                    *Piano Bar/Cabaret*
Eighth Avenue (at 45th St.)
(212) 581-0500

Intimate, relaxed piano bar with comedy acts at times.

| | |
|---|---|
| AVERAGE DRINK | $2.25 |
| COVER OR MINIMUM | $5.00 per person Friday and Saturday |
| PLASTIC | AE, DC, MC, V |
| CROWD | Eclectic crowd of all ages |
| DRESS | Casual |
| OPEN | 10:30 P.M. to 3 A.M., Tuesday or Wednesday through Saturday |
| FOOD | Light menu, with dinner ranging from $5.00 to $9.00 |

**Carnegie Tavern**                    *Restaurant/Bar/Piano Bar*
165 W. 56th Street (corner of Seventh Ave.)
(212) 757-9522

Not specifically a singles bar—but many singles do feel comfortable
here. The piano comes to life at 8 P.M. from Monday through Saturday. The room is dimly lit, cozy, and attractive, with an enclosed
sidewalk café. Reservations are recommended.

| | |
|---|---|
| AVERAGE DRINK | $2.50 |
| COVER OR MINIMUM | $7.95 from 8 to 10 P.M., and $5.95 from 10 P.M. to midnight |
| PLASTIC | AE, DC, MC, V |
| CROWD | Many TV and network executives and actors, celebrities, and professional people in their 30s |
| DRESS | Jackets are worn but not required |
| OPEN | 11:30 A.M. to 1 A.M.; closed Sunday; during July and August it's closed Saturday and Sunday |
| FOOD | American/Continental; dinner prices start at $7.95 from 8 to 10 P.M., and at $5.95 from 10 P.M. to midnight; lunch available from 11:30 A.M. to 4 P.M. |
| SPECIALS | Free hot hors d'oeuvres during cocktail hour from 4 to 8 P.M. |

**Charlies'**                              *Restaurant/Bar*
263 W. 45th Street (between Broadway and Eighth Ave.)
(212) 354-2911

Brick walls, blue and white checkered tablecloths and wood floors
make the room warm and casual. It seats 110 people plus a small
bar and cocktail tables. Sociability is the password here, with singles as well as some couples.

| | |
|---|---|
| AVERAGE DRINK | $1.75 |
| COVER OR MINIMUM | None |
| PLASTIC | AE, MC, V |

| CROWD | People who are either going to the theater or are in it; all ages |
|---|---|
| DRESS | Casual |
| OPEN | Seven days, 11:30 A.M. to 4 A.M. |
| FOOD | American menu, with "a little bit of everything," served from lunchtime to 1:30 A.M.; dinner entrées are about $6.00 to $7.95 |

## Chilie's                                        *Supperclub*
142 W. 44th Street (between Ave. of the Americas and Broadway)
(212) 840-1766

The big thirty-five-foot bar is where you'll find the singles that go to Chilie's, although there are many couples there, too. Live jazz and contemporary music.

| AVERAGE DRINK | $1.80 |
|---|---|
| COVER OR MINIMUM | $3.00 |
| PLASTIC | AE, CB, DC, MC, V |
| CROWD | Professional and business people in the 25 to 40 age range |
| DRESS | Casual |
| OPEN | Monday through Saturday, noon to 2 or 3 A.M. |
| FOOD | American/Mexican; dinners range from $5.95 to $11.50; lunch available |
| SPECIALS | Happy Hour from 4 to 6:30 P.M., Monday through Friday, with free hors d'oeuvres |

## Colbeh Club 56                          *Village-Type Nightclub*
304 W. 56th Street (off Eighth Ave.)
(212) 581-8496

Many couples, some singles. Bar seats fifteen plus standing, and the restaurant seats sixty-five. Live jazz Friday and Saturday. Talent showcase on Tuesday.

| | |
|---|---|
| AVERAGE DRINK | $1.75 |
| COVER OR MINIMUM | Saturday $3.00 with a two drink minimum |
| PLASTIC | AE, DC |
| CROWD | Theater and local people from 25 to 40 |
| DRESS | Casual |
| OPEN | Seven days, from noon to 2, 3, or 4 A.M. |
| FOOD | International and Continental cuisine; dinner entrées run from $7.00 to $14.50 |

**The Fives**                             *Restaurant/Bar*
555 W. 57th Street (between Tenth and Eleventh Aves.)
(212) 757-4303

A large, quiet place with a long bar and tables. Some couples, some singles. But the accent is on the show. Catch some well-known artists, or see a showcase of a vocalist on the way up. The entertainment schedule varies, so call first.

| | |
|---|---|
| AVERAGE DRINK | $2.00 |
| COVER OR MINIMUM | $3.00 to $5.00 |
| PLASTIC | AE, DC, MC, V |
| CROWD | Many CBS employees, in the 30 to 45 age bracket |
| DRESS | Casual |
| OPEN | Monday through Friday from 11 A.M. to midnight-ish |
| FOOD | Lunch and dinner; small meals or large entrées; dinner from $5.95 to $11.95 |

**High Roller**                                *Roller Disco*
617 W. 57th Street (between Eleventh and Twelfth Aves.)
(212) 247-1530

A large roller disco with live d.j. spinning discs. The ratio of singles to couples varies, but why not put on your skates and give it a try?

| | |
|---|---|
| AVERAGE DRINK | No liquor |
| COVER OR MINIMUM | $7.00 to $9.00 plus $3.00 skate rental |

| PLASTIC | None |
| CROWD | All types, all ages |
| DRESS | Anything |
| OPEN | Seven days; call for times |
| FOOD | Snacks |
| SPECIALS | Monday is 2-for-1 night; Sunday from 6 to 8 P.M. is Early Bird Special; call for other specials |

## Joe Allen                                   *Restaurant/Bar*
326 W. 46th Street (between Eighth and Ninth Aves.)
(212) 581-6464

A haven for theater-district singles and couples, the mood is laid-back and casual with brick walls, red and white checkered tablecloths, theater posters and sports pictures on the walls. It's like the ground floor of a brownstone, with two rooms—one for the bar area (which includes tables) and another for dining (or you can eat at the bar if you can't bear to leave it). A lovely skylight in the back adds to the mood.

| AVERAGE DRINK | $2.00 to $2.25 |
| COVER OR MINIMUM | None |
| PLASTIC | MC, V |
| CROWD | Working and nonworking actors and celebrities of all ages |
| DRESS | Casual |
| OPEN | Sunday, Monday, Tuesday, Thursday, and Friday from noon to 3 A.M.; Wednesday and Saturday from 11:30 A.M. to 3 A.M. |
| FOOD | American food for lunch and dinner; reservations required; most expensive item on the a la carte dinner menu is $13.00 |

**Kenny's Steak Pub** · *Restaurant/Cocktail Lounge*
221 W. 46th Street (between Broadway and Eighth Ave.)
(212) 719-5799

Beautiful, brand new terraced room in the theater district, with white walls and flowers on the tables. The bar is large and long, with piano nightly from 6:30 to 11 P.M. Many couples, some singles.

| | |
|---|---|
| AVERAGE DRINK | $2.50 to $2.75 |
| COVER OR MINIMUM | None |
| PLASTIC | AE, MC, V |
| CROWD | Theater crowd |
| DRESS | Proper attire requested |
| OPEN | Seven days, noon to 1 A.M. |
| FOOD | American menu with dinner ranging from about $15.00 to $20.00; lunch served also |
| SPECIALS | Hors d'oeuvres from 5:30 to 7:30 |

**La Ronde** *Cabaret/Lounge with Dancing*
(in the Sheraton Centre)
Seventh Avenue and 52nd Street
(212) 581-1000

Sophisticated room with couples and singles. Vegas lounge acts at 10:30 and 12:30. Live disco music and dancing from 9:30.

| | |
|---|---|
| AVERAGE DRINK | $3.00 to $5.00 |
| COVER OR MINIMUM | Two drink minimum |
| PLASTIC | AE, CB, DC, MC, V |
| CROWD | Mixed crowd, all ages |
| DRESS | Neat |
| OPEN | Monday through Saturday 9 P.M. to 2 A.M.; closed Sunday |
| FOOD | None |

**La Rousse**                                                    *Restaurant/Bar*
414 W. 42nd Street (between Ninth and Tenth Aves.)
(212) 736-4913

Formerly a massage parlor, this cozy little place is smack in the center of the off-Broadway theater district. There's a mural of a naked woman on the wall (left over from the old days), a zinc bar, and a tin ceiling. Singles, couples.

|  |  |
|---|---|
| AVERAGE DRINK | $2.50 |
| COVER OR MINIMUM | None |
| PLASTIC | AE, CB, DC, MC, V |
| CROWD | Actors, students, theater-goers; all ages |
| DRESS | Casual |
| OPEN | Monday through Friday, noon till closing; Saturday 5 P.M. till closing; Sunday 4:30 P.M. till closing |
| FOOD | French Provincial; a la carte dinner entrées run from $7.00 to $15.00 |


**Micky's**                                          *Bar/Restaurant/Cabaret*
44 W. 54th Street (between Fifth Ave. and Ave. of the Americas)
(212) 247-2979

A casual, friendly theater district place. Enjoy comedy, music, and revues. Some couples, some singles, many groups. Reservations suggested.

|  |  |
|---|---|
| AVERAGE DRINK | $1.50 |
| COVER OR MINIMUM | Varies |
| PLASTIC | AE, CB, DC, MC, V |
| CROWD | All types, 25 and up |
| DRESS | Casual |
| OPEN | Monday through Friday, noon to 1 or 2 A.M.; Saturday 4 P.M. to midnight |
| FOOD | American; dinner is from $5.00 to $10.95; lunch served also |
| SPECIALS | Free hors d'oeuvres with cocktails |

**The Oak Bar**                                          *Lounge*
(in the Plaza Hotel)
Fifth Avenue and 59th Street
(212) 759-3000

Here's where you go to catch up on your *Wall Street Journal* or
your London *Times*, to impress your business clients or your
mother, or to ponder politics while sipping a fine Scotch and sitting
in a deep black leather chair. The elegance of the room is further
enhanced by windows which face onto Central Park, and wall
murals by the famed American artist Everett Shinn. The crowd is a
blend of couples, business people of undetermined marital status,
and groups of singles at the tables rather than at the bar.

| | |
|---|---|
| AVERAGE DRINK | $4.50 |
| COVER OR MINIMUM | None |
| PLASTIC | AE, CB, DC, MC, V |
| CROWD | Sophisticated business people and executives, from 30 to 80 |
| DRESS | Jackets required, ties preferred |
| OPEN | Seven days, from 11:30 A.M. to 2 A.M.; Sunday 11:30 A.M. to 1 A.M. |
| FOOD | Lunch only; about $14.00; dinners available in the Plaza Hotel restaurants |

**O'Lunney's**                                    *Restaurant/Pub*
12 W. 44th Street (between Fifth Ave. and Ave. of the Americas)
(212) 840-6688

A singer/guitarist adds to the cozy pub atmosphere where couples
and singles relax and socialize.

| | |
|---|---|
| AVERAGE DRINK | $2.25–$3.50 |
| COVER OR MINIMUM | None |
| PLASTIC | AE, DC, MC, V |
| CROWD | All types of office people in all kinds of professions, plus people in the arts; 20s and up |
| DRESS | Casual, some suits and ties |

| | |
|---|---|
| OPEN | Monday through Friday from lunch on; Saturday night from dinner on |
| FOOD | American menu, with dinners from $3.50 to $10.95 |

**O'Neals' and O'Neals' Times Square** *Restaurant/Nightclub*
60 W. 57th Street (at Ave. of the Americas)
(212) 399-2357

147 W. 43rd Street (between Broadway and
Ave. of the Americas)
(212) 869-4200

Be part of the busy midtown or Times Square crowd in the pub on the main floor. Or relax and enjoy the soft jazz and other entertainment (call for schedule). Many singles, some couples, very sociable.

| | |
|---|---|
| AVERAGE DRINK | $2.25 |
| COVER OR MINIMUM | Variable |
| PLASTIC | AE, CB, DC, MC, V |
| CROWD | Business people at lunch, an after-work crowd later |
| DRESS | Casual—many jeans with jackets, many suits and ties |
| OPEN | 11:30 A.M. to midnight, Monday through Thursday; 11:30 A.M. to 1 A.M. Friday, Saturday, and Sunday. Times Square room opened Monday through Friday, 11:30 A.M. to 1 A.M.; Saturday 4 P.M. to 1 A.M.; closed Sunday |
| FOOD | American menu, with dinners from $4.00 to $16.00 |

**Plato's Retreat** *Sex Club*
509 W. 34th Street (between Tenth and Eleventh Aves.)
(212) 947-0111

In the world of sex clubs, Plato's remains a classic, known from coast to coast. People in Aberdeen, Washington, have been known to take visiting New Yorkers aside and, with eyes wide and curious, ask in hushed tones, "Is it *really* like *that*?" The answer is yes. And more so. Plato's is an experience in another dimension; a sociological phenomenon; an underground world capable of redefining reality; guaranteed to drop the jaw of the uninitiated from chin to floor, permanently. Here's the thing—men must have a date to get in. Women may go solo. Now ordinarily that would preclude a place from being listed in this book. But in this case you and your date are free to go your separate ways once you're inside. So it really becomes a singles scene. Well, singles, couples, groups, masses—who's counting. Lavish facilities in this 23,000-square-foot space include a big swimming pool, hot tub, two movie rooms, many "other" rooms, a Jacuzzi, an entire disco, and more. Loud disco music permeates everything. This is not the sort of place where a chance meeting with your boss would prove fruitful.

| | |
|---|---|
| AVERAGE DRINK | No liquor |
| COVER OR MINIMUM | $55.00 per couple at the door the first time; $40.00 on subsequent visits; $15.00 for unescorted women |
| PLASTIC | None |
| CROWD | All types, all ages |
| DRESS | Just don't worry about it |
| OPEN | 9 P.M. to 4 A.M. weekdays; 9 P.M. to 6 A.M. weekends; closed Monday |
| FOOD | Huge buffet |
| SPECIALS | Varies—includes mud wrestling, male strippers, S & M parties, etc. |

**Possible 20**                               *Restaurant/Bar with Music*
**Restaurant and Bar**
253 W. 55th Street (between Broadway and Eighth Ave.)
(212) 541-9350

The lounge is upstairs, the food is downstairs, the music is mostly upstairs from Wednesday through Saturday. A contemporary decor with mirrors and chrome and a small but friendly bar give the place an atmosphere of "elegant party." Mostly couples, but singles are made to feel welcome.

| | |
|---|---|
| AVERAGE DRINK | $2.00 |
| COVER OR MINIMUM | $4.00 |
| PLASTIC | AE, CB, DC, MC, V |
| CROWD | Artists, musicians and others with the upstairs age range of 30 to 40ish |
| DRESS | Casual |
| OPEN | Seven days; Monday through Friday noon to 4 A.M.; Saturday and Sunday 5 P.M. to 4 A.M. |
| FOOD | American and Chinese, with an average dinner price of $5.00 to $9.00 |

**Rainer's**                                                                 *Restaurant*
(at the Sheraton Centre Hotel)
Seventh Avenue and 52nd Street
(212) 581-1000

Entering this elegant room is like entering a private library—with sofas, divans, little marble tables, a little bar, and then a number of dining rooms. Thick carpeting, wood paneling, the works. The lounge is in a separate area but you can still hear the piano Monday through Saturday 7 to 11 P.M. Couples, some singles.

| | |
|---|---|
| AVERAGE DRINK | $3.50 |
| COVER OR MINIMUM | None |
| PLASTIC | AE, CB, DC, MC, V |
| CROWD | Professionals from 30 to 50 |
| DRESS | Jackets and ties required |
| OPEN | Seven nights, 5:30 P.M. till . . . |
| FOOD | Northern Italian cuisine till 11:30 P.M.; a prix-fixe dinner is available at $25.00 |

**Red Parrot**                                                    *Nightclub*
617 W. 57th Street (between Eleventh and Twelfth Aves.)
(212) 247-1530

If you want to do the West Side in style or impress out-of-town
visitors with the diversity that is New York, maneuver your way
past the limousines and the doorman into this airplane hangar of a
room. Once inside you can dance or listen to the music (which
ranges from disco to classical to country-western in one set) or
socialize with other singles in the soundproof lounge. If you find
yourself temporarily alone, you can do a Vulcan mind-probe on
one of the many big, colorful macaws, to see what they think of all
this. Not to be missed: the twelve-piece Red Parrot Orchestra,
which alternates sets with the disco.

| | |
|---|---|
| AVERAGE DRINK | $4.00 |
| COVER OR MINIMUM | $15.00 Wednesday and Thursday; |
| | $20.00 Friday and Saturday |
| PLASTIC | None |
| CROWD | Everyone; all ages |
| DRESS | Fashionable, trendy, elegant, campy— |
| | whatever suits your mood |
| OPEN | Wednesday through Saturday, 10 P.M. to |
| | closing |
| FOOD | None |

**Roseland**                                    *Ballroom/Disco/Restaurant*
239 W. 52nd Street (just west of Broadway)
(212) 247-0200

The historic, majestic Roseland is a New York experience not to be
missed. Remember dance marathons, jazz weddings, real art deco,
and big bands of the 1920's? It happened at Roseland. And today,
with a 3500-person capacity and a dance floor a half a block wide,
they still house some of the best bands around. Older singles, couples, and groups feel especially comfortable.

| | |
|---|---|
| AVERAGE DRINK | $2.00 |
| COVER OR MINIMUM | $6.00 |

| | |
|---|---|
| PLASTIC | AE, MC, V |
| CROWD | People from all over; all ages |
| DRESS | Proper attire |
| OPEN | Wednesday at 5:30—try the unlimited hot and cold buffet for $12.00, which also includes a dance show and lesson, ballroom dancing, and disco from 11 P.M. to 4 A.M.; Thursday doors open at 2:30 P.M. for ballroom dancing till 11, then disco till 4 A.M.; Friday the action starts at 6:30 P.M. and the disco begins at midnight; dancing begins on Saturday at 2:30, disco from midnight; Sunday dancing is from 2:30 to midnight |
| FOOD | American cuisine at the Terrace Restaurant, with a la carte dinner entrées up to $10.75 |

**Sally's**                                                      *Disco*
Seventh Avenue and 56th Street, in the
New York Sheraton Hotel
(212) 484-3361

Activities here are dancing and socializing, in that order. Strobe lights provide most of the decor, and the small bar is always crowded. Live music begins at 9:30 P.M. nightly.

| | |
|---|---|
| AVERAGE DRINK | $4.00 |
| COVER OR MINIMUM | Two drink minimum |
| PLASTIC | AE, CB, DC, MC, V |
| CROWD | Chic and sophisticated, and everyone else, too; all ages |
| DRESS | Fashionable |
| OPEN | Monday through Friday, 4 P.M. to 2:30 A.M.; Saturday and Sunday, noon to 2:30 A.M. |
| FOOD | None |

**Sha Sha House**                                      *Restaurant/Cabaret*
338-40 W. 39th Street, ninth floor (near Ninth Ave.)
(212) 736-7547

Live jazz, swing, and bebop bands with singers. Dancing is OK.
Rustic, loft atmosphere with a small informal restaurant area. Seventy to 80 percent singles.

| | |
|---|---|
| AVERAGE DRINK | International beers and wines $1.00 |
| COVER OR MINIMUM | $5.00 |
| PLASTIC | None |
| CROWD | Sophisticated and lively crowd from 19 to 60 |
| DRESS | Casual |
| OPEN | Thursday, Friday, Saturday 8 P.M. to 1 A.M., but call—it changes |
| FOOD | Vegetarian/International/Southern/Island when available; call for details (When you call, don't worry about the answering service greeting you with "Doctor's office"—it must make sense to someone.) |

**Studio 54**                                                      *Disco*
254 W. 54th Street (between Broadway and Eighth Ave.)
(212) 489-7667

Though it's his job to say this, the Studio's publicist may not be that
far off when he describes the club as the "world's most well-known
and popular disco." Indeed, when it re-opened a year ago, it made
headlines in Japan. Converted from a real studio, the room is
basically one huge, mammoth open space packed with people—all
kinds of people, including many many singles. One patron described it as "so crowded you can't see a thing!" Music is primarily
recorded, with a live d.j.; but from time to time they have bands. If
"in" spots are your thing and you don't mind possibly waiting on
line outside, then Studio 54 is an adventure that should be on your
agenda.

| | |
|---|---|
| AVERAGE DRINK | $3.00 or $4.00 |
| COVER OR MINIMUM | $15.00 during the week, $18.00 on weekends |

| | |
|---|---|
| PLASTIC | None |
| CROWD | All kinds of chic people; all ages |
| DRESS | Fashionable, up-to-the-minute outfits |
| OPEN | Tuesday through Sunday, 10 P.M. to 4 A.M. |
| FOOD | None |
| SPECIALS | Call |

**Sybil's**                                                    *Supperclub*
(in the New York Hilton)
101 W. 53rd Street (between Ave. of the Americas and
Seventh Ave.)
(212) 977-9898

A sophisticated room with live entertainment for dinner and dancing Monday, Tuesday, Wednesday and Friday till 11 P.M., then
disco after 11. Thursday is Talent Shownight. Saturday is dinner
and dancing to a live band till midnight, then disco. Many couples,
enough singles.

| | |
|---|---|
| AVERAGE DRINK | $4.00 |
| COVER OR MINIMUM | Weekdays $5.00, weekends $10.00 |
| PLASTIC | AE, CB, DC, MC, V |
| CROWD | Professional, chic; mid 30s |
| DRESS | Jackets required |
| OPEN | Seven days, 11:30 A.M. to 4 A.M. |
| FOOD | Dinners 8 to 11 P.M. with a la carte entrées from $14.00 to $24.00; buffet brunch served also, seven days |

**Thursday's 24**                       *Restaurant with Dancing Later*
57 W. 58th Street (near Ave. of the Americas)
(212) 371-7777

A three-level place with the dance floor suspended between two
dining rooms. Many trees, plants, and Tiffany lamps. Singles and
couples dance from 10 P.M. on with a d.j. presiding.

| | |
|---|---|
| AVERAGE DRINK | $2.75 |
| COVER OR MINIMUM | None |

92                                                    *Places to Go*

|          |                                              |
|----------|----------------------------------------------|
| PLASTIC  | AE, CB, DC, MC, V                            |
| CROWD    | Varied; ages 25 to 50                        |
| DRESS    | Casual but neat                              |
| OPEN     | Seven days: 11:45 A.M. to 2 A.M. Sunday through Thursday; 11:45 A.M. to 3 A.M. Friday and Saturday |
| FOOD     | American/Continental, with a la carte dinner entrées from $5.00 to $13.00 |
| SPECIALS | Hors d'oeuvres Monday through Friday 5 to 7 P.M. |

## Tyson's                                                Restaurant/Cabaret
755 Ninth Avenue (at 51st St.)
(212) 397-9027

Theatrical but intimate atmosphere with show posters on the walls and a large copper-topped bar. The room seats eighty couples and singles. Entertainment nightly with jazz on Monday, a showcase on Thursday, and piano and/or guitar other nights.

|                   |                                              |
|-------------------|----------------------------------------------|
| AVERAGE DRINK     | $2.00                                        |
| COVER OR MINIMUM  | None                                         |
| PLASTIC           | AE, MC, V                                    |
| CROWD             | Actors, theater people, and a neighborhood crowd from 22 to 52 |
| DRESS             | Casual                                       |
| OPEN              | Seven days, 4 P.M. to 4 A.M.                 |
| FOOD              | Dinner from 5 P.M. to midnight during the week, and till 1 A.M. weekends; $3.95 for a burger, $12.95 for a steak |

## West Bank Café                                          Restaurant/Bar
407 W. 42nd Street (between Ninth and Tenth Aves.)
(212) 695-6909

The main floor has a restaurant and a huge bar with cocktail tables. Eating is allowed at the bar. The bottom floor is for private parties. Many singles (perhaps 80 percent), some couples.

| | |
|---|---|
| AVERAGE DRINK | $2.00 |
| COVER OR MINIMUM | None |
| PLASTIC | AE, MC, V |
| CROWD | Actors and people in the arts; all ages |
| DRESS | Casual |
| OPEN | Seven days from noon; closes at varied times |
| FOOD | Wide range of Continental entrées, till 1 A.M.; evening prices range from $5.95 to $12.95 |

## East Side

FROM 14TH TO 34TH STREETS, EAST OF FIFTH AVENUE

**Annie Oakley's Saloon**                                    *Bar/Restaurant*
275 First Avenue (between 15th and 16th Sts.)
(212) 674-9429

Get ready for a good time in this cozy but lively little place. There's a small dance floor and live country-western music from time to time. Owner Barbara Ann Oakley has it done up tastefully in western decor.

| | |
|---|---|
| AVERAGE DRINK | $1.75 |
| COVER OR MINIMUM | $2.00 |
| PLASTIC | They only used real money back then |
| CROWD | Cowpersons from 21 to 40ish; employees of the many nearby hospitals let their hair down at Annie's after work |
| DRESS | Anything, although you see a fair share of boots and hats on weekends |
| OPEN | Seven days, from lunch to 4 A.M. |
| FOOD | American food for lunch, country-western food till 10 P.M.; dinner prices go from $4.95 to about $7.50 |

**Buchbinders Greenhouse Café**                    *Restaurant/Bar*
Third Avenue and 27th Street
(212) 683-6500

An open, spacious atmosphere with high ceilings and different levels. The bar seats twenty-five to thirty plus standing, and looks out onto the two floors of dining rooms. Enjoy live piano music nightly, or chamber music at brunch on weekends. Many singles, lots of socializing.

|  |  |
|---:|:---|
| AVERAGE DRINK | $2.50 |
| COVER OR MINIMUM | None |
| PLASTIC | AE, MC, V |
| CROWD | All ages, from 25 to 60; all types, from neighborhood to business executives |
| DRESS | Casual but neat |
| OPEN | Seven days, noon to 3 A.M. |
| FOOD | Continental; brunch on Saturday and Sunday; dinner goes from $6.00 to $14.50 |

**Café Society**                                   *Restaurant/Disco*
43 E. 20th Street (between Park and Broadway)
(212) 673-8885

Meet other singles on Friday and Saturday night. Plenty of conversation and dancing. Live d.j. spins oldies, rock, new wave and disco on weekends.

|  |  |
|---:|:---|
| AVERAGE DRINK | $2.50 |
| COVER OR MINIMUM | Friday and Saturday after 11 P.M., $5.00 |
| PLASTIC | AE, MC, V |
| CROWD | A mixed crowd in their late 20s and 30s |
| DRESS | Anything |
| OPEN | Noon to 4 A.M. daily except Sunday |
| FOOD | Lunch, dinner till 11 P.M.; you can spend about $14.50 to $16.50 for dinner |

**Chelsea Park**                                    *Bar/Restaurant*
495 Second Avenue (at 28th St.)
(212) 684-9153

The bar seats twenty-six in this cozy, comfortable room. Live piano or guitar on weekends, and some big name talent on occasion. The singles are basically an after-work or neighborhood crowd, so many people know each other already. It's a friendly, lively place, though, and not hard to fit in.

| | |
|---|---|
| AVERAGE DRINK | $1.75 |
| COVER OR MINIMUM | None |
| PLASTIC | AE, MC, V |
| CROWD | Young people and hospital personnel from 25 to 50 |
| DRESS | Casual |
| OPEN | Seven days, from 11 A.M. to 4 A.M. |
| FOOD | American and Continental; $7.00 or $8.00 for dinner |

**Fat Tuesdays**                                         *Jazz Room*
190 Third Avenue (at 17th St.)
(212) 533-7902

A sophisticated jazz club with top name talent. It's mainly a listening rather than a socializing situation, but that shouldn't stop you from going if you love good jazz. Other singles love good jazz, too.

| | |
|---|---|
| AVERAGE DRINK | $2.25–$2.50 |
| COVER OR MINIMUM | $7.50 cover, $5.00 minimum; $8.00 to sit at the bar (includes 1 drink) |
| PLASTIC | AE, MC, V |
| CROWD | Jazz lovers in the 20s and 30s |
| DRESS | Neat and casual |
| OPEN | Tuesday through Sunday; doors open at 8:30 P.M., shows at 9 and 11; Friday and Saturday shows are 9, 11, and 1 |
| FOOD | All kinds; see *Tuesdays*, in this section |

**Harley Street** *Restaurant/Lounge/Piano Bar*
547 Second Avenue (between 30th and 31st Sts.)
(212) 685-9659

Lovely piano bar Tuesday through Saturday. Some singles, some couples.

| | |
|---|---|
| AVERAGE DRINK | $2.25 |
| COVER OR MINIMUM | None |
| PLASTIC | AE, MC, V |
| CROWD | Many medical people from nearby New York University Hospital, plus other professionals; there's an 18-to-30 age group, and a 40-to-60 age group—take your pick |
| DRESS | Casual |
| OPEN | Seven days, from 11:30 A.M. to 4 A.M. |
| FOOD | Continental; expect to spend $8.95 and up for dinner |
| SPECIALS | Happy Hour Monday through Friday 4:30 to 7:00 P.M. |

**The Orchid** *Restaurant/Bar*
81 Lexington Avenue (at 26th St.)
(212) 889-0960

"Art deco dining and drinking establishment." Small room, large bar, and live jazz Saturday night at 10.

| | |
|---|---|
| AVERAGE DRINK | $2.25 |
| COVER OR MINIMUM | $3.50 Saturday night at bar tables; modest minimum during peak lunch and dinner hours |
| PLASTIC | AE, DC, MC, V |
| CROWD | Professionals and neighborhood people |
| DRESS | Casual |
| OPEN | Sunday through Thursday noon to 11:30 P.M.; Friday noon to 12:30 A.M.; Saturday 5 P.M. to 12:30 A.M. |

| | |
|---|---|
| FOOD | Unique pub menu; dinner prices range from $4.50 to $12.95 |
| SPECIALS | Sunday brunch with unlimited special drinks; Sunday evening free hors d'oeuvres at the wine tasting party |

**The Park Ten Restaurant** *Restaurant/Cocktail Lounge*
10 Park Avenue (at 34th St.)
(212) 889-1310

Beautiful, two-tiered room with an intimate atmosphere and piano nightly from 5 P.M. Vocalists entertain from 9 P.M., and you can see and hear the entertainment from the bar area. Couples and singles.

| | |
|---|---|
| AVERAGE DRINK | $3.00 |
| COVER OR MINIMUM | None |
| PLASTIC | AE, DC, MC, V |
| CROWD | Professional people and Park Avenue residents; ages 30 to 55 |
| DRESS | Coat and tie atmosphere |
| OPEN | Monday through Saturday 11:30 A.M. to 2 A.M.; Sunday 5:30 P.M. to 2 A.M. |
| FOOD | French nouvelle cuisine; a la carte entrées run from $8.00 to $19.00; reservations necessary |

**Shelter** *New York Bar*
540 Second Avenue (at 30th St.)
(212) 684-4207

A cozy and intimate atmosphere with a mahogany bar, leather booths, terra-cotta floors, and tables in the back. The staff is exceptionally friendly, and singles feel very comfortable.

| | |
|---|---|
| AVERAGE DRINK | $2.00 |
| COVER OR MINIMUM | None |
| PLASTIC | AE, DC, MC, V |

| | |
|---|---|
| CROWD | Neighborhood people, including doctors, nurses and other personnel from nearby hospitals; age span 22 to 35 |
| DRESS | Casual |
| OPEN | Seven days, 11:30 A.M. to 4 A.M. |
| FOOD | New York menu; dinner ranges from $4.25 to $7.95 |
| SPECIALS | Free special drinks at brunch |

## Tom O'Reilly's Pub                  *Traditional Irish*
75 Lexington Avenue (between 25th and 26th Sts.)
(212) MU 4-9164

Friendly and intimate pub with traditional Irish music Friday, Saturday and Sunday from 9:30 P.M. Singles and couples.

| | |
|---|---|
| AVERAGE DRINK | $2.00 |
| COVER OR MINIMUM | None |
| PLASTIC | None |
| CROWD | All types, all ages |
| DRESS | Casual |
| OPEN | Seven days, 8 A.M. to 4 A.M. |
| FOOD | Pub fare, lunches only, no dinner; $1.25 for chili to $3.95 for burgers |

## Tramps                           *Music Club*
125 E. 15th Street (between Third Ave. and Irving Pl.)
(212) 777-5077

Many singles and some couples do a lot of dancing and socializing. Here's the rundown. Monday is "Mod Monday" featuring reggae, Motown, and new African music. Tuesday is "Uptown Horns Party" with a nine-piece rhythm and blues band and a big crowd. Wednesday you can hear reggae direct from Jamaica. Thursday and Saturday there will often be blues bands from such authentic blues cities as Chicago. Friday is "Native Rhythm Night" with new, progressive rock bands that are on the scene. And Sunday is "Show-case Night" with just about any style of music. As the owner said, "Every night is an event."

| | |
|---|---|
| AVERAGE DRINK | $2.50 |
| COVER OR MINIMUM | Wednesday and Thursday, $4.00 to $5.00; weekends, $5.00 to $7.00 |
| PLASTIC | AE |
| CROWD | Musicians, celebrities, rock stars from 22 on up |
| DRESS | Monday most people will show up in trendy attire; Tuesday through Sunday you'll see fashionable and new wave dress, some casual outfits and some regular suits |
| OPEN | Seven days, 11 A.M. to 4 A.M. |
| FOOD | Pub fare; lunch, dinner; average dinner price, $4.00 or $5.00 |
| SPECIALS | Free admission Monday and Tuesday |

**Tuesdays**                                                     *Bar/Restaurant*
190 Third Avenue (at 17th St.)
(212) 533-7900

Saloon nostalgia with a cozy, casual Tiffany lamp atmosphere. Mixed couples and singles. **Fat Tuesdays,** downstairs, is listed separately.

| | |
|---|---|
| AVERAGE DRINK | $2.25 |
| COVER OR MINIMUM | Varies |
| PLASTIC | AE, MC, V |
| CROWD | Neighborhood people from 20 to 30ish |
| DRESS | Casual |
| OPEN | Seven days, 11:30 A.M. to closing |
| FOOD | Dinner prices range from $3.95 to $12.95; lunch available also |

**W. J. Flywheel**                                    *Restaurant/Bar*
359 Second Avenue (at 21st St.)
(212) 473-8908

A charming room in brick-and-beams decor with an oak floor and
a 100-year-old bar. Not a pickup place, but there are singles. Couples, too.

| | |
|---|---|
| AVERAGE DRINK | $2.25 to $2.50 |
| COVER OR MINIMUM | None |
| PLASTIC | DC, MC, V |
| CROWD | All types, many neighborhood people who already know each other; all ages |
| DRESS | Casual |
| OPEN | Seven days, lunch to 4 A.M. |
| FOOD | Hamburger-to-steak till 12:30 A.M.; average dinner $6.00 to $9.00 |

---

## Chelsea

FROM 14TH TO 34TH STREETS, WEST OF FIFTH AVENUE

---

**Angry Squire**          *Restaurant with Jazz Club Atmosphere*
*on Weekends*
216 Seventh Avenue (between 22nd and 23rd Sts.)
(212) 242-9066

Singles and others come to sit in this warm, intimate pub to eat,
drink, talk, and listen to top name jazz groups on Friday and Saturday. Nautical decor and a casual mood contribute to the friendliness.

| | |
|---|---|
| AVERAGE DRINK | $2.00 |
| COVER OR MINIMUM | None at the bar; $2.00 music charge plus two drink minimum at tables (no drink minimum with an entrée) |
| PLASTIC | None |

| | |
|---|---|
| CROWD | All types of people from 24 to 35, plus ageless jazz club dwellers |
| DRESS | Casual |
| OPEN | Seven days, noon to 2 A.M.; weekends till 4 A.M. |
| FOOD | Full American and English menu, light and heavy dishes; champagne brunch Saturday and Sunday; dinner is from $4.95 to $6.95 |

## Black Beans Music Studio *Concerts*
132 W. 24th Street (between Ave. of the Americas and
Seventh Ave.)
(212) 243-2979

Brazilian music and jazz are the forces that bind people together at
Black Beans' concerts. Depending on the entertainment, it can be
anything from a strict seating concert to a party-and-dancing situation. The studio seats about 125 people.

| | |
|---|---|
| AVERAGE DRINK | No liquor, but you can have soft drinks, tea, and coffee |
| COVER OR MINIMUM | Varies, count on from $2.00 to $5.00 |
| PLASTIC | AE, CB, DC, MC, V |
| CROWD | All types |
| DRESS | Casual |
| OPEN | Call for concert times and dates |
| FOOD | Brazilian food every Monday from 3 P.M. to 11 P.M., for about $7.00 |

## Botany Rocks *Bar*
806 Avenue of the Americas (between 27th and 28th Sts.)
(212) 741-9184 or 9182

A cozy place with some singles and some couples. Seats forty-plus
at the bar. Social, but casual.

| | |
|---|---|
| AVERAGE DRINK | $1.90 |
| COVER OR MINIMUM | $3.00 to $4.00 |
| PLASTIC | None |

| | |
|---|---|
| CROWD | Young professionals, artists, and writers, mostly in their 20s |
| DRESS | Casual |
| OPEN | Seven days, 8 A.M. to 2 A.M. |
| FOOD | None |

## Chelsea Commons                                      *Bar/Restaurant*
Tenth Avenue and 24th Street (near the Hudson Guild Theatre)
(212) 929-9424

Singles feel comfortable here, but it's not specifically a singles place. The crowd is mixed and the bar seats fourteen. Go for Sunday brunch and listen to live piano if you want to enjoy a relaxed, Chelsea neighborhood atmosphere.

| | |
|---|---|
| AVERAGE DRINK | $1.75 |
| COVER OR MINIMUM | None |
| PLASTIC | None |
| CROWD | Neighborhood people of all types and ages |
| DRESS | Casual |
| OPEN | Seven days, noon to 4 A.M. |
| FOOD | Light, homemade meals; Sunday brunch; average dinner about $4.00 |

## Club 51                                              *Sex Club*
51 W. 19th Street (between Fifth Ave. and Ave. of the Americas)
(212) 675-8013

Live S & M shows, unique dungeon parties, and Kinky Clan Club on Friday. And more. Only in New York, folks. Call for information.

## Club "O" at Fantasy Manor                            *Sex Club*
31 W. 21st Street, second floor (between Fifth Ave. and
Ave. of the Americas)
(212) 439-4583

Imagine all your wildest "O" fantasies come true—need we continue? Undressing is optional, and there is a disco, steam room, shower, lockers, and lots of other things.

| | |
|---|---|
| AVERAGE DRINK | Complimentary liquid refreshments and buffet. No liquor |
| COVER OR MINIMUM | $20.00 for couples, $15.00 for single men, $5.00 for single women |
| PLASTIC | Call them |
| CROWD | All types, all ages |
| DRESS | Does it really matter? |
| OPEN | Wednesday and Thursday at 8 P.M. is Club "O"; Friday and Saturday from 9 P.M. is plain old ordinary swinging sex |
| FOOD | Buffet |

**Cody's**                                        *Country-Western Club*
579 Avenue of the Americas (at 16th St.)
(212) 620-0377

Live country-rock nightly, with dining upstairs and dancing downstairs. Comfortable atmosphere, holding about 260 people.

| | |
|---|---|
| AVERAGE DRINK | $2.25 |
| COVER OR MINIMUM | $3.00 |
| PLASTIC | AE, MC, V |
| CROWD | Big cross section of people, from professionals to students; ages 19 to 50 |
| DRESS | From cowperson outfits and jeans to three-piece suits |
| OPEN | Seven days: Monday through Thursday 11:30 A.M. to 3 A.M.; Friday 11:30 A.M. to 4 A.M.; Saturday 6:30 P.M. to 4 A.M.; Sunday 6:30 P.M. to 3 A.M.—Got that? |
| FOOD | Steaks, burgers, salads, etc.; $4.50 to about $9.50 |
| SPECIALS | Free hot hors d'oeuvres Monday through Friday, 5 to 7 P.M. |

**Danceteria**                    *Dance/Nightclub/Restaurant*
30 W. 21st Street (between Fifth Ave. and Ave. of the Americas)
(212) 620-0516

You can get anything you want at Danceteria! The slick, clean, sophisticated mood permeates all three floors. On the ground floor is dancing, a d.j., live music (call to find out when), and a bar. The second floor is a disco and bar. And when hunger sets in, go up one more flight to the restaurant and cocktail lounge.

| | |
|---|---|
| AVERAGE DRINK | $3.00 |
| COVER OR MINIMUM | $5.00 to $10.00 |
| PLASTIC | None |
| CROWD | Artists, designers, music industry people, TV executives, models, photographers, etc.; 18 to 30 |
| DRESS | You can wear a suit or something weird, as long as it's fashionable |
| OPEN | Wednesday through Sunday, 9:00 P.M. to dawn |
| FOOD | Northern Italian cuisine; $3.00 to $7.00 |
| SPECIALS | Many unannounced specials—call to find out |

**The Eagle Tavern**                    *Bar/Restaurant*
355 W. 14th Street (off Ninth Ave.)
(212) 924-0275

A comfortable Village-style music place, with the accent on eating during the day and drinking and listening at night. At present you can enjoy an Irish "seisun" (jam session) on Monday, folk music from the British Isles on Wednesday, bluegrass on Thursday (bring your banjo just in case), country-western music on Saturday, and Sunday of course is for the blues. (No entertainment Tuesday and Friday.)

| | |
|---|---|
| AVERAGE DRINK | $1.50 |
| COVER OR MINIMUM | Varies from free to about $2.50 |
| PLASTIC | MC, V |
| CROWD | Many professionals, from 25 to 45 |

| | |
|---|---|
| DRESS | Casual |
| OPEN | Seven days, 8 A.M. to 4 A.M. |
| FOOD | Lunch, no dinner (the dining room turns into the entertainment room at night); $2.00 to $6.00 |

**The Empire Diner** *Diner*
Tenth Avenue and 22nd Street
(212) 243-2736

Where else but in New York can you get what we have affectionately termed Nouvelle Diner cuisine? This exquisitely campy place is open twenty-four hours and serves eggs at any time, "and everything else, too" says the manager. But beware: If you go there for an emergency egg at 3 A.M. it's going to be crowded. And it's no wonder, the contemporary truck-stop decor, done in stainless steel, shiny black tiles, and candlelight makes it a fun, friendly place to be. (The diner used to be a real truck stop, built in the 1930's, and the stainless steel is the original.) There's a piano player nightly during dinner and on weekends during the day. Mixed couples and groups of singles.

| | |
|---|---|
| AVERAGE DRINK | $2.75 |
| COVER OR MINIMUM | None |
| PLASTIC | AE over $15.00 |
| CROWD | This covers just about every age, type, and profession in New York, though there is sometimes a concentration of the 20-to-40-year-olds; we also have the after-theater crowd, the post-disco set, the dessert-and-coffee crew, and the early breakfasters who have either been out all night or who got up awfully early |
| DRESS | People wear whatever they were wearing when they were doing whatever they were doing before they came here |
| OPEN | All the time |

| | |
|---|---|
| FOOD | Just about anything |
| SPECIALS | Happy Hour Monday through Friday from 5 to 7 P.M. |

## The Fun House                    *Disco/Entertainment*
526 W. 26th Street (between Tenth and Eleventh Aves.)
(212) 691-0621

The name of the game is party. The place holds up to 2000 people, in what has been described as a "wild" atmosphere with dancing, a game room, big name performers, circus acts, and a d.j. with records.

| | |
|---|---|
| AVERAGE DRINK | $2.50 |
| COVER OR MINIMUM | "Girls" free Friday and Saturday till 12, then $12.00; men $12.00 |
| PLASTIC | None |
| CROWD | Mixed from 18 |
| DRESS | Jeans |
| OPEN | Friday and Saturday 10 P.M. till . . . |
| FOOD | Snacks and ice cream |

## Jazz Gallery                          *Jazz Room*
55 W. 19th Street (between Fifth Ave. and Ave. of the Americas)
(212) 924-5026

This is really the home of a New York sculptor, but call or check the paper to see who's playing there and when. Or you can write and ask to be on the free mailing list. Write "Jazz Coalition, 56 Fifth Ave., Suite 817, New York, N.Y. 10010." A must for jazz fans.

## Jazzmania                              *Jazz Club*
40 W. 27th Street (between Broadway and Ave. of the Americas)
(212) 532-7666

People who love jazz, love Jazzmania. Top name local and national talent, plus a ten-piece Brazilian band perform in this comfortable, cozy room. Couples and singles.

| | |
|---|---|
| AVERAGE DRINK | Call to see if liquor is being served |
| COVER OR MINIMUM | $7.00 at the door, $3.50 minimum at tables |
| PLASTIC | None |
| CROWD | Jazz lovers of all types, all ages |
| DRESS | Casual |
| OPEN | Wednesday through Saturday from 8 P.M. |
| FOOD | Sunday brunch available |
| SPECIALS | All night ticket available for $10.00 at the door; reduced door rates after 12:30 A.M.; after-hours jam sessions occasionally from 1 to 3 A.M. |

## Les Mouches                                    *Restaurant/Disco*
260 Eleventh Avenue, fourth floor (between 26th and 27th Sts.)
(212) 695-5190

The disco is large and sophisticated, with the lights and big sound system. (The restaurant is mostly couples or groups.)

| | |
|---|---|
| AVERAGE DRINK | $3.00 |
| COVER OR MINIMUM | Disco $10.00 Friday, $15.00 Saturday |
| PLASTIC | AE, CB, DC, MC, V |
| CROWD | All types, really; all ages, too |
| DRESS | Fashionable disco attire; designer jeans OK |
| OPEN | Friday and Saturday (other nights sometimes) from 11 P.M. till . . . |
| FOOD | In the restaurant; dinners range from $7.95 to about $20.00 |

## McFeely's                                      *Victorian Saloon*
565 W. 23rd Street (at Eleventh Ave.)
(212) 929-4432

Eighteen-nineties decor with original pieces and piano/vocal nightly from 8 P.M. The bar area holds about eighty people, some couples and some singles, with the dining room seating 200.

| | |
|---|---|
| AVERAGE DRINK | $2.50 |
| COVER OR MINIMUM | None |

|        |                |
|--------|----------------|
| PLASTIC | AE, MC, V |
| CROWD | Entertainers and professionals; 20s and 30s |
| DRESS | Casual |
| OPEN | Seven days, from 4 P.M. to 1 A.M.; Sunday noon to 1 A.M. |
| FOOD | American/Continental; dinners and Sunday brunch; $7.95 to $15.50 |

## Peppermint Lounge

*Rock/Dance Club*

100 Fifth Avenue (corner 15th St.)
(212) 989-9505

If you're the multimedia type, here's your place. Lots of different activities going on in different parts of the room, with dancing, a lounge area, an extensive video system, live bands, and a d.j.

|        |                |
|--------|----------------|
| AVERAGE DRINK | $2.25 to $2.50 |
| COVER OR MINIMUM | $5.00 weekdays; $7.00 to $10.00 weekends |
| PLASTIC | None |
| CROWD | A good mixture of people from 20 to 35 |
| DRESS | Casual to punk |
| OPEN | Wednesday through Monday, 10 P.M. to 4 A.M. |
| FOOD | None |
| SPECIALS | "Blue Monday" has a low cover—usually $3.00 |

## Public Access Synthesizer Studio

*Concerts*

16 W. 22nd Street, Room 902 (between Fifth Ave. and
Ave. of the Americas)
(212) 989-2060

A small, informal studio seating seventy, with experimental, avant garde, and electronic music concerts.

|        |                |
|--------|----------------|
| AVERAGE DRINK | No beverages served |
| COVER OR MINIMUM | $3.00 |
| PLASTIC | None |

| CROWD | Musicians, composers, artists, students; 18 to 50 years old |
|---|---|
| DRESS | Casual |
| OPEN | Monday nights from October to May; call them for specific schedules or check the newspapers |
| FOOD | None, but you can bring your own |

**Roxy** *Roller Skating*
515 W. 18th Street (between Tenth and Eleventh Aves.)
(212) 675-8300

A live d.j., sophisticated atmosphere, and good music bring many singles around for an evening of fun.

| AVERAGE DRINK | Varies |
|---|---|
| COVER OR MINIMUM | $8.00 weeknights, $12.00 Friday and Saturday, and $3.00 for skate rental |
| PLASTIC | None |
| CROWD | Fashionable, sophisticated, mainly in the late 20s |
| DRESS | No jeans during evening sessions |
| OPEN | Tuesday, Wednesday, Thursday, and Sunday from 8 P.M. to 3 A.M.; Friday and Saturday from 9 P.M. to 4 A.M. |
| FOOD | Snacks and pastries |
| SPECIALS | Adults and children are the special people on Saturday and Sunday from noon to 6 P.M. |

**s.n.a.f.u.** *Rock/Cabaret*
676 Avenue of the Americas (at 21st St.)
(212) 691-3535

Pub atmosphere in hi-tech style. Owned by the former owner of Reno Sweeney's, s.n.a.f.u. has been called "a bar with a mind of its own." Decor was done by photographer Robert Mapplethorpe and some of his work is on the walls. Live bands put on cabaret shows nightly to a listening audience of singles and couples.

| | |
|---|---|
| AVERAGE DRINK | $2.75 |
| COVER OR MINIMUM | $5.00 |
| PLASTIC | AE, DC, MC, V |
| CROWD | All types of people from 20 to 60 |
| DRESS | Casual |
| OPEN | Seven days, noon to 2 A.M. |
| FOOD | Quiche, pizza, and other light meals; $2.50 to $4.00 |
| SPECIALS | Monday is dollar night |

**Squat**                                                           *Theater Club*
256 W. 23rd Street (between Seventh and Eighth Aves.)
(212) 691-1238

Small, comfortable room with various forms of live theater and film productions. Call or check the paper to see what's playing.

| | |
|---|---|
| AVERAGE DRINK | No liquor |
| COVER OR MINIMUM | $6.00 to $8.00 |
| PLASTIC | None |
| CROWD | Varies with the band |
| DRESS | Casual |
| OPEN | Friday and Saturday from 11 P.M. to 3 or 4 A.M. |
| FOOD | Nonalcoholic beverages available |

# Greenwich Village

FROM HOUSTON STREET TO 14TH STREET, EAST AND WEST

**Arthur's Tavern**                                                  *Piano Bar*
57 Grove Street (near Sheridan Square)
(212) 242-9468

Arthur's has a very friendly crowd of singles, and a coziness that kind of happens when a place has been in the family for thirty-seven years. For instance: all the holiday decorations are on the wall all year. Once a decoration goes up, it stays there until it gets really bad. The main activities are talking and listening to the music. The Grove Street Stompers have been playing Dixieland there for eighteen years, and can be heard on Monday from 9:30 P.M. to 1 A.M. Tuesday and Wednesday Al Bundee on piano/vocal from 9:30 to 3:30 A.M. takes requests. Thursday, Friday and Saturday Mabel Godwin entertains as she has been for twenty years, with lots of bluesy, gutsy old tunes, and there's other talent as well.

| | |
|---|---|
| AVERAGE DRINK | $1.75 and up |
| COVER OR MINIMUM | Two drinks, more or less |
| PLASTIC | None |
| CROWD | Lots of young people coming back to hear the old music, but the ages range from 25 to 45 |
| DRESS | Casual |
| OPEN | Seven nights, 8:30 P.M. to 4 A.M. |
| FOOD | None |

**Bradley's**                                                     *Jazz Room*
70 University Place
(212) 228-6440

Live piano/bass from 9:45 P.M. with some of the top names in the New York jazz scene. Plenty of other singles to talk to and listen with, in this cozy and intimate room.

| | |
|---|---|
| AVERAGE DRINK | $2.00 |
| COVER OR MINIMUM | None |
| PLASTIC | AE, DC |
| CROWD | Neighborhood people, professionals, musicians in the 20 to 30 age range |
| DRESS | Casual |
| OPEN | Seven days, from lunch till . . . |
| FOOD | Dinner from 6 P.M. to 12:30 A.M., prices from $4.25 to $13.75; Saturday and Sunday brunch available |

**Buffalo Roadhouse**                                        *Restaurant/Bar*
87 Seventh Avenue South (between Bleecker and Christopher Sts.)
(212) 243-8000

A friendly, comfortable room in the heart of Greenwich Village.
Many singles.

| | |
|---|---|
| AVERAGE DRINK | $1.80 to $2.00 |
| COVER OR MINIMUM | None |
| PLASTIC | None |
| CROWD | All types, ages 20 to 50 |
| DRESS | Casual |
| OPEN | Seven days, 10 A.M. to 3 A.M. |
| FOOD | American menu for lunch and dinner, with dinner prices ranging from $6.00 to $10.95 |

**CBGB**                                                        *Concerts*
315 Bowery (at Bleecker St.)
(212) 982-4052

Live music each night in this casual East Village club with its punk/
new wave atmosphere. The sound system is amazingly loud, so
don't expect to have any in-depth conversations. On the other
hand, there are many singles, and by just being there you automat-
ically have something in common with them.

| | |
|---|---|
| AVERAGE DRINK | $2.75 |
| COVER OR MINIMUM | $4.00 during the week, $5.00 on weekends |
| PLASTIC | None |
| CROWD | Punk fans around 19 or 20ish |
| DRESS | Jeans |
| OPEN | Seven nights, from 8 P.M. to 4 A.M. |
| FOOD | None |

**City Limits**                                        *Country-Western Club*
125 Seventh Avenue South (near W. 10th St.)
(212) 243-2242

Country-western knows no limits at City Limits—a big, loud room
with a big, happy dance floor and a generous bar. Practice your

two-step because you'll hear some of the best country-western dance bands around, from 10 P.M. to 3 A.M.

| | |
|---|---|
| AVERAGE DRINK | $2.25 |
| COVER OR MINIMUM | $2.00 on Sunday and Monday, $3.00 on Tuesday, Wednesday, and Thursday, and $5.00 on Friday and Saturday |
| PLASTIC | None |
| CROWD | Age range—20s and 30s; the country-western fan comes from all professional and socioeconomic backgrounds |
| DRESS | Cowperson outfits and jeans |
| OPEN | Seven nights: Sunday through Thursday 6 P.M. to 4 A.M.; Friday and Saturday 8 P.M. to 4 A.M. |
| FOOD | Free peanuts |

**Club 57**                                   *Dancing and "Anything Goes"*
57 St. Mark's Place (East Village)
(212) 475-9671 (Call eves. if you can't reach them during the day.)

The general public is invited to this membership club. Live music once or twice a week, plus recorded music at other times. All styles. Lots of dancing, parties, movies. The best thing to do is call or write (zip code is 10009) for their monthly calendar.

| | |
|---|---|
| AVERAGE DRINK | $2.00 |
| COVER OR MINIMUM | $3.00 to $5.00 |
| PLASTIC | None; no traveler's checks |
| CROWD | Artists and new wave fans, many under 25 |
| DRESS | Casual or outrageous |
| OPEN | Usually seven days |
| FOOD | None |
| SPECIALS | Call them |

**Coco's**                                            *Roller/Disco*
75 Christopher Street (corner of Seventh Ave. South)
(212) 255-0249

Five thousand square feet is considered a medium-sized rink. It
holds up to 450 people, with a low ceiling and intimate decor. Live
d.j. every night.

| | |
|---|---|
| AVERAGE DRINK | No liquor at the present time |
| COVER OR MINIMUM | $7.00 |
| PLASTIC | None |
| CROWD | A mixed crowd from 18 to 35 years old |
| DRESS | Casual |
| OPEN | Seven nights: 8 P.M. to midnight Sunday through Thursday; 8 P.M. to 1 A.M. Friday and Saturday |
| FOOD | Munchies |
| SPECIALS | Sunday is Men's Night; Monday is two-for-one; Tuesday is Ladies' Night |

**The Cookery**                                         *Jazz Club*
21 University Place (at 8th St., 1 block east of Fifth Ave.)
(212) 674-4450

A great Greenwich Village jazz club with well-known talent. Couples and singles.

| | |
|---|---|
| AVERAGE DRINK | $2.00 |
| COVER OR MINIMUM | $3.00 to $5.00 |
| PLASTIC | MC, V |
| CROWD | All kinds of people from the 20s on up |
| DRESS | Casual |
| OPEN | Six days, 11 A.M. to 1 A.M.; closed Monday |
| FOOD | All kinds; dinner from about $7.00 to $13.00; lunch available also |

**Dan Lynch**                                              *Blues Club*
221 Second Avenue (between 13th and 14th Sts.)
(212) 473-8807

If you love the blues, why not meet someone else who loves the blues, too? The atmosphere here is not geared toward singles—it's geared toward the music. But there are single people that go and feel very comfortable. At least you'll have something in common to talk about right from the start. Thursday, Friday and Saturday are the most lively nights.

|  |  |
|---|---|
| AVERAGE DRINK | $1.75 |
| COVER OR MINIMUM | None |
| PLASTIC | None; no traveler's checks |
| CROWD | Blues lovers from 18 to 50 |
| DRESS | Anything |
| OPEN | Seven days; music usually starts around 9 or 9:30 P.M. and goes until 2 A.M. weeknights and 3 A.M. weekends; send a self-addressed stamped envelope (zip code is 10003) and ask for their monthly schedule |
| FOOD | Sandwiches |
| SPECIALS | Happy Hour from 5 to 6:30 P.M. |

**El Coyote**                                           *Restaurant/Bar*
774 Broadway (between Ninth and Tenth Sts.)
(212) 677-4291

Pleasant Mexican cantina flavor with wooden booths, rough plaster walls, and a big mural. The bar seats twenty-five plus. Half singles, half couples.

|  |  |
|---|---|
| AVERAGE DRINK | $2.00 |
| COVER OR MINIMUM | $5.00 minimum |
| PLASTIC | AE, MC, V |
| CROWD | Neighborhood people and professionals |
| DRESS | Casual |

Sunday through Thursday 11:30 A.M. to
11:30 P.M.; Friday and Saturday 11:30 A.M. to
midnight

FOOD Tex-Mex; dinners run from $5.25 to $10.95

## Farkas                                          *Restaurant/Bar*
60 E. 8th Street (corner of Broadway)
(212) 228-4117

After movies and theater, singles can be found at the forty-chair bar
in the middle of the large floor. Tiffany lamps and soft background
music set the mood.

| | |
|---|---|
| AVERAGE DRINK | $1.85 |
| COVER OR MINIMUM | None |
| PLASTIC | AE, MC, V |
| CROWD | Business people in their 20s, 30s, and 40s |
| DRESS | Most are dressed up |
| OPEN | Seven days, 11 A.M. to 1 A.M. |
| FOOD | Continental and Greek cuisine; dinner prices range from $4.00 to $13.00 |

## Folk City                                      *Folk Music Club*
130 W. 3rd Street (between MacDougal and Ave. of the
Americas)
(212) 254-8449

Hosts top talent in rock, country-western, new wave, blues, folk,
and "new folk" music. They describe themselves as a "historic
music room for over twenty years." Couples and singles.

| | |
|---|---|
| AVERAGE DRINK | Varies |
| COVER OR MINIMUM | Free to about $2.00 |
| PLASTIC | None |
| CROWD | Varies with the band |
| DRESS | Casual |
| OPEN | Call for recorded information or check the paper |
| FOOD | None |

## 14 Christopher Street                                  *Restaurant/Bar*
14 Christopher Street (near Ave. of the Americas)
(212) 620-9594

The bar seats twelve but is often three-deep. Not predominantly a singles bar, but singles can be found there on weekends. Live piano music.

| | |
|---|---|
| AVERAGE DRINK | $2.50 |
| COVER OR MINIMUM | None |
| PLASTIC | AE, MC, V |
| CROWD | All types of people "from leather-and-chains to mink coats," says the owner; most in their 20s |
| DRESS | If your leather is at the cleaners and your mink in storage, jeans would be fine |
| OPEN | Tuesday through Friday 5 P.M. on; Saturday and Sunday noon on |
| FOOD | American/Continental; dinners range from $6.95 to $15.95; lunch available on Saturday, brunch on Sunday |

## The Front                                             *Restaurant/Bar*
91 Seventh Avenue South (between Grove and Barrow Sts.)
(212) 691-3430

The bar seats fifteen plus standing, and the singles infiltration can vary from zero to 60 percent. Live folk music Friday and Saturday, and classical music Sunday afternoon and evening.

| | |
|---|---|
| AVERAGE DRINK | $2.00 |
| COVER OR MINIMUM | None |
| PLASTIC | AE, MC, V |
| CROWD | Professionals from 25 to 50 |
| DRESS | Neat but casual |
| OPEN | Seven days, from 11 A.M. to 3 A.M. during the week and from 11 A.M. to 4 A.M. on weekends |
| FOOD | Lunch, dinner; entrées at night range from $7.00 to $13.00 |

**Garvin's** *Restaurant/Bar*
19 Waverly Place (between Broadway and Fifth Ave.)
(212) 473-5261

Live piano with other instruments occasionally. Garvin's is more of a listening and eating place than a socializing room, yet there are singles there on weekends.

| | |
|---|---|
| AVERAGE DRINK | $2.00 |
| COVER OR MINIMUM | None |
| PLASTIC | AE, CB, DC, MC, V |
| CROWD | All types, 19 to about 24 |
| DRESS | Anything |
| OPEN | Seven days, lunch to 2 A.M. |
| FOOD | French/Continental; dinners range from about $10.00 to $15.00 |

**Googies** *Bar with Kitchen*
237 Sullivan Street (near West 3rd St.)
(212) 673-0050

A good neighborhood saloon with a good jukebox and some good conversation. Not a meat rack by any means.

| | |
|---|---|
| AVERAGE DRINK | $1.75 |
| COVER OR MINIMUM | None |
| PLASTIC | None |
| CROWD | NYU students, professional people of all ages |
| DRESS | Casual but respectable; no muscle beach or tank tops |
| OPEN | Seven days: Monday through Saturday 11 A.M. to 4 A.M.; Sunday noon to 4 A.M. |
| FOOD | Grill and salad; dinner from about $3.00 to $5.00; lunch available, too |

**Great Gildersleeves**                                        *Rock Club*
331 Bowery (between 2nd and 3rd Sts. in the East Village)
(212) 533-3940

A large room, holding about 500 people. Live rock and dancing.

|  |  |
|---|---|
| AVERAGE DRINK | $2.50 |
| COVER OR MINIMUM | Varies |
| PLASTIC | None |
| CROWD | Depends on who's playing; most in their 20s, though |
| DRESS | Anything |
| OPEN | Seven nights, times vary |
| FOOD | Snacks |

**Horn of Plenty**                          *Restaurant/Bar/Music Room*
91 Charles Street (at Bleecker St.)
(212) 242-0636

A large, contemporary place with a dining room downstairs, a nightly piano bar, and a separate music room. Enjoy country-western music on Monday, watch a showcase audition Tuesday, see the showcase itself on Wednesday. Jazz or cabaret acts appear Thursday, with some top name talent on Friday and Saturday. Sunday is jazz.

|  |  |
|---|---|
| AVERAGE DRINK | $3.00 |
| COVER OR MINIMUM | $2.00 to $4.00 |
| PLASTIC | AE, CB, DC, MC, V |
| CROWD | All kinds, all ages |
| DRESS | Casual |
| OPEN | Seven nights from 5 P.M. to 2, 3, or 4 A.M. |
| FOOD | Dinner from 6 P.M., with entrées ranging from $9.00 to $14.00 and up |
| SPECIALS | Happy Hour seven days, from 5 to 7 |

**Jazz Forum**                                          *Jazz Room*
648 Broadway, fifth floor (at Bleecker)
(212) 477-2655

It's a huge loft, holding 400 people, but it's friendly and you'll enjoy big name and local talent.

| | |
|---|---|
| AVERAGE DRINK | Beer and wine for now at about $1.50 a glass; full bar soon |
| COVER OR MINIMUM | $5.00 Wednesday through Sunday, TDF accepted; includes a drink |
| PLASTIC | None |
| CROWD | Jazz lovers |
| DRESS | Casual |
| OPEN | Seven nights: Monday, workshop from 5 P.M. to midnight; Tuesday, jam night from 9 P.M. to 1:30 A.M.; Wednesday, Big Bands; Thursday, smaller ensembles; Friday, Saturday, and Sunday, well known groups; call for showtimes |
| FOOD | Light snacks, calzone |

**Jimmy Days**                                      *Bar/Restaurant*
186 W. 4th Street (one block east of Seventh Ave. South on Sheridan Square)
(212) 929-8942

Huge bar with old dark wood and a very friendly crowd. Good, casual socializing rather than heavy hitting.

| | |
|---|---|
| AVERAGE DRINK | $1.75 to $2.50 |
| COVER OR MINIMUM | $4.00 minimum at tables |
| PLASTIC | None |
| CROWD | NYU students, Wall Street people, neighborhood people, from 19 to 55 |
| DRESS | Casual |
| OPEN | Seven days: Monday through Saturday 8 A.M. to 4 A.M., Sunday noon to 4 A.M. |

| | |
|---|---|
| FOOD | Burgers, roast beef, sandwiches; lunch is available, and dinner prices range from $3.00 to $7.95 |

## Kelly's Village West                                   *Bar/Cabaret*
46 Bedford Street (at Seventh Ave. South)
(212) 929-9322

The atmosphere is warm, personal, and friendly with an old wooden bar, stained glass, and red shag carpeting on the walls above the back bar. Live music Wednesday, Friday, Saturday, and Sunday—pop, ballads, rock, and country-western. Some couples, some singles.

| | |
|---|---|
| AVERAGE DRINK | $2.00 |
| COVER OR MINIMUM | $3.00 |
| PLASTIC | None |
| CROWD | Neighborhood people and entertainers, from 18 to 65 |
| DRESS | Casual |
| OPEN | Seven days, noon to 4 A.M. |
| FOOD | None |
| SPECIALS | Sunday buffet during the summer |

## Kenny's Castaways                                   *Showcase Club*
157 Bleecker Street (between Thompson and Sullivan Sts.)
(212) 473-9870 or 9871

An intimate listening club with a long bar and original music.

| | |
|---|---|
| AVERAGE DRINK | $2.50 |
| COVER OR MINIMUM | Two drink minimum at tables, one at the bar |
| PLASTIC | None |
| CROWD | Lots of neighborhood people, plus others from all over; ages 25 to about 35 |
| DRESS | Casual |
| OPEN | Seven days, noon to 4 A.M. |
| FOOD | Burgers and fries; lunch and dinner; evening prices range from $2.75 to $6.50 |

**La Tertulia** *Café/Latin/Jazz*
113 E. 12th Street (between Third and Fourth Aves.)
(212) 473-8691

Though singles are in the minority here, you still may meet someone else who enjoys Latin jazz, unusual theater events, and art
exhibitions. The bar and restaurant house the gallery, and the stage
is in a separate room.

| | |
|---|---|
| AVERAGE DRINK | $2.00 |
| COVER OR MINIMUM | $5.00 |
| PLASTIC | None |
| CROWD | Professionals, students, neighborhood people, from 27 up |
| DRESS | Casual |
| OPEN | Friday, Saturday, Sunday (sometimes Thursday) from 9:30 P.M. to 3 A.M. |
| FOOD | Snacks |

**The Lion's Head** *Bar/Restaurant*
59 Christopher Street (east of Seventh Ave. South on
Sheridan Square)
(212) 929-0670

Couples, singles, and everyone else. Usually crowded and very
social.

| | |
|---|---|
| AVERAGE DRINK | $1.85 to $2.25 |
| COVER OR MINIMUM | None |
| PLASTIC | AE, DC, MC, V |
| CROWD | Artists, newspaper and entertainment people, locals, tourists, celebrities |
| DRESS | Casual |
| OPEN | Seven days, noon to 4 A.M. |
| FOOD | International and American; dinner prices range from $7.00 to $13.00; lunch is available also |

**The Lone Star Café**                    *Dinner and Show Club*
61 Fifth Avenue (at 13th St.)
(212) 242-1664

With two bars, a 400-person capacity room, music every night
(country-western, blues, jazz), and a great mixture of couples,
groups, and singles, you can't help but have a good time.

| | |
|---|---|
| AVERAGE DRINK | $1.75 |
| COVER OR MINIMUM | $6.00 to $10.00 with a two-drink minimum |
| PLASTIC | AE, CB, DC, MC, V |
| CROWD | All types, all ages |
| DRESS | Casual |
| OPEN | Monday through Friday 11:30 A.M. to 3 A.M.; Saturday and Sunday 7:30 P.M. to 3 A.M. |
| FOOD | Tex-Mex cuisine; dinner entrées are $8.00 to $12.00 |

**Lush Life**                              *Jazz Club*
184 Thompson (at Bleecker St.)
(212) 228-3788

If you love top-name jazz but are not in the mood to rough it, make
a reservation and join the crowd. The maroon-velvet curtains and
cushions and the intimate candlelit tables make it an elegant place
to socialize with other couples and singles. If you want to get away
from the crowd, slip over to the back balcony area and enjoy the
show from there.

| | |
|---|---|
| AVERAGE DRINK | $2.00 and up |
| COVER OR MINIMUM | $6.00 to $10.00 music charge; $5.00 minimum at the tables; $6.00 to $10.00 minimum at the bar—these include the first drink |
| PLASTIC | AE, MC, V |
| CROWD | Jazz lovers of all ages |
| DRESS | From jeans and jackets to black ties and tuxedos |
| OPEN | Seven days, from 6 P.M. to 4 A.M. |

FOOD    Italian/Continental with entrées ranging from about $6.00 to $10.00; Sunday brunch noon to 4 P.M. with live music and no cover charge

**Montana Eve**                                              *Bar/Restaurant*
140 Seventh Avenue South
(212) 242-1200

Warm, turn-of-the-century atmosphere with an ornate but comfortable bar, an outdoor café and greenhouse, and an additional glass enclosed outdoor section. Busy, social mood.

| | |
|---|---|
| AVERAGE DRINK | $2.25 |
| COVER OR MINIMUM | None |
| PLASTIC | None |
| CROWD | Casual, professional crowd from 20 to 32 |
| DRESS | Neat and casual |
| OPEN | Seven days, noon to 3 or 4 A.M. |
| FOOD | Lunch and dinner; average dinner price range is $4.95 to $10.95 |

**One Fifth Avenue**                                    *Restaurant/Cabaret*
2 E. 8th Street (at Fifth Ave.)
(212) 260-3434

Art deco ship design gives a nice mood to singles and couples who socialize and listen to the nightly jazz from 9:30. A vocalist entertains Friday and Saturday with pop and contemporary tunes.

| | |
|---|---|
| AVERAGE DRINK | $2.75 |
| COVER OR MINIMUM | $6.50 minimum |
| PLASTIC | AE, CB, DC, MC, V |
| CROWD | Sophisticated, mid 30s |
| DRESS | Many suits and ties; casual is OK, too |
| OPEN | Seven days, from lunch till closing |
| FOOD | Continental; lunch, dinner, late supper, weekend brunch; a la carte dinner entrées range from $11.00 to $18.00 |

**The Other End**                                    *Restaurant/Cabaret*
147 Bleecker Street (three blocks east of Ave. of the Americas)
(212) 673-7030

A large room with a country/folk atmosphere. The bar in the restaurant serves couples and singles. Entertainment nightly, with a talent showcase on Monday.

| | |
|---|---|
| AVERAGE DRINK | $2.25 |
| COVER OR MINIMUM | In the cabaret, $4.00 to $7.00 |
| PLASTIC | None |
| CROWD | All types of people, 18 to 35; double ID may be required |
| DRESS | Casual |
| OPEN | 3 P.M. to 4 A.M. weekdays, 1 P.M. to 4 A.M. weekends |
| FOOD | Restaurant open till 3 A.M., café till 4; dinner prices range from $2.95 to $9.00 |

**Red River Rib Company**                                    *Restaurant/Bar*
28 W. 8th Street (at MacDougal)
(212) 777-2540

The many singles go to enjoy the live western music Thursday, Friday, and Saturday; the friendly bar; and the western cooking with Texas-size portions.

| | |
|---|---|
| AVERAGE DRINK | $2.00 |
| COVER OR MINIMUM | None |
| PLASTIC | AE, MC, V |
| CROWD | Village people and others, 17 to 70 |
| DRESS | Casual |
| OPEN | Seven days, noon to midnight or later |
| FOOD | Burgers, steaks, ribs, with dinner going from $8.00 to about $12.00 |
| SPECIALS | Perhaps the most unusual time for a Happy Hour anywhere in the city—11 P.M. to 2 A.M. |

**The Reggae Lounge**                                    *Dancing*
599 Broadway (at Houston)
(212) 431-8163

D.j. and dancing. Call for recorded information.


**Riviera Café**                                    *Restaurant/Bar*
225 W. 4th Street (at Seventh Ave. So.)
(212) 242-8732

Two bars and two good jukeboxes. Sports-minded singles watch
TV downstairs, while others socialize upstairs. A good time.

|                    |                                                        |
| ------------------ | ------------------------------------------------------ |
| AVERAGE DRINK      | $2.50                                                  |
| COVER OR MINIMUM   | None                                                   |
| PLASTIC            | None                                                   |
| CROWD              | Local workers during the day and evening; a party crowd at night; average age, 30 |
| DRESS              | Casual                                                 |
| OPEN               | Seven days, noon to 4 A.M.                             |
| FOOD               | Burgers, salads, sandwiches for lunch and dinner, with dinner going for about $5.00 to $8.00 |


**San Francisco Plum**                  *Cocktail Lounge/Restaurant*
544 Avenue of the Americas (at 15th St.)
(212) 924-9125

A comfortable atmosphere with natural wood and plants. Couples
and singles.

|                    |                                           |
| ------------------ | ----------------------------------------- |
| AVERAGE DRINK      | $1.75                                     |
| COVER OR MINIMUM   | None                                      |
| PLASTIC            | AE, CB, DC, MC, V                         |
| CROWD              | Professionals and others in their mid 20s |
| DRESS              | Casual                                    |
| OPEN               | Seven days, 11 A.M. to 4 A.M.             |

|       |                                                              |
|-------|--------------------------------------------------------------|
| FOOD  | American/Continental lunch and dinner; dinner is from $2.95 to $9.75 |
| SPECIALS | Happy Hour, 4 to 7 nightly; call for other specials |

## Seventh Avenue South                                    *Bar/Nightclub*

21 Seventh Avenue South (corner of Leroy; two blocks south of Bleecker St.)
(212) 242-4694

Two floors, with the bar downstairs and the show upstairs. Friendly, bright, airy—a refreshing change from the stereotypically dark, dingy jazz club. Live music nightly from 10 P.M.—jazz and fusion—with top name talent. Many singles, some couples.

|                    |                                             |
|--------------------|---------------------------------------------|
| AVERAGE DRINK      | $2.50                                       |
| COVER OR MINIMUM   | Varies                                      |
| PLASTIC            | MC, V                                       |
| CROWD              | Musicians, actors, neighborhood people; 20 to 40 |
| DRESS              | Casual                                      |
| OPEN               | Seven days, 4 P.M. to 4 A.M.                |
| FOOD               | Snacks and desserts                         |

## Star and Garter                                          *Jazz Club*

105 W. 13th Street (between Ave. of the Americas and Seventh Ave.)
(212) 242-3166

The white brick walls with mirrors, a raised dining area, and brass rails give the room an air of casual chic. A good mixture of singles and couples listen to jazz/blues piano and vocal music Sunday through Tuesday. Jazz duos and trios entertain Wednesday through Saturday.

|                    |                              |
|--------------------|------------------------------|
| AVERAGE DRINK      | $1.95                        |
| COVER OR MINIMUM   | $2.50 minimum at tables      |
| PLASTIC            | AE                           |

| | |
|---|---|
| CROWD | NYU students and neighborhood people; ages 21 to 35 |
| DRESS | Casual |
| OPEN | Seven days from noon to 4 A.M. |
| FOOD | Burgers to steaks; sandwiches at dinner are about $4.95, and a full-course meal goes for $7.95 to $12.95 |

## Sweet Basil                                      *Jazz Club*
88 Seventh Avenue South (between Barrow and Grove Sts.)
(212) 242-1785

An elegant jazz club with top name musicians. Small bar, many tables for drinks and/or dinner. Couples, groups, and some singles.

| | |
|---|---|
| AVERAGE DRINK | $2.50 to $3.00 |
| COVER OR MINIMUM | $6.50 |
| PLASTIC | AE, CB, DC, MC, V |
| CROWD | Jazz lovers and sophisticates from 20 to 60 |
| DRESS | Casual |
| OPEN | Seven days from noon till . . . |
| FOOD | American/Continental menu for lunch and dinner, with dinner ranging from $5.00 to $15.00; Sunday brunch available from 3 to 7 P.M. with live jazz and no cover |

## Village Corner                                  *Restaurant/Bar*
142 Bleecker Street (at La Guardia Place)
(212) 473-9762

Large and friendly with many couples and many singles. Jazz piano nightly. Quartet on Sunday from 2:30 to 5:30 P.M.

| | |
|---|---|
| AVERAGE DRINK | $2.00 to $2.50 |
| COVER OR MINIMUM | None |
| PLASTIC | None |
| CROWD | All types, all ages |
| DRESS | Casual |

OPEN   Seven days, 11 A.M. to 4 A.M.

FOOD   Chili, burgers, quiches, desserts; a burger is about $3.00

## Village Vanguard                                                *Jazz Club*
178 Seventh Avenue South (near 11th St.)
(212) AL 5-4037

Funky, basement atmosphere and the top names in jazz. Call or check the paper to find out who's playing.

| | |
|---|---|
| AVERAGE DRINK | $2.00 to $3.00 |
| COVER OR MINIMUM | $6.50 plus one drink |
| PLASTIC | None |
| CROWD | All types, early 20s to late 50s |
| DRESS | Anything |
| OPEN | Seven days; show times are 10 P.M., 11:30 P.M., and 1 A.M. |
| FOOD | None |

## West 4th Street Saloon                         *Restaurant/Bar/Cabaret*
174 W. 4th Street (between Ave. of the Americas and Seventh Ave. South)
(212) 255-0518

This warm and cozy room has multilevel dining, three fireplaces, and a large singles crowd. Classical guitar adds to the atmosphere on Sunday.

| | |
|---|---|
| AVERAGE DRINK | $2.25 |
| COVER OR MINIMUM | $2.00 per person on a busy night |
| PLASTIC | AE, CB, DC |
| CROWD | All kinds of people, mainly around 25 to 30 years old |
| DRESS | Casual |
| OPEN | Seven days, 11 A.M. to 4 A.M. |
| FOOD | Lunch, dinner, late supper, Sunday brunch; average dinner might run $8.95 |

**The Wild Bunch**                                    *Wine Bar*
82 Bank Street (at Bleecker)
(212) 929-8656

A casual, loose place with a nice horseshoe bar that's separated
from the restaurant, and offering a varied foreign beer selection.
Music seven nights, with jazz piano three nights and singers doing
blues, jazz, and rock four nights. Couples and singles.

|  |  |
|---|---|
| AVERAGE DRINK | $2.25 |
| COVER OR MINIMUM | None unless it's very crowded |
| PLASTIC | MC, V |
| CROWD | Local Village people, the H.B. Acting Studio crowd, and others; ages 22 to mid 40s |
| DRESS | Casual |
| OPEN | Seven days noon to 4 A.M. |
| FOOD | Lunch from noon to 5:30 P.M.; dinner costs about $6.95 or $7.95 and is served from 6 P.M. to 12:30 A.M. weeknights, till 2 A.M. weekends |

---

## Soho, Tribeca, and Lower Manhattan

EVERYTHING BELOW HOUSTON STREET

---

**Brass Moon Café**                                *Restaurant/Bar*
145 Duane Street (between Church St. and
W. Broadway, Tribeca)
(212) 227-3042

This cozy, warm, private room serves a business crowd during the
day, and more singles at night. The bar seats forty people so there's
lots of talking and socializing going on.

|  |  |
|---|---|
| AVERAGE DRINK | $1.75 |
| COVER OR MINIMUM | Varies |
| PLASTIC | AE, MC, V |

| | |
|---|---|
| CROWD | All kinds of people; the singles are from 28 to 35 |
| DRESS | Casual |
| OPEN | Seven days, from 11:30 A.M. to 4 A.M. |
| FOOD | Lunch, dinner till midnight; dinner prices range from $6.50 to $14.00; brunch is served on Saturday and Sunday |
| SPECIALS | Happy Hour from 4 to 6 P.M., Monday through Friday |

**Cantina Caffé de Medici** *Café*
475 W. Broadway (Soho)
(212) 982-7445

Comfortable setting, looking onto a garden. Singles and couples enjoy the sophisticated, highly intellectual atmosphere. Recorded jazz and classical music in the background never interferes with the major activity—conversation.

| | |
|---|---|
| AVERAGE DRINK | Wine and beer from $1.50; no hard liquor |
| COVER OR MINIMUM | None |
| PLASTIC | None |
| CROWD | The weekend crowd is in the 25 to 45 age range; during the week it's a little older; many celebrities frequent the place in addition to artists, gallery owners, and writers |
| DRESS | Anything except roller skates |
| OPEN | Noon to 1 A.M., seven days |
| FOOD | No hot food—but you won't go hungry with their selection of fruits, cheeses, salami, and other delights; many different coffees, and an excellent French and Italian wine menu |

**Central Falls**                                    *Bar/Restaurant/Gallery*
478 W. Broadway (Soho)
(212) 533-9481

Long railroad-car-shaped room. In one area is the gallery/restaurant which seats 80 to 100 people. In the front is the comfortable, handcarved bar which was brought down from Central Falls, Rhode Island. The bar area seats twenty to twenty-five plus cocktail tables. Easy, friendly atmosphere. Many couples, some singles.

| | |
|---|---|
| AVERAGE DRINK | $2.75 |
| COVER OR MINIMUM | Varies |
| PLASTIC | AE, MC, V |
| CROWD | Professionals in their mid 30s |
| DRESS | Casual |
| OPEN | Seven days: Monday through Friday 5 P.M. to 1 A.M.; Saturday noon to 2 A.M.; Sunday noon to about midnight |
| FOOD | Continental and American; burgers are $5.50, steaks to $17.50 |

**Ear Inn**                                                          *Pub*
326 Spring Street (Soho)
(212) 226-9060

An old, cozy pub seating fifty people for meals and twenty-five to thirty at the bar plus standing. The singles and couples go to hear the Saturday poetry readings and the jazz and contemporary music on Sunday.

| | |
|---|---|
| AVERAGE DRINK | $1.75 |
| COVER OR MINIMUM | None |
| PLASTIC | None |
| CROWD | Poets and artists of all ages |
| DRESS | Casual |
| OPEN | Seven days, usually noon to 4 A.M. |
| FOOD | Dinner goes from $3.00 to $6.50; lunch and dinner menus are both varied |

**Grand Street Bar**                              *Restaurant/Bar/Lounge*
55 Grand Street (corner W. Broadway, Soho)
(212) 966-4180

The bar/lounge has twenty stools plus standing room and the atmosphere is soft, low-keyed, and laidback. The decor is "Soho loft."

| | |
|---|---|
| AVERAGE DRINK | $2.00 |
| COVER OR MINIMUM | None |
| PLASTIC | AE, MC, V |
| CROWD | Artists, writers, and actors in their 20s |
| DRESS | Stylish Soho clothing |
| OPEN | Seven nights, from 4 P.M. to 2 A.M. |
| FOOD | Chinese |

**Greene Street**                                   *Restaurant/Bar/Gallery*
101 Greene Street (between Prince and Spring Sts., Soho)
(212) 925-2415

Although the schedule is very flexible, the Greene Street bar and dining area has varied music nightly and the gallery, called Greene Space, has everything from experimental theater to music and dance programs.

| | |
|---|---|
| AVERAGE DRINK | $2.00 |
| COVER OR MINIMUM | Varies |
| PLASTIC | AE, MC, V |
| CROWD | Varied crowd of all ages |
| DRESS | Anything |
| OPEN | Seven days; noon to 2 or 3 A.M., Monday through Friday; from 6 P.M. on Saturday and Sunday; bar opens at 6 P.M. daily |
| FOOD | Full dinner menu; entrées from $16.00 to $20.00 |

**Kitchen Center**                                     *Gallery/Showcase*
484 Broome Street (Soho)
(212) 925-3615

A gallery and performing space, very avant garde. The perfor-
mances are informal, so there's lots of walking around socializing—
at times it's more like a party than a concert.

| | |
|---|---|
| AVERAGE DRINK | Beer and wine at some performances |
| COVER OR MINIMUM | $4.00 |
| PLASTIC | None |
| CROWD | Artists and others from 20 on up |
| DRESS | Casual |
| OPEN | Call for performance dates and times; gallery open Tuesday through Saturday 1 P.M. to 6 P.M. |
| FOOD | None |

**Laughing Mountain Bar and Grill**          *Restaurant/Bar*
148 Chambers Street (between W. Broadway and
Greenwich St., Tribeca)
(212) 233-4434

The thirty-foot bar and avant garde decor create a casual atmosphere. Live chamber music Sunday afternoon. Couples and
singles.

| | |
|---|---|
| AVERAGE DRINK | $2.25 |
| COVER OR MINIMUM | None |
| PLASTIC | AE, CB, DC, MC, V |
| CROWD | Young bohemian, from 18 to 48 |
| DRESS | Casual |
| OPEN | Seven days, 11:30 A.M. to 2 A.M. |
| FOOD | Dinner prices on the nouvelle cuisine menu range from $9.00 to $14.50; lunch and weekend brunch are also available |

**Mudd Club**                                    *Nightclub/Cabaret*
77 White Street (2 blocks south of Canal St. between Broadway and Lafayette, Tribeca)
(212) 227-7777

Constant live entertainment by a wide variety of rock/disco/fusion groups, and comedians. Dance to the music, or visit the art galleries on the third and fourth floors. Call for recorded information.

|  |  |
|---|---|
| AVERAGE DRINK | $2.50 |
| COVER OR MINIMUM | Free to $10.00 |
| PLASTIC | None |
| CROWD | The crowd varies tremendously depending on what group is playing, but the management likes to maintain a sophisticated mood; large groups of guys may be turned away |
| DRESS | Well-dressed |
| OPEN | Seven nights, usually from 9 P.M. to 4 A.M. but call first |
| FOOD | None |

**The Odeon**                                    *Restaurant/Bar*
145 W. Broadway (corner of Thomas, Tribeca)
(212) 233-0507

The large walnut-and-maple art deco bar takes up about a fourth of this sophisticated 3000-square-foot restaurant. Many singles.

|  |  |
|---|---|
| AVERAGE DRINK | $3.00 |
| COVER OR MINIMUM | None |
| PLASTIC | AE, MC, V |
| CROWD | Artists, movie stars, designers; all ages |
| DRESS | Casual but trendy |
| OPEN | Seven days, noon to 4 A.M. |
| FOOD | Nouvelle cuisine with dinner entrées from $8.00 to $22.00; Sunday brunch available from noon to 3:30 P.M. |

**162 Spring Street**                                    *Bar/Restaurant*
401 W. Broadway (at the corner of Spring St., Soho)
(212) 431-7637

The bar holds about fifty people and there's a good deal of socializing. When you get hungry, choose from three dining rooms.

| | |
|---|---|
| AVERAGE DRINK | $2.25 |
| COVER OR MINIMUM | None |
| PLASTIC | AE, MC, V |
| CROWD | Artists, art lovers; most in the 20s and 30s, but a fair number of 40s and 50s, too |
| DRESS | Casual |
| OPEN | Tuesday through Saturday, noon to 4 A.M.; Sunday and Monday, noon to 3 A.M. |
| FOOD | Tuesday through Saturday full menu till 2 A.M.; Sunday and Monday till 1 A.M.; dinners range from $6.95 to $15.00 |

**Ones**                                                        *Disco*
111 Hudson Street (between Franklin and North Moore Sts., Tribeca)
(212) 925-0011

The bar was built over 100 years ago, giving the room a nice antique feeling. Dance to d.j. and recorded music with many other singles and some couples. The room gets very crowded—a "mob scene" as one bartender put it.

| | |
|---|---|
| AVERAGE DRINK | $2.00 |
| COVER OR MINIMUM | $5.00 |
| PLASTIC | None |
| CROWD | Perhaps the most mixed group of people around; age range 21 to 40 |
| DRESS | Casual |
| OPEN | Thursday, Friday and Saturday from 9 P.M. to 4:30 A.M. |
| FOOD | None |
| SPECIALS | Call for details |

**Riverrun**                                    *Restaurant/Bar/Gallery*
176 Franklin Street (at Hudson St., Tribeca)
(212) 966-3894

A cozy room with live music and the *New York Times* at Sunday brunch.

| | |
|---|---|
| AVERAGE DRINK | $2.00 |
| COVER OR MINIMUM | None |
| PLASTIC | AE, MC, V |
| CROWD | "You name 'em, we got 'em," says the bartender; late 20s |
| DRESS | Casual |
| OPEN | Seven days, 11:30 A.M. to 2 or 3 A.M. |
| FOOD | Full American menu; dinner from $5.95 to $11.95; lunch available also |
| SPECIALS | Friday two-for-one from 5 to 7 P.M. |

**Skrambles**                                    *Bar with Restaurant*
402 W. Broadway (corner of Spring St., Soho)
(212) 966-6660

Rustic, cozy, comfortable, and social.

| | |
|---|---|
| AVERAGE DRINK | $2.00 |
| COVER OR MINIMUM | Variable minimum for dinner at certain times |
| PLASTIC | AE, DC |
| CROWD | Eclectic; 20 to 35 |
| DRESS | Everything |
| OPEN | Seven days, from 11:45 A.M. to 2 A.M. weekdays and 3 A.M. weekends |
| FOOD | Light meals and complete salad bar; average dinner is $11.00 |

**Smokestacks Lightnin'**                                    *Restaurant/Bar*
380 Canal Street (corner of W. Broadway, Soho)
(212) 226-0485

Comfortable, laidback atmosphere with lots of easy socializing.

| | |
|---|---|
| AVERAGE DRINK | $2.25 |
| COVER OR MINIMUM | None |
| PLASTIC | AE |
| CROWD | All types, from late 20s to 30s |
| DRESS | Casual |
| OPEN | Seven days, 11 A.M. to 4 A.M. |
| FOOD | Seafood, chicken, and other American dishes served till 2 A.M. weeknights, till 4 A.M. weekends; dinner prices range from $3.00 to $11.50 |

**South Street Seaport Museum District**                    *Concerts and Ships*
Pier 16, Fulton Street at the East River
(or write to:
203 Front St.
New York, NY 10038
Attn.: Public Relations)
(212) 766-9020

Imagine the divine delight of sitting on New York City's romantic, historic Pier 16 under the summer stars, listening to jazz. Free. If you do nothing else, be sure to call or write for their current schedule. There are other special events, too, as well as tours of the ships. The crowd is mostly couples and groups, so round up some friends before you go.

**Spring Street Natural Food Bar**                    *Restaurant/Bar*
149 Spring Street (at W. Broadway, Soho)
(212) 966-0290

Small bar, big restaurant, light, pleasant decor. Mixed couples and singles.

| | |
|---|---|
| AVERAGE DRINK | $2.25 |
| COVER OR MINIMUM | None |
| PLASTIC | AE, CB, DC, MC, V |
| CROWD | Young professionals and neighborhood people from 18 to 48 |

| DRESS | Casual |
| OPEN | Seven days, 11:30 A.M. to 2 A.M. |
| FOOD | Lunch, brunch, dinner with a huge health food menu; dinner entrées range from $5.50 to $10.00 |

**Stilwende**                                    *Dance Room and Cabaret*
225 W. Broadway (between Franklin and White, near Canal St., Tribeca)
(212) 431-1133

A lot happens here. With the bare walls and that clean, minimalist look that the designer describes as "direct architecture," the room is ready for whatever may occur. "Anything can take place," explains one of the artists connected with their weekend techno-cabaret troup called Andronyx. Tuesday, Wednesday, and Thursday there's a d.j. and dancing. Often they will have movie previews, art or photography gallery showings, and fashion previews.

| AVERAGE DRINK | $3.00 |
| COVER OR MINIMUM | $10.00 |
| PLASTIC | AE |
| CROWD | Uptown and downtown people, all ages |
| DRESS | Trendy and fashionable, leaning toward punk |
| OPEN | Tuesday through Saturday from about 10 P.M. to 4 A.M. |
| FOOD | None |

**Tenbrooks**                                             *Bar/Restaurant*
62 Reade Street (between Broadway and Church St., Tribeca)
(212) 349-5900

A small "trysting place" in a low key, peaceful neighborhood near Tribeca. Low lights and candles from 4 P.M. on. Couples and singles enjoy the friendly atmosphere.

| AVERAGE DRINK | $2.50 |
| COVER OR MINIMUM | None |

| PLASTIC | AE, MC, V |
|---|---|
| CROWD | Wall Street people, City Hall employees, lawyers, and others; all ages |
| DRESS | Neat but casual; not punk |
| OPEN | Monday through Friday from lunch till about 10:30 P.M.; Saturday dinner till about 11:30; Sunday brunch |
| FOOD | Very busy lunch (call for reservations); dinner prices range from $7.95 to $13.00; coffee-and-cognac people welcome |

## Two Eleven                                    *Bar/Restaurant*
211 W. Broadway (at Franklin St., Tribeca)
(212) 925-7202

A mixed, friendly crowd gathers in this converted warehouse with sixteen-foot windows, a big oak bar and marble slab tables. Chamber music at Sunday brunch.

| AVERAGE DRINK | $2.00 |
|---|---|
| COVER OR MINIMUM | None |
| PLASTIC | AE |
| CROWD | Lunch—people who work in the area; evenings—Soho and Tribeca residents, ages 23 to 40 |
| DRESS | Casual |
| OPEN | Seven days, noon to 3 A.M. |
| FOOD | Continental with a Middle Eastern flavor; lunch and dinner, with dinner entrées ranging from about $5.00 to $12.00 |

## Watts Happen Inn                              *Restaurant/Bar*
32 Watts Street (near Ave. of the Americas, Soho)
(212) 925-7693

Mostly couples, but some singles and very chatty. A tiny place holding nineteen people and described by the owner as a "late Victorian adventure."

| | |
|---|---|
| AVERAGE DRINK | $2.25 |
| COVER OR MINIMUM | None |
| PLASTIC | DC, MC, V with a $20.00 minimum only |
| CROWD | Artists, intellectuals, poets, industrialists; from 25 to 40 |
| DRESS | Casual |
| OPEN | Seven days: Monday through Friday from 4:30 P.M. on; Saturday and Sunday from noon on |
| FOOD | Ribs, chili and other specialty items; $5.75 to $7.75 |
| SPECIALS | Are you ready?—Kill-a-Watts Hour is from 4:30 to 7:30; free hors d'oeuvres on weekends |

**The Wine Bar** *Wine Bar*
422 W. Broadway (between Prince and Spring Sts., Soho)
(212) 431-4790

A London pub/French wine bar type of place. Friendly, sophisticated, many singles and couples. Nice, non-hassled atmosphere.

| | |
|---|---|
| AVERAGE DRINK | $2.00 |
| COVER OR MINIMUM | None |
| PLASTIC | None |
| CROWD | Entertainment, business people, celebrities of all ages; also just plain folks |
| DRESS | Anything |
| OPEN | Seven days from noon to about 4 A.M. |
| FOOD | Continental-type snacks and cheeses from $2.75 to $5.25 |

**Wings** *Restaurant/Bar*
76 Wooster Street (between Spring and Broome, Soho)
(212) 966-1300

If you like pink, you'll like Wings. It's all pink, even the piano (which is played nightly from 8 P.M. to midnight). The bar is on a balcony in the back of this ultra-contemporary room and looks out over the diners. Many singles, and quite friendly.

| | |
|---|---|
| AVERAGE DRINK | $3.25 |
| COVER OR MINIMUM | None |
| PLASTIC | AE |
| CROWD | Lawyers, brokers, artists, tourists; all ages |
| DRESS | From casual to formal, but must be neat |
| OPEN | Seven days, noon to 4 A.M. |
| FOOD | French/American/Nouvelle; dinner entrées run from $13.00 to $21.00; weekend brunch is available from noon to 4 P.M. |

# BROOKLYN

**Brown Derby**                                              *Lounge/Dancing*
9310 4th Avenue (Bay Ridge)
(212) 748-7200

A big elegant room with a gas fireplace in winter and a nice-sized
dance floor. Live music, all kinds. Couples and singles.

| | |
|---|---|
| AVERAGE DRINK | Varies |
| COVER OR MINIMUM | None |
| PLASTIC | None |
| CROWD | Neighborhood people, 25 and up |
| DRESS | Jackets |
| OPEN | Tuesday through Sunday, 7 P.M. to 4 A.M.; closed Monday |
| FOOD | Hamburgers and cheeseburgers served Friday and Saturday only |

**Café Galleria**                         *Café/Bar/Bakery/Restaurant*
174 Montague Street (Brooklyn Heights)
(212) 625-7883

The gloriously unique, international flavor of this charming art
deco café is highlighted by a thirty-foot mural of Montague Street
in the 1920's by Italian painter Giancarlo Impiglia.

| | |
|---|---|
| AVERAGE DRINK | $2.00 to $2.50 |
| COVER OR MINIMUM | None at the bar |
| PLASTIC | AE, DC, MC, V |
| CROWD | Writers, painters, Brooklyn Academy of Music people, and local brownstone residents who come in with their kids for ice cream; all ages |
| DRESS | Casual |

<dl>
<dt>OPEN</dt>
<dd>Monday through Thursday 8 A.M. to 11 P.M.; Friday 8 A.M. to midnight; Saturday 8 A.M. to 1 A.M.; Sunday 9 A.M. to 10 P.M.</dd>
<dt>FOOD</dt>
<dd>Breakfast, lunch, dinner by candlelight, and Sunday brunch, or feel free to stop in for a cappuccino and éclair; there's also a large selection of French and domestic wines; average dinner price, $3.95 to $10.00</dd>
</dl>

## Capulet's on Montague                                          *Pub*
151 Montague Street (Brooklyn Heights)
(212) 852-3128

Many singles frequent this "ale house and gathering place" to drink, socialize, and play darts. During the summer you can sit in the outdoor café—or indoors all year in the old English pub atmosphere. If you're there for Sunday brunch you'll be treated to live chamber music. And Saturday night during the winter months enjoy bluegrass.

| | |
|---|---|
| AVERAGE DRINK | $2.25 |
| COVER OR MINIMUM | None at the bar, $7.00 at tables |
| PLASTIC | None |
| CROWD | Brooklyn Heights and Park Slope people in their 20s and 30s |
| DRESS | Casual |
| OPEN | Thursday, Friday and Saturday from noon to 3 A.M.; Sunday through Wednesday noon to 1 A.M. |
| FOOD | Lunch, dinner, brunch on Sunday; dinner prices from $3.25 to $12.95 |

## Jolly Bull Pub                                                 *Pub*
2925 Avenue H (at the foot of Brooklyn College, Flatbush)
(212) 434-9522

A campus hangout in an English pub atmosphere, there are lots of singles during the winter and a mixture of singles and couples during the summer. They've been in business fifteen years, so you know they're doing something right.

| | |
|---|---|
| AVERAGE DRINK | $1.75 |
| COVER OR MINIMUM | Friday and Saturday $2.00 minimum at the tables |
| PLASTIC | None |
| CROWD | Students and others from 18 to 30 |
| DRESS | Casual—but you've gotta wear shoes; and no beach clothes |
| OPEN | Seven days, 4 P.M. to closing |
| FOOD | Full menu in the winter, hamburger menu in the summer; prices run from $2.00 to $6.50 |

**Pier 92** *Restaurant with Bar*
377 Beach (behind McDonald's, Rockaway Beach)
(212) 945-2200

Though there are mostly couples and only some singles, Pier 92 is right on the water with a panoramic view from Kennedy Airport to the Manhattan skyline. It's worth a drink there just to soak up the sight. Inside there's a thirty-three-foot bar and dark wood decor with a fireplace.

| | |
|---|---|
| AVERAGE DRINK | $1.75 |
| COVER OR MINIMUM | None |
| PLASTIC | AE |
| CROWD | Professionals and neighborhood people, many politicians; the age span is from the mid 20s on up |
| DRESS | Casual |
| OPEN | Seven days, noon to 11 P.M. |
| FOOD | American menu for lunch and dinner; dinner costs from $6.95 to $15.95 |

**Snooky's Pub**                                    *Restaurant/Pub*
140 7th Avenue (Park Slope)
(212) 788-3245

A popular singles haunt after 10:30 P.M.; Snooky's is comfortable, casual, and very social. With a 28-foot-long bar and table capacity for eighty, the room looks like a typical, earth-colored New York bar. But it's not. All the tables and the bar itself are made from the hatch covers of World War II liberty ships. They've used the actual wood, the handles, and all the original hardware. Why not drop by, take in a bit of history, and start a conversation about hatch covers?

| | |
|---|---|
| AVERAGE DRINK | $2.00 |
| COVER OR MINIMUM | None |
| PLASTIC | AE, DC, MC, V |
| CROWD | Professionals, actors, models; age 35 and under |
| DRESS | Casual |
| OPEN | Seven days, noon to 4 A.M. |
| FOOD | Hamburgers till 2 A.M. Friday and Saturday, and till 1 A.M. weeknights; dinners range from $3.25 to $10.00 |

**Two Steps Down**                                  *Restaurant/Pub*
240 DeKalb Avenue (Clinton Hill/Fort Green)
(212) 622-9041

Enjoy ambience and warmth in a rustic old brownstone. The street floor has the restaurant and kitchen, and upstairs on the second floor you'll find the pub and another dining room. There's also a small terrace for use during the summer. Couples and singles.

| | |
|---|---|
| AVERAGE DRINK | $2.00 to $2.25 |
| COVER OR MINIMUM | None |
| PLASTIC | AE, DC, MC, V |
| CROWD | Professionals, doctors, and lawyers; over 25 |
| DRESS | No shorts |
| OPEN | Seven days, 11:30 A.M. to 4 A.M. |
| FOOD | Seafood and Southern cuisine for lunch and dinner; dinner $6.50 to $9.25   [cont'd] |

SPECIALS Happy Hour is from 5 P.M. to 7, Monday
through Friday; also other specials as they
think them up

**United Skates of America**                    *Roller Skating*
6002 Fort Hamilton Parkway (Bay Ridge)
(212) 435-3221

Manager John Neilson tells us that Sunday night is the best night
for singles, but their schedule may fluctuate, so call. When the light
show is off, you'll see that you're in a big, contemporary room done
in earth tones. Lots of fun, music, and socializing.

| | |
|---|---|
| AVERAGE DRINK | No liquor |
| COVER OR MINIMUM | $3.50 plus $1.00 skate rental |
| PLASTIC | None |
| CROWD | Many students, 19 to 25 |
| DRESS | Casual but neat |
| OPEN | Call for schedule |
| FOOD | Full snack and soft drink menu |

**United Skates of America**                    *Roller Skating*
2402 86th Street (Bensonhurst)
(212) 373-1248

An adult rink done in silver, chrome, and black with mirror ac-
cents. Singles have special nights, so call to find out when they are.
All kinds of music and live d.j.s in a nightclub-like atmosphere.

| | |
|---|---|
| AVERAGE DRINK | No liquor |
| COVER OR MINIMUM | $3.00 |
| PLASTIC | Major credit cards accepted in the Pro Shop only |
| CROWD | All ages, call |
| DRESS | Casual but neat |
| OPEN | Call |
| FOOD | Snacks |
| SPECIALS | Call for details |

**Amber Lantern**                                  *Restaurant/Bar*
150th Street and Northern Boulevard, Flushing
(212) 445-9500

A pretty, friendly place with lanterns and that early English pub look. The large bar seats many couples and some singles who dance to the live music nightly.

|  |  |
|---|---|
| AVERAGE DRINK | $1.75 |
| COVER OR MINIMUM | None |
| PLASTIC | AE, CB, DC, MC, V |
| CROWD | All types of people in their late 30s and early 40s |
| DRESS | Jackets on weekends |
| OPEN | Seven days, noon to 4 A.M. |
| FOOD | Restaurant open till midnight and till 2 A.M. Friday and Saturday; dinner prices go from $8.50 to $10.50 till 7 P.M. weeknights, and slightly higher after 7 and on weekends; lunch available also |

**Beethoven's Restaurant and Pub**           *Restaurant/Pub*
271-11 Union Turnpike, New Hyde Park (just west of
Lakeville Rd.)
(212) 347-9565

As one might expect, the walls are decorated with all sorts of instruments, giving a musical motif to the heavy singles activity. It's a comfortable room with live jazz on Thursday, Top 40/rock and roll on Friday, and Beatles music on Saturday—mainly for listening rather than dancing.

| | |
|---|---|
| AVERAGE DRINK | $1.75 |
| COVER OR MINIMUM | $2.00 during live entertainment |
| PLASTIC | AE, MC, V |
| CROWD | Business crowd during the day, joined by the rest of the world at night; all ages |
| DRESS | Neat |
| OPEN | Seven days: Monday through Friday, noon to 2 A.M.; Saturday and Sunday 6 P.M. to 4 A.M. |
| FOOD | Light meals and Italian; dinners from $3.25 to $9.25 |
| SPECIALS | Happy Hour Monday through Friday, 5 to 7 P.M. |

## Camouflage  *Nightclub*
38-17 Bell Boulevard, Bayside
(212) 631-7656

Is there such a thing as a "rock disco"? You'll find out here, along with many other singles. Dance to top name and New York showcase bands in the brand new contemporary room—all done in greys, blacks and high gloss mica with air brush paintings on the walls. Or choose one of several side lounges—one with pillows, another with a mirrored area, and another separate bar area. It's an intimate situation with the bands set up right on the dance floor— you could reach right out and touch them if you were so inclined.

| | |
|---|---|
| AVERAGE DRINK | $2.50 |
| COVER OR MINIMUM | $1.00 on Wednesday, $3.00 on Thursday and Friday, $5.00 on Saturday |
| PLASTIC | None |
| CROWD | All types of people, mainly in their early to mid 20s |
| DRESS | Casual but neat |
| OPEN | Wednesday through Sunday till 4 A.M.; Wednesday, Thursday and Sunday doors open at 9:30 P.M., Friday and Saturday at 10 P.M. |

|            |                              |
|------------|------------------------------|
| FOOD       | Restaurant opening soon      |
| SPECIALS   | House drinks are 75¢ on Wednesday; Sunday is VIP Night with house drinks at $1.25 |

## Lemon Tree

*Disco*

70-34 Austin Street, Forest Hills
(212) 263-2850

Someone has finally invented a disco with an additional room where people can go to talk—and actually be heard! Lemon Tree is an intimate, romantic place with a d.j. spinning discs, and a predominantly singles crowd.

|                   |                              |
|-------------------|------------------------------|
| AVERAGE DRINK     | $2.75 to $3.50               |
| COVER OR MINIMUM  | $3.00 to $6.00 admission     |
| PLASTIC           | None                         |
| CROWD             | All types, over 21           |
| DRESS             | Neat and proper              |
| OPEN              | Wednesday through Sunday 9:30 P.M. to 4 A.M. |
| FOOD              | None                         |
| SPECIALS          | Call for details             |

## O.K. Corral

*Country-Western*

164-07 Northern Boulevard, Flushing (at 164th St.)
(212) 961-0846

The wild west has come to Queens. Here you can dance, listen to the live country-western music, or round up some of the many other singles and socialize. It's a real saloon atmosphere with authentic wagon wheels and other western items decorating the walls.

|                   |                              |
|-------------------|------------------------------|
| AVERAGE DRINK     | $2.00                        |
| COVER OR MINIMUM  | $3.00 admission              |
| PLASTIC           | None                         |
| CROWD             | Party people from 20 to 80   |
| DRESS             | Many country-western outfits, jeans |
| OPEN              | Wednesday through Saturday, 7 P.M. till . . . |

FOOD None
SPECIALS Call for their many specials such as
Jamboree Night

## O'Neill's                                              *Bar/Restaurant*
64-21 53rd Drive, Maspeth
(212) 429-9193, (212) 429-8289, (212) 429-9131

Many singles in the evenings, especially on Friday, Saturday, and
Sunday to hear the live guitarist with pop and rock sounds. The
dining rooms are rustic and cozy with fireplaces and the bar has
that intimate wood and brick feeling. Many couples, too.

| | |
|---|---|
| AVERAGE DRINK | $1.75 |
| COVER OR MINIMUM | None |
| PLASTIC | AE |
| CROWD | All types of people in their mid to late 20s |
| DRESS | Casual |
| OPEN | Seven days, 11:30 A.M. to 3 A.M. |
| FOOD | Steaks and seafood; an average dinner might cost you $8.00 or $9.00; lunch available also |

## One Station Plaza                            *Bar/Restaurant/Pub*
213th Street and 41st Avenue, Bayside
(212) 224-6520

A rustic, dark wood atmosphere with a fireplace that actually
works, art on the wall, and friendly people—many of whom are
single. A trio plays pop and country music every night.

| | |
|---|---|
| AVERAGE DRINK | $2.00 |
| COVER OR MINIMUM | None |
| PLASTIC | AE, CB, DC, MC, V |
| CROWD | Many professional people in their mid 30s |
| DRESS | Neat |
| OPEN | Seven days, 11 A.M. to 4 A.M. |
| FOOD | Large menu for lunch and dinner; dinner prices range from $5.95 to $23.95 |

**Poets**                                          *Nightclub*
147-28 Northern Boulevard, Flushing
(212) 359-0069

A big, friendly place with a fifty-four-foot bar and lots of dancing.
Live rock and roll nightly. Singles and couples.

| | |
|---|---|
| AVERAGE DRINK | $1.50 |
| COVER OR MINIMUM | $3.00 |
| PLASTIC | None |
| CROWD | All types, from 21 up |
| DRESS | Casual, but no sneakers or cutoffs |
| OPEN | Seven days, from 10 A.M. to 4 A.M. |
| FOOD | Pretzels on the bar |
| SPECIALS | Call for details |

**Rockaways**                                      *Nightclub*
113-20 Beach Channel Drive, Rockaway Park
(212) 474-5984

Here's the place to go to forget all your troubles and woes. It's
teeming with fun, music, singles, glamour, and live rock and blues
bands Wednesday through Saturday. The cocoa- and peach-colored
room holds 1000 people all ready to party. You can sit at a table,
socialize at the 150-foot bar, or join the crowd on the 1000-square-
foot tile dance floor. Rockaways describes itself as a "Rock and
Roll Video Club," and while there are lights and slides flashing on
and off most of the time, it has a contemporary but not impersonal
atmosphere.

| | |
|---|---|
| AVERAGE DRINK | $1.75 |
| COVER OR MINIMUM | $3.00 during the week, $5.00 on weekends |
| PLASTIC | None |
| CROWD | Women must be 18, men 21 |
| DRESS | Proper |
| OPEN | Wednesday through Saturday, 9 P.M. to 4 A.M. on weekends, 8 P.M. to 4 A.M. on weekdays; cocktail tables must be reserved |

|      |            |
|------|------------|
| FOOD | Peanuts    |
| SPECIALS | Here's the good part: Thursday is "I Want to Be Sedated Night" with, of course, certain drink specials; there are magic shows, various admission specials, and whatever else the management can dream up |

## Skateworld                                    *Roller Skating*
57-16 99th Street, Elmhurst
(at 57th Ave., near Alexander's)
(212) 271-1500/1

The 10,000 square feet includes a maple floor, Pro Shop, a carpeted rest area, a great sound system, and light shows. The d.j. keeps things going. Skateworld has many singles events, so call them to find out when you'd best fit in.

|      |            |
|------|------------|
| AVERAGE DRINK | No liquor |
| COVER OR MINIMUM | $2.50 to $4.00 plus $1.00 for skates |
| PLASTIC | None |
| CROWD | Friday and Saturday are Adult Nights— ID required |
| DRESS | Comfortable |
| OPEN | Call |
| FOOD | Snack bar |

## Sly Fox Inn                                    *Pub/Restaurant*
177-23 Union Turnpike, Flushing
(2 blocks east of St. John's University)
(212) 969-8169

Singles can be found in the pub on weekends. A d.j. hosts dancing in this early American room from Wednesday through Saturday.

|      |            |
|------|------------|
| AVERAGE DRINK | $1.50 |
| COVER OR MINIMUM | None |
| PLASTIC | AE, DC, MC, V |
| CROWD | Young professionals in their 20s |
| DRESS | Neat and casual |

<table>
<tr><td>OPEN</td><td>Seven days, from 11:30 A.M. to 4 A.M.</td></tr>
<tr><td>FOOD</td><td>Full American menu for lunch and dinner; a la carte dinner entrées range from $6.50 to $12.95</td></tr>
<tr><td>SPECIALS</td><td>Call for details</td></tr>
</table>

## United Skates of America                    *Roller Disco*
7117 Roosevelt Avenue, Jackson Heights
(212) 651-4301

The skate floor is like a track surrounding the large middle area with tables and the concession. You can dance with or without skates, the point is simply to have fun. Live d.j. hosts many adult and singles events, so call to find out what's happening when.

<table>
<tr><td>AVERAGE DRINK</td><td>No liquor</td></tr>
<tr><td>COVER OR MINIMUM</td><td>$3.50</td></tr>
<tr><td>PLASTIC</td><td>MC, V</td></tr>
<tr><td>CROWD</td><td>Good skaters and others from 21 to 35</td></tr>
<tr><td>DRESS</td><td>Neat</td></tr>
<tr><td>OPEN</td><td>Call for specifics</td></tr>
<tr><td>FOOD</td><td>Snacks</td></tr>
<tr><td>SPECIALS</td><td>Tuesday is College Night from 10 P.M. to 1 A.M.; call for other specials</td></tr>
</table>

## Waterfront Crab House                    *Restaurant/Bar*
2-03 Borden Avenue, Long Island City
(Van Dam exit off the Long Island Exp.
near the Midtown Tunnel)
(212) 729-4862

A large, roomy place with a thirty-foot bar and a mixed singles/couples crowd on Friday. Live music all week includes piano/vocal from Monday through Thursday, a band on Friday and Saturday, and Dixieland on Sunday. Dancing.

<table>
<tr><td>AVERAGE DRINK</td><td>$2.25</td></tr>
<tr><td>COVER OR MINIMUM</td><td>None</td></tr>
<tr><td>PLASTIC</td><td>AE, DC, MC, V</td></tr>
</table>

| | |
|---|---|
| CROWD | Professional and neighborhood people from 25 to 35 |
| DRESS | Casual |
| OPEN | Monday through Friday 11 A.M. till closing; Saturday and Sunday 2 P.M. to whenever |
| FOOD | Seafood and steak with a la carte dinner entrées ranging from $5.95 to $15.95; lunch available also |

## Woodstock                                                  *Rock Club*
Corner of Gates and Onderdonk, Ridgewood
(right near Glendale)
(212) 821-9346

National and local bands in a concert/listening situation. Intimate, modern decor done in black and yellow with artwork all over. Singles and couples.

| | |
|---|---|
| AVERAGE DRINK | $1.50 |
| COVER OR MINIMUM | $3.00 |
| PLASTIC | None |
| CROWD | All types of people from 18 to 25 |
| DRESS | Anything |
| OPEN | Tuesday through Saturday 7 P.M. to 4 A.M. |
| FOOD | Snacks |
| SPECIALS | Free admission with a Woodstock T-shirt |

**Century Inn**                                    *Rock Club*
4254 Arthur Kill Road
(212) 984-1202, (212) 984-2136

Live rock bands in a concert situation. Plus a pool table room, game room, potbelly lamps room, and the bar—which, by the way, was hand-carved out of pure mahogany in 1859. Mixed couples and singles.

|  |  |
|---|---|
| AVERAGE DRINK | $1.50 |
| COVER OR MINIMUM | $3.00 |
| PLASTIC | None |
| CROWD | Rock fans from 18 to 26 or 30; double ID required |
| DRESS | Neat, but as one person put it, "Let's face it, you can't have a dress code with rock" |
| OPEN | Wednesday, Friday and Saturday from 8 P.M. to 3 A.M. |
| FOOD | None |
| SPECIALS | Wednesday is Alabama Slammer Night |

**The Ground Round**                *Restaurant/Bar/Dance Room*
2655 Richmond Avenue (in the Staten Island Mall, upper level)
(212) 698-7002

Daytime and dinnertime it's mostly families. But later the singles and young couples come in to dance. Thursday, Friday, and Saturday there is live music from 9 P.M. to 1 A.M. (Top 40) and the atmosphere is cozy with Tiffany lamps, red and white checkered tablecloths, the seven-foot TV screen, and old time movies.

|  |  |
|---|---|
| AVERAGE DRINK | $1.70 |
| COVER OR MINIMUM | 10¢ extra per glass during entertainment |

| PLASTIC | AE, MC, V |
|---|---|
| CROWD | Business people and managers from the nearby stores; age span is about 19 to 30 |
| DRESS | Proper attire |
| OPEN | 11:30 A.M. to closing Monday through Saturday; noon to closing on Sunday |
| FOOD | Steaks, burgers, fried fish till 11 P.M. or later and till 2 A.M. on weekends; dinner prices range from $3.75 to $10.95 |
| SPECIALS | Drinks are $1.10 Monday through Saturday from 3 to 7 P.M. |

**Lancaster Cocktail Lounge**                    *Lounge/Dancing*
1075 N. Railroad Avenue (corner Midland Ave.)
(212) 667-9889, (212) 667-9138

Singles who like 1950's music should drop by on Friday or Saturday to dance to the live band. The main section seats 200 and the lounge area thirty, so it's a friendly, intimate situation. Many couples, too.

| AVERAGE DRINK | $1.00 |
|---|---|
| COVER OR MINIMUM | None |
| PLASTIC | None |
| CROWD | All types of people from 25 up |
| DRESS | Proper attire on weekends—that means no sneakers, etc. |
| OPEN | Seven days from 11 A.M. to 4 A.M. |
| FOOD | Snacks |
| SPECIALS | Happy Hour is from 4 to 6 P.M., Monday through Friday with 60¢ drinks and 20¢ tap beer! |

**The Office**                    *Lounge with Dancing*
Nelson Avenue and Amboy Road
(212) 948-9030, (212) 948-9033

For those of you who don't get enough office during the day, come to The Office at night to hear live three- and four-piece bands doing oldies from the 1950's and 1960's. It's a cozy room, seating about 200 couples and singles.

AVERAGE DRINK $2.50
COVER OR MINIMUM $6.00 per person minimum on Saturday
PLASTIC AE, DC
CROWD Professional people, lawyers, judges, from age 40 up
DRESS Jackets required
OPEN Seven nights from 9 P.M. to 4 A.M.
FOOD None

## Pennyfeathers
*Restaurant/Bar*
185 New Dorp Lane
(212) 667-9722

The mood is tropical with a Greenhouse Room, lots of light and plants. At present they are working on getting music in there—so call. Mixed couples and singles.

AVERAGE DRINK $1.75
COVER OR MINIMUM $2.00 minimum
PLASTIC AE, DC, MC, V
CROWD Lots of business and professional people and others of all ages
DRESS Proper casual attire
OPEN Seven days from 11:30 A.M. to 2 A.M.-ish
FOOD N.Y./American cuisine till 11:30 P.M. weekdays and 1:30 A.M. Friday and Saturday; nothing costs over $9.95

## Rustic Inn
*Restaurant/Lounge*
1675 Hylan Boulevard, Dongan Hills
(212) 667-9774

Like the man says, it's rustic. The atmosphere is cozy, warm, and friendly with a big lounge that's separated from the dining area. Live bands Wednesday through Sunday play folk/rock and country/rock. Mixed couples and singles.

| | |
|---|---|
| AVERAGE DRINK | $2.00 |
| COVER OR MINIMUM | None |
| PLASTIC | None |
| CROWD | All types of people from 19 up |
| DRESS | No sneakers or shorts on music nights |
| OPEN | Seven days, 11 A.M. to 4 A.M. |
| FOOD | Seafood, steaks, and Italian specialties, with the ceiling being about $11.25 for dinner; lunch available also |

## Snoopy's                                                        *Rock Concert Club*
100 Johnston Terrace
(212) 948-7093

Besides the fact that there is a big colored parachute hanging from the ceiling, Snoopy's claims to have the longest bar in the city of New York, checking in at 206 feet. Pictures of Snoopy characters and clouds and things on the walls, with live rock bands and a d.j.

| | |
|---|---|
| AVERAGE DRINK | $1.75 |
| COVER OR MINIMUM | $4.00 |
| PLASTIC | None |
| CROWD | Rock fans from 18 to 25 |
| DRESS | Dress jeans and T-shirts with the names of the rock groups on them |
| OPEN | Thursday, Friday, and Saturday from 8 P.M. to 4 A.M.; possibly adding on Wednesday and Sunday in the future—call |
| FOOD | Snack bar |

## Thunderbird Lounge                                        *Lounge/Restaurant*
990 Bay Street, Rosebank
(212) 447-9782

Small and cozy with live bands playing country-western, oldies, and some disco for dancing. Call for music schedule. Singles can be found there on weekends.

| | |
|---|---|
| AVERAGE DRINK | $2.00 |
| COVER OR MINIMUM | None |

PLASTIC   None
CROWD   Local business people and professionals from 25 up
DRESS   Casual
OPEN   Seven days from 11 A.M. to 4 A.M.
FOOD   Snacks, sandwiches, Italian dishes, and steak; average sandwich is $2.75; no food served after 4 P.M.

**Wagon Wheel**                    *Country-Western Nightclub*
35 Androvette Street (off Arthur Kill Rd.)
(212) 948-9642

See how well you do on the mechanical bull! Plus live country-western music six nights.

AVERAGE DRINK   $1.75 during entertainment, $1.25 during the day
COVER OR MINIMUM   Two drink minimum and three at the tables
PLASTIC   None
CROWD   Country-western fans of all ages
DRESS   Country
OPEN   Seven days from 11 A.M. to 4 A.M.
FOOD   Light meals; the average burger is $2.00

**Charlie's Inn**                                    *Restaurant/Bar*
2711 Harding Avenue (Throggs Neck)
(212) 931-9727

Many singles, some couples on Friday, Saturday and Sunday to hear the pop/jazz trio. Thursday listen to live Irish music or watch sports on the giant TV screen.

| | |
|---|---|
| AVERAGE DRINK | $1.25 |
| COVER OR MINIMUM | None |
| PLASTIC | AE |
| CROWD | Neighborhood and Queens, from age 40 up |
| DRESS | Proper |
| OPEN | Seven days, 9 A.M. to 4 A.M. |
| FOOD | German cuisine, with dinner averaging $6.95 to $9.95 |

**Geppeto's Restaurant**                          *Restaurant/Lounge*
2010 Williamsbridge Road (2 blocks south of Pelham Pkwy.)
(212) 828-6220

Singles can be found in the lounge on weekends. Live music nightly except Monday—disco and oldies with some dancing. Intimate and cozy atmosphere. Many couples, too.

| | |
|---|---|
| AVERAGE DRINK | $2.00 |
| COVER OR MINIMUM | None |
| PLASTIC | AE, MC, V |
| CROWD | Professional people in their 30s and 40s |
| DRESS | Jackets and ties |
| OPEN | Tuesday through Sunday from 8 P.M. to 4 A.M.; closed Monday |

Italian menu with dinner starting at $8.00

SPECIALS  Hot and cold buffet in the lounge

## Skate Key Roller Rink                              *Roller Disco*
2424 White Plains Road (near Pelham Pkwy.)
(212) 547-0700

A big rink, friendly atmosphere, and Pro Shop are just for openers. Singles can choose from Ladies Nights, Lovers Nights, TGIF Parties, Adult Nights, Weekend Parties and more. There's even a Parent-Children event, and occasional live entertainment. Call them to find out their most recent schedule. If you fall, someone is sure to pick you up.

|  |  |
|---|---|
| AVERAGE DRINK | No liquor |
| COVER OR MINIMUM | $2.00 to $6.00 |
| PLASTIC | None |
| CROWD | All types, all ages; it depends on the event |
| DRESS | Casual but no T-shirts or bare feet |
| OPEN | Morning, noon and night; call for details |
| FOOD | Large snack bar area |

## Skatin Palace                                    *Roller Skating*
930 Soundview Avenue (near Bruckner Blvd.)
(212) 542-7030

There's something for everyone, including Ladies Nights and Lovers Nights. Call for their most recent schedule. Live d.j. hosts the fun.

|  |  |
|---|---|
| AVERAGE DRINK | No liquor |
| COVER OR MINIMUM | $2.00 to $7.00 |
| PLASTIC | None |
| CROWD | All types all ages; call to find out when you'd fit in best |
| DRESS | Neat |
| OPEN | Tuesday through Sunday approximately 10 A.M. to 4 A.M., but again, call |
| FOOD | Snacks |

**Stardust Room**                                        *Ballroom*
3435 Boston Post Road (between Fish and Seymore Sts.)
(212) 654-0200

Remember Maureen Stapleton's movie, *Queen of the Stardust Ball-room*? Well, this is it. The lounge is on a big balcony which over-looks what the manager says is the largest dance floor in the Bronx, checking in at 1750 square feet. And the lounge itself has a smaller dance floor. Occasional live music—some name groups and some local. Mixed couples and singles.

|  |  |
|---|---|
| AVERAGE DRINK | $2.00 |
| COVER OR MINIMUM | $5.00 to $20.00 |
| PLASTIC | None |
| CROWD | People from all over from 23 up |
| DRESS | Jackets required in the winter, more casual in the summer |
| OPEN | Wednesday through Sunday during the winter, just Friday and Saturday during the summer; 9 P.M. to 4 A.M. |
| FOOD | Snacks |

# LONG ISLAND

**Alda's**                                                *Supperclub*
2158 Jericho Turnpike, Commack (Suffolk)
(516) 462-5757

A multilevel supperclub done in natural wood with plants, ceramic tiles, and an awning over the bar. Downstairs is a lounge; upstairs is the live entertainment, another lounge, and the restaurant. Have a drink and socialize under the skylight or enjoy the show (singers, comedians, revues). Many singles scattered throughout the lounges, mostly couples in the dining area.

|                   |                                                   |
|-------------------|---------------------------------------------------|
| AVERAGE DRINK     | $1.75 to $2.50                                    |
| COVER OR MINIMUM  | None                                              |
| PLASTIC           | AE, CB, DC, MC, V                                 |
| CROWD             | All kinds of people from 25 up                    |
| DRESS             | Neat and casual                                   |
| OPEN              | Seven nights, 7 P.M. to 4 A.M. upstairs on Thursday, Friday, and Saturday |
| FOOD              | Italian from 11:30 A.M. to 11 P.M. (till midnight on weekends); average dinner ranges from $4.95 to $11.95 |

**The Apartment**                              *Lounge with Dancing*
1828 Sunrise Highway, Merrick (Nassau)
(516) 623-4449

Oddly enough, it's done in "apartment decor." That means there are eighteen couches, a fireplace, a chandelier, bookcases, and pictures on the walls. In "The Den" there are more couches and another fireplace. Although most of us don't have live music in our apartments, this one does—with Top 40, disco, and oldies for dancing or just plain listening. It's about 60 percent singles.

| | |
|---|---|
| AVERAGE DRINK | $2.00 |
| COVER OR MINIMUM | None |
| PLASTIC | None |
| CROWD | All types of people, from 28 to 35; you must be 23 to get in |
| DRESS | Casual but proper—no faded jeans |
| OPEN | Seven nights, 8 P.M. to 4 A.M. |
| FOOD | None |

## Apple Annie's                                   *Restaurant/Bar*
242 Maple Avenue, Westbury (Nassau)
(516) 334-1600

The huge bar is usually wall-to-wall singles, and there's a separate
dining room if all the activity makes you hungry.

| | |
|---|---|
| AVERAGE DRINK | $2.00 |
| COVER OR MINIMUM | None |
| PLASTIC | AE, CB, DC, MC, V |
| CROWD | Professionals and others, from 20 to 35 |
| DRESS | Casual, neat |
| OPEN | Seven days, 11:30 A.M. to 2 A.M. |
| FOOD | American/Continental menu for lunch and dinner; dinner prices range from $3.75 to $12.95 |
| SPECIALS | Call for details |

## Apple Orchard                          *Restaurant/Lounge/Disco*
1750 Northern Boulevard, Roslyn (Nassau)
(516) 621-2800

If you're in an elegant mood, this is the place to be. The main floor
is done up with mirrors and velvet, and features live dance music
from Wednesday through Saturday. The downstairs has a contemporary chrome-mirror look and a disco with live d.j. from Tuesday
through Sunday. There are some couples, but many singles. If you
go in alone and need some pampering, ask for Jack or Herb, the
owners—they'll make you feel right at home.

| | |
|---|---|
| AVERAGE DRINK | $2.50 |
| COVER OR MINIMUM | Varies—could be $5.00 |
| PLASTIC | AE, CB, DC, MC, V |
| CROWD | Professionals and executives from 25 to 55, with 40ish being the average age |
| DRESS | Casual but neat |
| OPEN | Tuesday through Sunday 5 P.M. to 4 A.M.; closed Monday |
| FOOD | Continental steak and seafood, with average dinner price ranging from $6.50 to $14.95 |
| SPECIALS | "Super Single Saver Special" on Wednesday and Thursday means that for $5.00 you get a drink and a free buffet dinner; Wednesday is the bigger night of the two |

**Arrows**                                                           *Bar*

547 Bedford Avenue, Bellmore (Nassau, ¼ mile north of
Sunrise Highway)
(516) 785-8955

The live music on Tuesday, Friday and Saturday adds to the lively,
party atmosphere. Mostly rock, some jazz. Mostly socializing,
some dancing. Mostly singles.

| | |
|---|---|
| AVERAGE DRINK | $1.25 |
| COVER OR MINIMUM | $2.00 on weekends when the band is playing |
| PLASTIC | None |
| CROWD | Local people and commuters; after work the age range is in the 30s and 40s, at night the 20s take over |
| DRESS | Casual |
| OPEN | Seven days: Sunday through Friday 3 P.M. to 4 A.M.; Saturday 7 P.M. to 4 A.M. |
| FOOD | Peanuts |
| SPECIALS | Beer Blasts, etc. |

**The Back Barn**                                                    *Cabaret*
164 Hicksville Rd., Bethpage (Nassau)
(516) 731-5590

210 Sunrise Highway, Valley Stream (Nassau)
(516) 825-7272

A cozy cabaret with a pub/barn atmosphere. Checkered tablecloths, candles, wood, and beams. Choose from a ninety-item wine list and listen to original folk and rock music with lots of other singles.

| | |
|---|---|
| AVERAGE DRINK | $1.75 |
| COVER OR MINIMUM | None |
| PLASTIC | None |
| CROWD | Local people from 20 to 25 |
| DRESS | Casual |
| OPEN | Seven days, 8 P.M. to 4 A.M. |
| FOOD | Homemade crepes, quiches, Italian food, desserts and exotic coffees till 3 A.M.; dessert and coffee till 4; dinner is about $6.00 to $8.00 |
| SPECIALS | Bar specials nightly |

**The Barefoot Peddler**                                     *Restaurant/Bar*
37 Glen Cove Road, Greenvale (Nassau, near Northern Blvd.)
(516) 621-4840

A cozy, casual, very friendly pub, often packed with singles at the bar.

| | |
|---|---|
| AVERAGE DRINK | $1.75 |
| COVER OR MINIMUM | $4.00 at the tables |
| PLASTIC | AE, DC, MC, V |
| CROWD | All types, many local people; all ages, many in their 20s |
| DRESS | Casual |
| OPEN | Monday through Saturday 11:30 A.M. to 4 A.M.; Sunday the bar is open from 3 P.M. to closing |

| FOOD | Pub fare till 2 A.M. with the a la carte entrées going from $2.00 up; brunch on weekends |
|---|---|
| SPECIALS | Attitude Adjustment Hour is from 5:30 to 7:30 P.M., Monday through Friday |

## Bobby Van's — *Restaurant/Bar*
Main Street, Bridgehampton (Suffolk)
(516) 537-0590

Summer is the main season for Bobby Van's fans, but weekends are busy year-round with a jazz duo of piano and bass for entertainment. Couples and singles (about half and half) enjoy the dining room and the forty-two-foot bar. Lots of dark wood makes the atmosphere warm and comfortable.

| AVERAGE DRINK | $2.00 |
|---|---|
| COVER OR MINIMUM | None |
| PLASTIC | None |
| CROWD | Neighborhood people and professionals, summer people and weekenders; age range is 25 to 70 |
| DRESS | Casual |
| OPEN | Seven days, 11:30 A.M. till at least 2 A.M.; if you're there at 2 A.M. having a great time, they won't kick you out |
| FOOD | Seafood/steak for lunch and dinner; dinner prices range from $8.00 to $13.00 |

## Bombay Bicycle Club — *Restaurant/Bar*
477 Old Country Road, Westbury (Nassau)
(516) 334-5856

A great old pub done up in light wood, with Tiffany lamps and artificial plants. The big two-sided bar has seen the beginnings of many a friendship. If you can't think of anything to say to the stranger next to you, just comment on the large old-fashioned bicycles that are on display. Hungrier singles hang out in the separate dining area.

| | |
|---|---|
| AVERAGE DRINK | $1.85 during the day, $2.00 at night |
| COVER OR MINIMUM | $3.50 during the day, none at night |
| PLASTIC | CB, DC, MC, V |
| CROWD | Professionals and people from the neighborhood; ages 25 and up |
| DRESS | Casual |
| OPEN | Seven days, 11:30 A.M. to 4 A.M. |
| FOOD | Lunch and dinner, American food; dinner ranges from $4.95 for a salad to $16.95 for a broiled steak |
| SPECIALS | Happy Hour Monday through Friday, 4 to 6 P.M. |

**The Bunnery Pub** *Restaurant/Bar*
514 Park Boulevard, Massapequa Park (Nassau, south of railroad station)
(516) 798-9851

Most of the singles can be found at the big bar, and dancing to the live music on Friday and Saturday. The atmosphere is friendly, casual, and quite cozy. Couples too.

| | |
|---|---|
| AVERAGE DRINK | $1.50 |
| COVER OR MINIMUM | None |
| PLASTIC | None |
| CROWD | All types of people in their mid 20s |
| DRESS | Proper and neat |
| OPEN | Seven days: weekdays 11 A.M. to 10 P.M. or midnight; weekends, lunch to 2 or 3 A.M. |
| FOOD | American menu with dinner prices ranging from $5.00 to $9.00 |
| SPECIALS | Unlimited beer and wine with meals Monday through Wednesday |

**Camelot Inn**                                            *Disco and More*
267 Mineola Boulevard, Mineola (Nassau, just south of
Jericho Turnpike)
(516) PI 6-9664

Dance to live music three nights and a d.j. spinning disco and Top
40 the rest of the week in this old London, England, style room. A
medium-sized disco holding about 300 people, many of whom are
single.

| | |
|---|---|
| AVERAGE DRINK | $1.75 |
| COVER OR MINIMUM | $4.00 minimum on Saturday |
| PLASTIC | None |
| CROWD | All types of people from 21 to 35 |
| DRESS | Casual but neat |
| OPEN | Seven days, 3 P.M. to 4 A.M. |
| FOOD | None |
| SPECIALS | From 3 to 7 P.M. all drinks are $1.00; after-work disco Friday afternoon |

**Chandler's**                                          *Restaurant/Bar*
106 Main Street, Port Jefferson (Suffolk, at the corner of Rt. 25A)
(516) 928-4188

Aside from the fireplace in the bar and in the dining room, this cozy
gathering spot is decorated to look like the stern of a ship. Many
singles, friendly atmosphere.

| | |
|---|---|
| AVERAGE DRINK | $2.25 |
| COVER OR MINIMUM | None |
| PLASTIC | AE, MC, V |
| CROWD | Locals and tourists from 21 up |
| DRESS | Casual |
| OPEN | Seven days, 11:30 A.M. to 4 A.M. |
| FOOD | Burgers, seafood, and steak with dinner ranging from $3.50 to $7.25; lunch available also |

**Channel 80**                                          *Restaurant/Disco*
80 Waterfront Boulevard, Island Park (Nassau)
(516) 432-2400

A big room with a comfortable atmosphere and attractive cocktail
lounge. A d.j. begins the disco action at 11 P.M. nightly with many
singles and some couples sharing the modest-sized dance floor.
Weekend outdoor afternoon disco is open during the summer
months—times fluctuate, so call first.

| | |
|---|---|
| AVERAGE DRINK | $2.00 and up |
| COVER OR MINIMUM | No admission charge if you're having dinner; $10.00 per person if you're just dancing |
| PLASTIC | AE, DC, MC, V |
| CROWD | All types, all ages |
| DRESS | Jackets required on Friday and Saturday nights; during the week jeans are OK but no sneakers |
| OPEN | Tuesday through Sunday from 5 P.M.; closed Monday |
| FOOD | American/Continental menu; a la carte dinner entrées go from $7.95 to $19.95 |

**Cheers**                                              *Rock Nightclub*
1258 Deer Park Avenue (Rt. 231), North Babylon
(Suffolk, Exit 39N on Southern State Pkwy., or Exit 51
off the Long Island Exp.)
(516) 586-8989

A large, fun club with live entertainment nightly and big name
groups Wednesday through Saturday. Mostly singles.

| | |
|---|---|
| AVERAGE DRINK | $1.50 |
| COVER OR MINIMUM | $3.00 |
| PLASTIC | None |
| CROWD | Many students and others in their 20s |
| DRESS | Nice jeans, no sneakers |
| OPEN | Seven days, 8:30 P.M. to 3 or 4 A.M. |

| | |
|---|---|
| FOOD | Hot dog wagon |
| SPECIALS | 10¢ drinks till 10 P.M. nightly! |

## Cinnamon                                        *Restaurant/Nightclub*
330 New York Avenue, Huntington (Suffolk)
(516) 673-2870

A nicely decorated, comfortable room with some couples, some singles. All kinds of live music every night.

| | |
|---|---|
| AVERAGE DRINK | $1.50 |
| COVER OR MINIMUM | $2.00 |
| PLASTIC | AE, CB, DC, MC, V |
| CROWD | All types, 25 and up |
| DRESS | Casual but neat |
| OPEN | Seven days: Monday through Friday 11:30 A.M. to 4 A.M.; Saturday and Sunday noon to 4 A.M. |
| FOOD | American menu with dinner ranging from $4.95 to $8.95; lunch available also |

## C.J.'s                                               *Restaurant/Bar*
479 Bay Walk, Ocean Beach (Suffolk, on Fire Island)
(516) 583-9890

A popular late-night spot for many singles, C.J.'s is right near Ocean Beach Ferry, giving it a casual waterfront atmosphere. The crowd has been known to get happy, and though there's no band, one waitress explained that "there's plenty of room between the bar and the tables if people want to dance."

| | |
|---|---|
| AVERAGE DRINK | $2.50 |
| COVER OR MINIMUM | None |
| PLASTIC | None |
| CROWD | All kinds of people, all ages |
| DRESS | Casual |
| OPEN | Seven days, noon to 4 A.M. |
| FOOD | Light meals for lunch and dinner; $2.00 to $4.00 |

**Clark Smathers** *Restaurant/Bar/Disco*
69 N. Service Road, Lake Success (Nassau, Exit 33 off
the Long Island Exp.)
(516) 829-9818

A d.j. hosts the many singles who gather in this large disco to dance.
There are two bars with a dance floor in front of each one, and a
separate area for dining.

| | |
|---|---|
| AVERAGE DRINK | $2.75 |
| COVER OR MINIMUM | $5.00 Wednesday, Friday, Saturday; includes one drink |
| PLASTIC | AE, CB, DC, MC, V |
| CROWD | A young, party crowd at night; ladies must be 23, gentlemen 25; you can be in your mid 30s and still fit in |
| DRESS | Dress jeans OK, but no sneakers |
| OPEN | Seven days: Monday through Friday 11 A.M. to 3 A.M.; Saturday and Sunday 5 P.M. to 3 A.M. |
| FOOD | Continental; dinner runs from $5.95 to $13.95; lunch served weekdays |
| SPECIALS | $1.00 drinks until 8 P.M. |

**Colonie Hill Top o' the Hill Lounge** *Lounge/Disco*
1717 Motor Parkway, Hauppauge (Suffolk, Exit 57 off
the Long Island Exp.)
(516) 234-7800

Lots of friendly singles dance to the live music Wednesday through
Saturday.

| | |
|---|---|
| AVERAGE DRINK | $2.00 |
| COVER OR MINIMUM | None |
| PLASTIC | AE, CB, DC, MC, V |
| CROWD | Professional people of all ages |
| DRESS | Casual |
| OPEN | Seven nights, from 6:30 P.M. on |

|   |   |
|---|---|
| FOOD | Free buffet Wednesday, hors d'oeuvres on Friday |
| SPECIALS | Happy Hour Friday, 9 to 10 P.M. |

## Copperfield's *Disco/Lounge*
2337 Jericho Turnpike, Garden City Park (Nassau)
(516) 746-8166

Live d.j. orchestrates the many singles from Wednesday through Saturday with disco music, a comfortably sized dance floor, and three bars on Friday and Saturday. The rest of the week you can enjoy the lounge with its three-sided bar. Lots to do and a good time is almost guaranteed.

|   |   |
|---|---|
| AVERAGE DRINK | $1.75 and up |
| COVER OR MINIMUM | $3.00 at the door Friday and Saturday |
| PLASTIC | None |
| CROWD | You must be at least 22; all types of people |
| DRESS | Designer jeans are OK if they're neat; no raggy jeans, sneakers, or T-shirts |
| OPEN | Seven nights, 8:30 P.M. to 4 A.M. |
| FOOD | None |
| SPECIALS | Thursday is Las Vegas Night—gamble for play money and win prizes |

## The Cruiser Club *Nightclub*
Canal Road, Hampton Bays 11946 (Suffolk, east bank of Shinnecock Canal)
(516) 728-0666

If you're on vacation in the Hamptons, are looking for a great time, and can hold your own on a crowded dance floor, here's your place! Live bands—local and top name—play disco, Top 40 and soft rock so you can party. This has been going on for the past twelve years, so they've got it down to an art. Nautical decor with wood and brick. Mostly singles with a smattering of couples on the side.

| | |
|---|---|
| AVERAGE DRINK | $2.25 |
| COVER OR MINIMUM | $5.00 |
| PLASTIC | None |
| CROWD | Vacationers; average age is 25 |
| DRESS | Casual proper attire |
| OPEN | From Memorial weekend to mid-June they are open weekends; summers through Labor Day weekend you can go Thursday through Monday; hours are 9 P.M. to 4 A.M. |
| FOOD | None |
| SPECIALS | "Blue Chip Thursdays"—buy a drink, and get a blue chip good for a complimentary drink; "TGIF"—Happy Hour Friday night from 9 P.M. to 11 P.M. with no admission charge before 11 |

**Davy Jones** *Restaurant/Bar*
1 Julian Place, Island Park (Nassau, near Long Beach Rd.)
(516) 432-9264

Say you're in the Long Beach section of the Island. What could be better than sitting on a spacious, elevated outdoor veranda in the summer, sipping a tall drink, and looking out over the channel? Or you could go to the lower deck, eat clams from the clam bar and watch the sailboats and yachts. If the weather gets chilly, you could always go inside and be entertained on Friday and Saturday by a guitarist or pianist. If you do all these things, it's doubtful you'll do them alone. The room is busy and social and often quite single.

| | |
|---|---|
| AVERAGE DRINK | $1.75 |
| COVER OR MINIMUM | None |
| PLASTIC | AE, DC, MC, V |
| CROWD | People who like water, aged 25 and up |
| DRESS | From shorts to tuxedos |
| OPEN | Seven days, 8 A.M. to 4 A.M. |
| FOOD | Seafood with a French touch; dinners go from $6.50 to $16.50; lunch available also |
| SPECIALS | Free barbeque on Sunday during the summer |

**Decameron** *Disco/Restaurant*
2890 Hempstead Turnpike, Levittown (Nassau)
(516) 579-4466

Imagine the social possibilities that could occur at an elegant 180-foot bar! Or you could try their huge dance floor for disco on Wednesday and Friday, Greek music and more disco on Thursday, and a big band sound and disco on Saturday.

| | |
|---|---|
| AVERAGE DRINK | $2.50 |
| COVER OR MINIMUM | $5.00 |
| PLASTIC | AE, CB, DC, MC, V |
| CROWD | All kinds of people from 21 to 70 |
| DRESS | Saturday night, jackets no jeans; other nights, neat but casual |
| OPEN | Wednesday through Saturday, 2 P.M. to 4 A.M. |
| FOOD | Northern Italian/Continental from 7:30 P.M. to 4 A.M.; a la carte dinner entrées go from $9.75 to $14.00 |
| SPECIALS | Call for details |

**Dering Harbor Inn** *Lounge/Restaurant*
13 Winthrop Road, Shelter Island Heights (Suffolk)
(516) 749-0900

A relaxed, dignified nightspot on a marina with a scenic 300-foot pier. The dining room seats 100 and the lounge seats fifty—mostly couples but a fair share of singles on weekends. Live music nightly with dancing. (Live music on Saturdays only during September.) Closed during the winter months.

| | |
|---|---|
| AVERAGE DRINK | $2.25 |
| COVER OR MINIMUM | None |
| PLASTIC | AE, MC, V |
| CROWD | Many vacationers, many boat people docking for dinner; age range, 35 to 55 |

DRESS    Jackets are preferred but not required; fashion jeans are OK, but no sloppy clothes or faded jeans

OPEN    Mid-May through mid-October, seven days a week, noon to 2 A.M.

FOOD    Availability varies, so call first

**Dublin Pub**                           *Rock and Dance Room*
2002 Jericho Turnpike, New Hyde Park (Nassau)
(516) 354-9349

Live music nightly, a big dance floor, and lots of singles.

| | |
|---|---|
| AVERAGE DRINK | $1.50 |
| COVER OR MINIMUM | $2.00 |
| PLASTIC | None |
| CROWD | Many students and others in their 20s |
| DRESS | Casual but no sneakers or T-shirts |
| OPEN | Seven nights, 6:30 P.M. to 4 A.M. |
| FOOD | None |

**East Side Comedy Club**                   *Comedy Club*
326 W. Jericho Turnpike, Huntington (Suffolk)
(516) 271-6061

Many couples, some singles (the bar seats ten but holds thirty), and good entertainment. Local and big name comedians perform at 9:30 P.M. during the week and at 8:30 and midnight on weekends.

| | |
|---|---|
| AVERAGE DRINK | $2.25 |
| COVER OR MINIMUM | $4.00 |
| PLASTIC | None |
| CROWD | Varied crowd of all ages |
| DRESS | Casual |
| OPEN | Tuesday through Sunday from 6 P.M. on; closed Monday |
| FOOD | Fish, steaks; Friday and Saturday dinner prices run from $6.00 to $10.00; there's a more limited menu during the week |

**Emanon** *Nightclub*
1096 Route 112, Arcade Shopping Plaza, Port Jefferson Station
(Suffolk)
(516) 473-7799

Done up in "contemporary plus," this 5000-square-feet-of-party
houses many fun-loving singles—with a 140-foot bar adding
friendly spirits. Formerly called "Hounds and Foxes," Emanon for
some reason is "Noname" backwards. Saturday night you can
catch big name live acts like Vicki Sue Robinson and Beatlemagic.
Other nights you can dance to records and d.j.

| | |
|---|---|
| AVERAGE DRINK | $2.50 |
| COVER OR MINIMUM | $3.00 if any |
| PLASTIC | None |
| CROWD | Local people, small business owners, and others from 23 to 33 |
| DRESS | Casual neat |
| OPEN | Tuesday through Saturday, 9 P.M. to 4 A.M.; closed Sunday and Monday |
| FOOD | None |

**Fearn's** *Showcase*
1431 Old Northern Boulevard, Roslyn (Nassau)
(516) 484-5380

A beautiful, turn-of-the-century, city-ish room with fifty or sixty
people at the bar (many of whom are single, but some are spoken
for). Small ensembles provide original music, with comedy acts on
Wednesday.

| | |
|---|---|
| AVERAGE DRINK | $1.75 |
| COVER OR MINIMUM | $1.00 |
| PLASTIC | None |
| CROWD | Many students from Post College and others in their 20s and 30s |
| DRESS | Casual |
| OPEN | Seven nights, 8 P.M. to closing |
| FOOD | Light snacks |

**Feathers** *Disco*
3601 Hempstead Turnpike, Levittown (Nassau)
(516) 796-0255

A large room with two bars, a big dance floor, special effect lighting, and casual wood decor just waiting for a party to happen! Join
the multitude of singles and the d.j. nightly.

| | |
|---|---|
| AVERAGE DRINK | $2.00 |
| COVER OR MINIMUM | $3.00 on weekends |
| PLASTIC | None |
| CROWD | Many students from 19 to 25 |
| DRESS | Casual but neat |
| OPEN | Seven nights from 8 P.M. to 4 A.M. |
| FOOD | None |
| SPECIALS | Monday is the dance contest; Tuesday is "All You Can Drink" night; Thursday is "2-for-1 Night"; call for more specials |

**The Fifth Amendment** *Cocktail Lounge*
639F Commack Rd., Commack (Suffolk, 1 mile north of
Long Island Exp.)
(516) 499-5554

Couples and singles enjoy the intimate, friendly atmosphere, the
large bar and the cozy dance floor. Live music Friday and Saturday.

| | |
|---|---|
| AVERAGE DRINK | $2.00 |
| COVER OR MINIMUM | None |
| PLASTIC | None |
| CROWD | All types of people from 25 up |
| DRESS | Neat casual |
| OPEN | Seven days from 12:30 P.M. to 4 A.M. |
| FOOD | None |
| SPECIALS | Happy Hour 4 to 7 P.M. and 1 A.M. to 4 A.M. on weekdays |

**Fox Hollow Inn**
See **Singles Playground Ltd.**, page 257.

180 *Places to Go*

**The Gazebo**                                    *Restaurant/Lounge*
177 Mineola Avenue, Roslyn (Nassau, Exit 37 off
Long Island Exp.)
(516) 621-0550

Tri-level dining surrounded by luscious plants, greenery, skylights,
and a fireplace. Couples and many singles enjoy the live music
nightly, with Irish tunes Tuesday, contemporary music Wednesday
and Saturday, and all styles on Friday.

| | |
|---|---|
| AVERAGE DRINK | $2.00 |
| COVER OR MINIMUM | None |
| PLASTIC | AE, CB, DC, MC, V |
| CROWD | A sophisticated crowd from 21 to 40 |
| DRESS | Casual |
| OPEN | Seven days, 11:30 A.M. to 4 A.M. |
| FOOD | American menu; dinner prices range from $7.95 to $15.95; lunch available |
| SPECIALS | Happy Hour nightly from 4:30 to 7 P.M. with half-priced drinks; another Happy Hour, if you should miss this one, is on Tuesday from 9:30 P.M. to 11 P.M. |

**Goodtimes**                                          *Rock Club*
122 Mayfair Plaza, Jericho Turnpike, Commack (Suffolk)
(516) 864-2278

131 Front St., Massapequa Park (Nassau)
(516) 799-8861

Live rock nightly with a loud, rowdy atmosphere—your basic good
time. Many singles.

| | |
|---|---|
| AVERAGE DRINK | $1.50 |
| COVER OR MINIMUM | $3.00 |
| PLASTIC | None |
| CROWD | Many students, 18 and up; double proof may be required |
| DRESS | Neat and casual |

| OPEN | Tuesday through Saturday from 9 P.M. to 4 A.M. |
| FOOD | None |
| SPECIALS | Call for details |

## Gurney's Inn/Gurney's Inn International Health and Beauty Spa
*Like It Says*

Old Montauk Highway, Montauk (Suffolk)
(516) 668-2345

We've actually got three things going on here: a lounge, a dining area, and a separate health and beauty facility. Most of the singles can be found keeping themselves ready for action at the spa, which offers Universal gym equipment, herbal wraps, exercise classes, yoga, and much more. The lounge area in the Inn itself has a small cozy bar and a large, ninety-foot bar, both of dark wood. Here you'll find more couples but still some singles. For dinner it's mostly couples. Gurney's is open year-round, with band music nightly during the in-season summer months. Off-season there's a piano player weeknights and a band on weekends.

| AVERAGE DRINK | $2.25 to $2.50 |
| COVER OR MINIMUM | None |
| PLASTIC | AE, DC, MC, V; good at the Inn or the Spa |
| CROWD | Professionals from 30 on up |
| DRESS | Jackets required in the lounge |
| OPEN | Seven days, 6 P.M. to 3 A.M. in the bar; call for specific Spa times |
| FOOD | Full dinner menu from 6 to 10 P.M.; a la carte dinner entrées range from $10.75 to $15.75 |

**Hammerheads** *Rock Nightclub*

135 Sunrise Highway, West Islip (Suffolk, Exit 40 off
Sunrise Highway, ⅛ mile east of Rt. 231; or Southern State Pkwy.,
Exit 39S to Sunrise Highway, Rt. 27 east)
(516) 669-3460

An enormous club with live music and three bars in the shape of
ships. Management claims it's the biggest club in New York State—
why not go and find out? You'll be among many other singles.

| | |
|---|---|
| AVERAGE DRINK | $1.50 |
| COVER OR MINIMUM | $3.00 at the door on weekends, $1.00 on weekdays |
| PLASTIC | None |
| CROWD | Students and others from 18 to 25 or 30 |
| DRESS | Neat and casual |
| OPEN | Six nights from 8:30 P.M. to 4 A.M.; closed Monday |
| FOOD | Snacks |
| SPECIALS | Call for details |

**Harlequin** *Restaurant/Café*

39 Roslyn Avenue, Seacliff (Nassau)
(516) 676-1641

A cosmopolitan café atmosphere with room for fifty to eat and
fifteen at the bar. Classical guitar Saturday night. Couples and
singles.

| | |
|---|---|
| AVERAGE DRINK | $2.25 |
| COVER OR MINIMUM | None |
| PLASTIC | AE, DC |
| CROWD | Professionals and executives from 23 to 65 |
| DRESS | Proper attire |
| OPEN | Tuesday through Sunday from 5:30 P.M. |
| FOOD | American/Continental till 11 P.M.; dinner prices range from $8.95 to $13.95 |

**Heads and Tails**                                    *Restaurant/Pub*
1362 Old Northern Boulevard, Roslyn (Nassau)
(516) 621-5675

Warm, cozy English pub atmosphere with some singles, some couples. Very friendly.

| | |
|---|---|
| AVERAGE DRINK | $2.00 |
| COVER OR MINIMUM | None |
| PLASTIC | AE, CB, DC, MC, V |
| CROWD | All types of people in their 20s |
| DRESS | Casual to dressy |
| OPEN | Seven days from 11:30 A.M. to about 3 A.M. |
| FOOD | Continental menu for lunch and dinner till midnight weekdays and till 1 A.M. weekends; dinner prices run from $4.00 to $8.00 |
| SPECIALS | Happy Hour from 3 P.M. to 7, Monday through Saturday, with a buffet |

**Heckle and Jeckle's**                              *Rock Nightclub*
1039 Park Boulevard, Massapequa Park (Nassau)
(516) 798-9672

A large and lively bar seats eighty-five friendly people, some singles, some couples. Dance floor and tables hold 400 more, with live music nightly.

| | |
|---|---|
| AVERAGE DRINK | $1.25 |
| COVER OR MINIMUM | $1.00 |
| PLASTIC | None |
| CROWD | All types, from 18 to 29 |
| DRESS | Casual but neat |
| OPEN | Seven days from noon to 4 A.M. |
| FOOD | None |
| SPECIALS | Call for details; ask about "Wild and Woolly Night" |

**Henry Afrika Café**                                    *Rock Club*
231 Main Street, Northport Village (Suffolk)
(516) 754-9719

Visit this casual and friendly room with a good-sized bar and nice
wood decor, and you'll find that almost everyone else there is single, too. Live music nightly except Monday.

| | |
|---|---|
| AVERAGE DRINK | $1.75 |
| COVER OR MINIMUM | $1.00 to $2.00 |
| PLASTIC | None |
| CROWD | Many college students and other from 25ish |
| DRESS | Casual |
| OPEN | Seven days, noon to 4 A.M. |
| FOOD | None |
| SPECIALS | Happy Hour nightly from 4 to 7 P.M. |

**Hoolihan's Old Place**                          *Restaurant/Lounge*
Roosevelt Field Mall, Garden City (Nassau, southeast corner of
the mall)
(516) 742-3003

Half restaurant/half lounge/all singles. A comfortable atmosphere,
done up in "California decor"—that means plants, old movie star
photos on the walls and artifacts all around. The bar is big and
sociable and, as the hostess put it, "It's the kind of place where you
can come in jeans or dressed to the hilt. You can order a hamburger
or escargot." There's a small dance floor and the d.j. begins spinning discs at 9 P.M. nightly, with disco, rock, new wave, and pop
music.

| | |
|---|---|
| AVERAGE DRINK | $2.00 to $2.50 |
| COVER OR MINIMUM | None |
| PLASTIC | AE, DC, MC, V |
| CROWD | Young professionals from 21 to 25 at night, and from 25 to 30 during Happy Hour |
| DRESS | Neat casual; men must wear collared shirts in the lounge |
| OPEN | Seven days, 11ish A.M. to 2 A.M. |

FOOD    Large or small menu from 11:30 A.M. to 11 P.M. Monday through Thursday, 11:30 A.M. to 12:30 A.M. Friday and Saturday, and 11 A.M. to 10:30 P.M. on Sunday; dinner averages out to $10.00

SPECIALS    Happy Hour weekdays from 4 to 7 P.M. with hot and cold hors d'oeuvres; other specials sporadically—call to find out

## Hot Skates                                       *Roller Skating*

14 Merrick Road, Lynbrook (Nassau, corner of Ocean Ave.)
(516) 593-1300

A casual, adult atmosphere with occasional live music. Call for information on singles nights.

| | |
|---|---|
| AVERAGE DRINK | Soft drinks, no liquor |
| COVER OR MINIMUM | $3.00 |
| PLASTIC | None |
| CROWD | All types, from 18 up |
| DRESS | Neat but casual |
| OPEN | Tuesday, Thursday, and Sunday nights; call for details |
| FOOD | Snacks |

## The Iron Horse                                      *Bar/Restaurant*
## (formerly Peter Piper's)

6 Railroad Avenue, Glen Head (Nassau, located in the Glen Head Railroad Station)
(516) 676-9272

This nice casual homey bar has many singles and lots to do. If you're there on the first or third Wednesday of each month you can have Stella read your palm. She might predict that you will hear music there, some oldies, some country-western (check your Penny Saver or local paper for details if you can't find Stella). And there's a large screen TV at the bar with football on Monday, Islanders on Tuesday, and free movies on Sunday.

| | |
|---|---|
| AVERAGE DRINK | $1.25 to $2.00 |
| COVER OR MINIMUM | None |
| PLASTIC | None |
| CROWD | Neighborhood people, about 25 to 35 years old |
| DRESS | Casual but neat |
| OPEN | Seven days 11 A.M. till empty |
| FOOD | Sandwiches, clams, burgers, etc.; lunch and dinner; average dinner runs $4.00 to $6.00 |
| SPECIALS | Happy Hour Monday through Friday from 4 to 7 P.M. |

## John Peele Room (at the Island Inn) *Restaurant/Pub*
Old Country Road, Westbury (Nassau)
(516) 741-3430

Beams and chandeliers give a sophisticated English look to the dining room, while a fireplace adds warmth and comfort to the separate pub area. The bar seats eighty-five with room for forty to fifty standees. Many couples, some singles. A four-piece band plays popular music for listening and dancing Tuesday through Saturday.

| | |
|---|---|
| AVERAGE DRINK | $2.50 |
| COVER OR MINIMUM | None |
| PLASTIC | AE, CB, DC, MC, V |
| CROWD | All types of people from 30 on up |
| DRESS | Casual, with many men wearing jackets |
| OPEN | Seven days, usually from 5 P.M.; times vary so you might want to call |
| FOOD | American/Continental/English; $10.25 to $21.50; Sunday brunch available |

## J. T. Bullitt *Restaurant/English Pub/Bar*
611 Port Washington Boulevard, Port Washington (Nassau)
(516) 883-2587

The decor is "casual New York wood" and the crowd is single and friendly. There's a pub area, a separate dining room, and occasional live music in the background.

| | |
|---|---|
| AVERAGE DRINK | $2.00 |
| COVER OR MINIMUM | None |
| PLASTIC | AE, MC, V |
| CROWD | Professionals and employees from the nearby hospitals; 23 to 35 |
| DRESS | Proper attire |
| OPEN | Seven days, 11 A.M. to 4 A.M. |
| FOOD | American/English food, Sunday brunch; dinner prices range from $4.95 to $12.95 |
| SPECIALS | Happy Hour happens seven days, 4 to 6 P.M., with drinks half-priced |

## King of Hearts                              *Disco/Nightclub*

475 Sunrise Highway, West Babylon (Suffolk, ¼ mile west of Sunrise Hwy. Exit 38; or Exit 37S off the Southern State Pkwy.) (516) 422-1781

Whether or not Henry VIII had a 76-foot bar and a disco with light show in his palace remains a question for historians. But this place, done in "castle decor," does. It's got a medieval feel with a red leather bar, black chairs, red velvet on the walls, lots of wrought iron and chandeliers. There's another, more contemporary looking lounge next to the dance floor. Some live music entertains the crowd (half singles half couples) on Friday and Sunday, but you can call for recorded, up-to-the-minute information.

| | |
|---|---|
| AVERAGE DRINK | $2.25 |
| COVER OR MINIMUM | $5.00 Friday and Saturday |
| PLASTIC | None |
| CROWD | A good cross section of people, ages 23 to 35 and up |
| DRESS | Jackets required September to June |
| OPEN | Call for exact days; doors usually open at 9 P.M. |
| FOOD | Snacks and munchies |
| SPECIALS | Free admission until 10 P.M. |

**Laces**                             *Roller Skating Center*
3345 Hillside Avenue, New Hyde Park (Nassau)
(516) 742-8161

The 30,000-square-foot rink is as lavish and plush as any disco, with light shows, a game room, pro shop, and once a month parties. Call to find out when the "Adult Sessions" for twenty-one and over are.

| | |
|---|---|
| AVERAGE DRINK | Soft drinks available |
| COVER OR MINIMUM | $3.75 |
| PLASTIC | MC, V |
| CROWD | Sophisticated adults |
| DRESS | Chic, disco clothing |
| OPEN | It varies, so call |
| FOOD | Snack bar |

**Levittown Roller Rink**              *Roller Skating*
Hempstead Turnpike and Wantaugh Parkway, East Meadow (Nassau)
(516) 731-6200

Many adult sessions for eighteen and over—call for days and times.

| | |
|---|---|
| AVERAGE DRINK | No liquor |
| COVER OR MINIMUM | $2.50 plus 75¢ for skates |
| PLASTIC | None |
| DRESS | Designer jeans OK if neat; no tank tops or jeans with holes |
| OPEN | Call for specifics |

**The Library**                              *Restaurant/Bar*
541 Port Washington Boulevard, Port Washington (Nassau)
(516) 883-3122

A casual singles spot done in dark wood and plants, with a dining room in the back and a bar with cocktail tables in front. The bar seats fifteen, but after 9 P.M. there are more drinkers than eaters, and you can sit in the dining room for "just drinks."

| | |
|---|---|
| AVERAGE DRINK | $2.00 |
| COVER OR MINIMUM | None |
| PLASTIC | AE, CB, DC, MC, V |
| CROWD | Mixed, with college students and others; mean age, 24 |
| DRESS | Casual |
| OPEN | Seven days, 11 A.M. to 4 A.M. |
| FOOD | Hamburgers, steaks, seafood; dinner from $4.25 to $10.50 |

**Lime Tree Lounge**                                          *Lounge/Disco*
Exit 64 Long Island Expressway and Route 112,
Medford (Suffolk)
(516) 654-3000

A friendly and intimate atmosphere in a large room with live music
and a d.j. Friday and Saturday and recorded music for dancing the
rest of the week.

| | |
|---|---|
| AVERAGE DRINK | $2.50 |
| COVER OR MINIMUM | None |
| PLASTIC | AE, CB, DC, MC, V |
| CROWD | All types, all ages |
| DRESS | Neat and casual; designer jeans OK, but no crummy jeans |
| OPEN | Seven days, noon to closing |
| FOOD | None |

**The Lone Piper**                                                    *Pub*
1 Village Square, Glen Cove (Nassau)
(516) 759-1770

A homey atmosphere with a fireplace in the winter and an outdoor
patio in the summer. The bar seats about twenty, and the separate
lounge area has comfortable couches and non-fussy cocktail tables.
The crowd is a friendly but non-hassling group of singles and couples (Friday more singles, Saturday more couples, you know how
that works, it's pretty much standard) with a nice protective bartender. Live entertainment weekends.

| | |
|---|---|
| AVERAGE DRINK | $1.75 to $2.50 |
| COVER OR MINIMUM | $3.00 during 1950's Night; other times no cover, no minimum |
| PLASTIC | AE, MC, V |
| CROWD | Nurses, neighborhood people and students from 25 to 30ish |
| DRESS | Casual |
| OPEN | Tuesday through Sunday, 11:30 A.M. to 4 A.M.; closed Monday |
| FOOD | Light meals ($3.00 to $7.00) available all the time; dinners feature American/Scottish cuisine and are available from 5 P.M. to 10 P.M. Monday through Thursday, and 5 P.M. to 2 A.M. Friday and Saturday ($6.95 to $13.95); Sunday brunch, noon to 3:30 |
| SPECIALS | Happy Hour 4 to 7 P.M., Tuesday through Friday, featuring regular-priced drinks but a free hot buffet |

**The Mad Hatter**                    *Nightclub with Dancing*
2192 Nesconset Highway, Stony Brook (Suffolk)
(516) 751-6953, (516) 751-6922

Live new wave and rock and roll music for the listening and dancing pleasure of the many singles who party up a storm in this enormous place. Tiffany lamps give it a pub look, and two big bars promote lots of socializing.

| | |
|---|---|
| AVERAGE DRINK | $1.50 |
| COVER OR MINIMUM | Free to $4.00 depending on the entertainment |
| PLASTIC | None |
| CROWD | It varies with the entertainment, but the manager tells us that many people have met at The Mad Hatter, married, and still come back; age range is 19 to 25 |
| DRESS | Proper attire |

| | |
|---|---|
| OPEN | Five to seven nights, depending on the season; 8:30 P.M. to 4 A.M.; call for exactitudes |
| FOOD | Munchies |
| SPECIALS | Call |

### The Mad Hatter East                    *Nightclub with Dancing*

East Quogue (it's not that big a town), in the Hamptons (Suffolk)
(516) 653-8766, (516) 653-6885

A friendly, good-time atmosphere with live music (new wave and rock and roll) for dancing. Couples, singles, and vacationers have been patronizing this huge room with Tiffany lamps and wood walls, for years.

| | |
|---|---|
| AVERAGE DRINK | $2.00 |
| COVER OR MINIMUM | Varies |
| PLASTIC | None |
| CROWD | Regulars and newcomers contribute to a party atmosphere; age range 25 to 35 |
| DRESS | Proper attire |
| OPEN | Closed during the winter; call for exact opening dates; hours are usually 8:30 P.M. to 4 A.M. |
| FOOD | Munchies |
| SPECIALS | Call |

### Malibu                                   *Rock and Dance Club*

Lido Boulevard, Lido Beach (Nassau)
(516) 432-1600

Beach club decor with three bars, a big game room, live music occasionally, and many other suntanned singles.

| | |
|---|---|
| AVERAGE DRINK | $1.75 to $2.00 |
| COVER OR MINIMUM | $5.00 |
| PLASTIC | None |
| CROWD | All types, mainly from 18 to 25 |

192                                         *Places to Go*

|  |  |
|---|---|
| DRESS | Neat and casual—no sneakers |
| OPEN | Wednesday through Sunday, from 9:30 P.M. to 4 A.M. |
| FOOD | Hot dog stand |
| SPECIALS | Lifeguard Nights during the summer—call them |

## Millennium                                            *Nightclub*

Route 110, Huntington (Suffolk, at the shopping center)
(516) 673-0301

A shiny, modern, "New York-ish" club with eighteen-foot ceilings, steel beams, and that chic, factory/warehouse look. Holds 500 people, 90 percent of whom are single. A d.j. spins disco and rock and people can either dance or drink at the 100-foot bar.

|  |  |
|---|---|
| AVERAGE DRINK | $2.25 |
| COVER OR MINIMUM | Varies |
| PLASTIC | None |
| CROWD | All types, from all over, from 18 to 27 |
| DRESS | Dress jeans and nice casual clothes |
| OPEN | Wednesday through Sunday 9 P.M. to 4 A.M. |
| FOOD | None |
| SPECIALS | Call for details |

## Millie's                                            *Restaurant/Bar*

25 Middle Neck Road, Great Neck (Nassau)
(516) 482-4223

A "Manhattan style café" with wood, brick, and brass decor, and lots of mirrors for that contemporary look. Many, many singles and an occasional piano player. The back room is decorated like an outdoor garden.

|  |  |
|---|---|
| AVERAGE DRINK | $2.75 |
| COVER OR MINIMUM | $3.50 minimum at the tables |
| PLASTIC | AE, DC, MC, V |
| CROWD | All types of people, ages 20 to 45 |
| DRESS | No sleeveless shirts |

## Moonraker                                    *Restaurant/Bar*
650 Jericho Turnpike, Syosset (Nassau)
(516) 364-2555

Adjectives that fit here: dark and intimate, though spacious and elegant. The dining room and the lounge are two separate entities, with a mixture of couples and singles in the lounge. Sit at the long, dark wood bar and enjoy live piano Sunday and Monday from 8:30, or a band Tuesday and Wednesday from 9, and Thursday through Saturday from 9:30.

| | |
|---|---|
| AVERAGE DRINK | $1.90 to $2.50 |
| COVER OR MINIMUM | None |
| PLASTIC | AE, DC, MC, V |
| CROWD | Executives and other professionals from 25 to 65 |
| DRESS | Casual but neat; many wear jackets, though it's not required |
| OPEN | Seven days; weekdays, noon to 1 A.M.; Saturday, 5 P.M. to 1:30 A.M.; Sunday, 11 A.M. to 11 P.M. |
| FOOD | Continental/American, with dinner running from $8.50 to $19.95 |
| SPECIALS | Gully Whumper Time is from 4 to 7 P.M. Monday through Friday; think about it |

## Mushrooms Pub                                    *Pub*
1 Cuttermill Road, Great Neck (Nassau)
(516) 466-2454

Your basic friendly Tudor-style pub containing a large percentage of singles and a big bar. Easy, casual mood.

| | |
|---|---|
| AVERAGE DRINK | $1.75 to $2.00 |
| COVER OR MINIMUM | None |

|           |                        |
|-----------|------------------------|
| PLASTIC   | AE, DC, MC, V          |
| CROWD     | All types, aged 20 to 60; how can you go wrong? |
| DRESS     | Neat casual; dress jeans OK |
| OPEN      | Seven days: Monday through Saturday, 11:30 A.M. to 3 A.M.; Sunday 5 P.M. to 3 A.M. |
| FOOD      | Burgers, etc., for about $4.00 |

## My Father's Place                                    *Nightclub*
19 Bryant Avenue, Roslyn Village (Nassau)
(516) 621-8700

It used to be a bowling alley, and now the tables are made out of the old bowling alley floor. That's economy for you! The atmosphere is friendly and comfortable, with comedians, rock and roll bands, raggae and jazz to entertain you and the other couples and singles.

|                   |                          |
|-------------------|--------------------------|
| AVERAGE DRINK     | $1.75                    |
| COVER OR MINIMUM  | $7.00 cover charge for shows |
| PLASTIC           | None                     |
| CROWD             | Mid 20s; varies depending on who's playing |
| DRESS             | Casual                   |
| OPEN              | Seven nights, from 7:30 P.M. to 2:30 A.M. |
| FOOD              | American menu, $2.00 to $5.00 |
| SPECIALS          | Call to find out when Video Nights are |

## Northstage Theatre/Restaurant            *Cabaret/Concert Club*
96 School Street, Glen Cove (Nassau)
(516) 676-8500

A beautiful, old restored vaudeville theater with two large bars and a dining room. Entertainment varies from concerts, variety shows, and country-western groups to pop music and oldies. A good mixture of couples and singles.

|                   |                          |
|-------------------|--------------------------|
| AVERAGE DRINK     | $2.00                    |
| COVER OR MINIMUM  | $10.00 to $13.50 if you're watching the show but not having dinner; there's a minimum of $24.50 if you're having dinner, too |

| | |
|---|---|
| PLASTIC | AE, CB, DC, MC, V |
| CROWD | Depends on the show |
| DRESS | Casual but neat |
| OPEN | Friday and Saturday and some weeknights |
| FOOD | An a la carte hamburger is about $5.00; the dinner starts at $24.50 |

## October's                                        *Disco/Lounge*
260-1 Smithtown Boulevard, Nesconset (Suffolk)
(516) 265-9613

Like the man says, it's autumn on Long Island with trees and rustic colors. And many many singles. Dance to recorded music and a d.j. from 9 P.M. nightly.

| | |
|---|---|
| AVERAGE DRINK | $2.00 |
| COVER OR MINIMUM | None |
| PLASTIC | None |
| CROWD | A casual crowd from 21 to 30 |
| DRESS | Proper attire |
| OPEN | Seven days, from 3 P.M. to 4 A.M. |
| FOOD | Light snacks |
| SPECIALS | Drinks are half-priced on weekends from 9:30 to 10:30 P.M.; call for other specials |

## On Broadway                                *Musical Restaurant*
1201 Broadway, North Massapequa (Nassau, Exit 30N off Southern State, 1 mile on the left)
(516) 249-8822

You "sound" freaks will delight in the acoustic baffles that were put up by a recording engineer in order to establish perfect sound distribution throughout the room. You singles will delight in the room, too, with local and big name talent. Rock, jazz, fusion. No dancing.

| | |
|---|---|
| AVERAGE DRINK | $2.00 |
| COVER OR MINIMUM | $3.00; no minimum at the tables |
| PLASTIC | AE, CB, DC, MC, V |

| | |
|---|---|
| CROWD | All types, from 21 to 40 |
| DRESS | Neat casual |
| OPEN | Wednesday, Friday, and Saturday from 9 P.M. to 3 A.M. |
| FOOD | Omelets, quiches, soups; from $5.00 to $15.00 |

## Pastime Pub                                             *Rock Room*
140 Merrick Road, Amityville (Suffolk)
(516) 691-9655

Top Long Island bands play rock and roll for listening and dancing seven nights a week, in this big, airy room. Everything is huge—the crowds (1200 capacity, mostly single), the dance floor, the rectangular bar, the long concert tables. The decor is rustic with pine and tablecloths and the mood is very friendly. "It's a big party," confides Mike the barmaid. "We're not sophisticated at all."

| | |
|---|---|
| AVERAGE DRINK | $1.25 |
| COVER OR MINIMUM | $2.00 weekdays, $3.00 weekends |
| PLASTIC | None |
| CROWD | All types of people, 18 to 22 |
| DRESS | Casual but neat |
| OPEN | Seven days, 1 P.M. to 4 A.M. |
| FOOD | Potato chip machine |
| SPECIALS | Happy Hour, Friday and Saturday, 4 to 10 P.M. |

## Printer's Devil                                             *Pub*
105 Wynn Lane, Port Jefferson (Suffolk, off Main St.)
(516) 928-7171

Converted from an old printer's workshop, this small, cozy room is decorated with many fine antiques, brass lamps, chandeliers, a beautiful flagstone floor, and lots of glass—including the original windows. It's a Dublin/London old world atmosphere with many singles and live Irish music on Friday night.

| | |
|---|---|
| AVERAGE DRINK | $2.00 |
| COVER OR MINIMUM | $5.00 at the tables |

| | |
|---|---|
| PLASTIC | AE, CB, DC, MC, V |
| CROWD | Local people, all ages |
| DRESS | No cut-offs |
| OPEN | Seven days, from 11:30 A.M. to 2 or 3 A.M. |
| FOOD | American pub cuisine; chicken is $7.95, filet mignon is $13.95 |
| SPECIALS | Happy Hour Monday through Friday from 4 to 6 P.M. |

## Quarterdeck Pub                                     *Rock Club*
1543 Montauk Highway, Oakdale (Suffolk, 1 mile east of
intersection of Sunrise and Montauk highways)
(516) 589-4747

Live rock and roll with a nautical decor and about 90 percent
singles.

| | |
|---|---|
| AVERAGE DRINK | $1.25 |
| COVER OR MINIMUM | $2.00 |
| PLASTIC | None |
| CROWD | Business crowd in the afternoons, younger 20s crowd at night |
| DRESS | Neat casual |
| OPEN | Monday, Tuesday and Wednesday from 2 P.M. to 4 A.M.; Thursday, Friday and Saturday from 11 A.M. to 4 A.M.; closed Sunday |
| FOOD | Snacks |
| SPECIALS | 25¢ bar drinks on Monday, Tuesday, and Wednesday night; Friday and Saturday from 9 P.M. to 10 and from 1 A.M. to 3, "Two-fers"; Friday afternoon, free cold buffet from 11:30 A.M. to 2:30 P.M. |

**Raffles**                                         *Restaurant/Bar*

Go to Roslyn in Nassau County and ask someone where the
Clock Tower is.
(516) 484-4518

Warm and friendly pub atmosphere with many singles and some
couples.

| | |
|---|---|
| AVERAGE DRINK | $2.00 |
| COVER OR MINIMUM | None |
| PLASTIC | AE, CB, DC, MC, V |
| CROWD | Local people from 21 (must be 21) to 35 |
| DRESS | Informal |
| OPEN | Seven days, noon to 2 A.M. |
| FOOD | American menu for lunch and dinner; dinner prices range from $4.25 to $14.00 |

**Red Fox Inn**                      *Restaurant/Bar/Outdoor Patio*

6 Parlato Drive, West Hampton Beach (Suffolk)
(516) 288-1040

The bar, which seats twenty, is mostly singles, and although it's
open year-round, the best crowds happen in the summer. Pub decor
is enhanced with stained glass lampshades and an ethnogeo-
graphical map of Ireland.

| | |
|---|---|
| AVERAGE DRINK | $2.00 |
| COVER OR MINIMUM | Seldom any |
| PLASTIC | MC, V |
| CROWD | Locals and vacationers, professionals and executives; age range 22 to 35 |
| DRESS | Casual proper |
| OPEN | Seven days 11 A.M. to 4 A.M. |
| FOOD | American/Continental lunch and dinner till 11 P.M.; dinner is about $7.95 and up |
| SPECIALS | Happy Hour from 4 to 7 P.M. daily, plus many varied specials in the summer |

**Reinhard's**                                          *Restaurant/Bar*

Reinhard's Park, Bayville Avenue, Bayville (Nassau)
(516) 628-8766

How divine to have a leisurely lunch or dinner on the deck over-looking Long Island Sound! Or to swim on their beach in the summer and then come on up to one of the three bars for a long, cool drink. If life could only be like this all the time! Friday and Saturday there's a piano bar to top it off, with occasional combos. Many couples, some singles—summer, as you may have guessed, is the best time to go.

| | |
|---|---|
| AVERAGE DRINK | $2.00 |
| COVER OR MINIMUM | $5.00 parking fee on weekends |
| PLASTIC | AE, DC, MC, V |
| CROWD | Professionals from 21 up to 60 |
| DRESS | Casual or formal, whatever makes you happy |
| OPEN | Seven days, 11 A.M. to 4 A.M. |
| FOOD | Seafood—what else?—lunch, dinner, brunch on Sunday; dinner prices range from $5.95 to $14.95 |

**Remsen's Garden Restaurant**                         *Restaurant/Bar*

450 Wheatley Plaza, Greenvale (Nassau, off Northern Blvd.)
(516) 621-8451

The plush, spacious bar is separated from the large dining area, and has a 50/50 singles-to-couples ratio on weekends. The decor is elaborate and Victorian, with lots of brass and polish. Live music may be in the works for the future.

| | |
|---|---|
| AVERAGE DRINK | $2.75 |
| COVER OR MINIMUM | None |
| PLASTIC | AE, CB, DC, MC, V |
| CROWD | Professionals, business people, local residents; late 20s to about 45 |
| DRESS | Proper fashionable attire |
| OPEN | Seven days, from 11:30 A.M. to 2 A.M. |

| FOOD | Lunch and dinner, American/Continental; average a la carte dinner entrée is $9.00 or $10.00 |
| SPECIALS | Hors d'oeuvres in the afternoon (sounds like a good title for a movie) |

## Ricky's
*Restaurant/Bar*

88 Mineola Avenue, Roslyn Heights (Nassau)
(516) 484-0555

An elegant but calm, low-profile room with singles and couples (50/50) at the bar on weekends. The bar seats over thirty people who enjoy piano music on Friday and Saturday and sip champagne cocktails out of elegant crystal. The dining area compliments the mood with that "white linen/flowers on the table" look.

| AVERAGE DRINK | $2.00 to $2.50 |
| COVER OR MINIMUM | None |
| PLASTIC | AE, CB, DC, MC, V |
| CROWD | Local people, professionals, all ages |
| DRESS | Proper attire; many men wear jackets |
| OPEN | Tuesday through Sunday 11:30 A.M. until the customers leave; closed Monday |
| FOOD | Northern Italian/Continental cuisine served from lunch till 11 P.M. Tuesday through Friday, 1 P.M. to 9 P.M. Sunday, and dinner only on Saturday from 5 P.M. to 11 P.M.; dinner prices range from $6.00 to $14.00 |

## Riddles
*Bar/Restaurant with Dancing*

533 Old Country Road, Westbury (Nassau)
(516) 997-8666

Made with 125-year-old wood from a real Vermont barn, the atmosphere is casual and friendly with singles and couples. Live Top 40 and rock music Wednesday through Saturday, with dancing.

| AVERAGE DRINK | $2.00 |
| COVER OR MINIMUM | None |

| | |
|---|---|
| PLASTIC | AE, DC, MC, V |
| CROWD | All types, all ages |
| DRESS | Casual |
| OPEN | Seven days: Monday through Friday 11:30 A.M. to 4 A.M.; Saturday and Sunday noon to 4 A.M. |
| FOOD | American/Italian; dinners go from $3.95 to $8.50 |
| SPECIALS | Happy Hour Monday through Friday from 4 to 7 P.M. |

**Rumrunner of Oyster Bay**                    *Rock Club*
200 Pine Hollow Road, Oyster Bay (Nassau, Long Island Exp. to Exit 41N, to Rt. 106)
(516) 922-1197

A large room with nautical decor and two large bars. Live music and dancing nightly. Mostly singles.

| | |
|---|---|
| AVERAGE DRINK | $2.00 |
| COVER OR MINIMUM | $3.00 |
| PLASTIC | None |
| CROWD | Many students and others from 19 through mid 20s |
| DRESS | Casual |
| OPEN | Tuesday through Sunday from 9 P.M. to 4:30 A.M.; closed Monday |
| FOOD | Burgers, pizza, hot dogs; to about $4.00 |
| SPECIALS | Wednesday pay $5.00 at the door from 9 P.M. to 11 and get all you can drink; call for other specials |

**Silver Dollar Music Saloon**          *Country-Western Club*
9 South Park Avenue, Bay Shore (Suffolk, 1 block south of Main St.)
(516) 665-8645

You can get anything you want here, from dancing to the live bands nightly except Monday, to riding on the mechanical bull! There's a

202                                        *Places to Go*

Bronco Shop in case you forgot your cowboy hat, and saddles all over. The mood is accented by a thirty-foot air brush mural of a desert sunset scene. Couples and singles.

| | |
|---|---|
| AVERAGE DRINK | $1.75 |
| COVER OR MINIMUM | $2.00 to $3.00 |
| PLASTIC | None |
| CROWD | From 18 to 30, but it really depends on the band |
| DRESS | Country-western outfits and jeans; no T-shirts |
| OPEN | Seven days, from 8 P.M. to 4 A.M. |
| FOOD | Nuts and popcorn |
| SPECIALS | They boast the longest running Budweiser Beer Blast: free beer on Wednesday from 8 to 10 P.M. and 25¢ beer from 10 to closing; other specials vary, so call |

## Strawberry's                                    *Restaurant/Lounge/Bar*
661 Northern Boulevard, Great Neck (Nassau)
(516) 466-9100

Pretty, airy, "outdoor" garden decor with a large bar area, a friendly clientele of both singles and couples, and live popular music nightly. Feel free to chat at the bar or join the fun on the dance floor.

| | |
|---|---|
| AVERAGE DRINK | $2.75 |
| COVER OR MINIMUM | None at the bar; $7.50 at the tables when the entertainment starts |
| PLASTIC | AE |
| CROWD | Many professionals and others from 30 to 50 years old |
| DRESS | Neat casual |
| OPEN | Seven days, from 11:30 A.M. to 4 A.M. |
| FOOD | Full menu till 2 A.M.; dinner runs $6.50 to $13.00 |
| SPECIALS | Happy Hour Monday through Friday from 4 to 7 P.M. with a hot buffet |

**Strawberry's Sidewalk Café**                    *Restaurant/Café*
378 New York Avenue, Huntington Village (Suffolk)
(516) 673-3888

A tiny, comfortable room with cedar, brick, brass, mirrors, plants, murals, and awnings. Singles and couples.

| | |
|---|---|
| AVERAGE DRINK | $1.75 |
| COVER OR MINIMUM | None |
| PLASTIC | Major credit cards are in the process of being accepted |
| CROWD | Business people; men must be 25, women 23 to get in |
| DRESS | Jackets worn but not required |
| OPEN | Seven days, from 11:30 A.M. to 4 A.M. |
| FOOD | Steaks, sandwiches, seafood for lunch and dinner; dinner prices range from $3.50 to $12.95 |
| SPECIALS | Happy Hour 5 to 6 P.M. |

**"The Subway" Roller Disco**              *Roller Disco/Bowling*
**at Royal Lanes**
120 Hempstead Avenue, West Hempstead (Nassau)
(516) 485-7400

There are party nights and various adult nights to suit any kind of single. Call for the schedule. Live d.j. nightly, plus a game room, lounge, and bowling.

| | |
|---|---|
| AVERAGE DRINK | $1.80 |
| COVER OR MINIMUM | Varies around $3.50 plus $1.00 for skates |
| PLASTIC | None |
| CROWD | Depends on what's going on that night |
| DRESS | Neat but casual |
| OPEN | 9 A.M. to whenever, seven days |
| FOOD | Snack bar with a big menu; $1.95 will get you recharged |
| SPECIALS | Call them |

**Sugar Mountain Lodge**                                    *Pub*
315 Merrick Avenue, East Meadow (Nassau, corner of Front St.,
1 mile north of Exit 24 on Southern State Pkwy.)
(516) 542-9539

A nice, warm fireplace and a friendly, very single crowd. Mellow
rock and roll on Thursday, Friday, and Saturday nights.

| | |
|---|---|
| AVERAGE DRINK | $1.50 |
| COVER OR MINIMUM | None |
| PLASTIC | None |
| CROWD | Business people during the day, and a younger crowd at night |
| DRESS | Neat, proper attire; men must have collars on their shirts |
| OPEN | Monday through Saturday 11 A.M. to 4 A.M.; Sunday noon to 4 A.M. |
| FOOD | Burgers, etc., for $2.00 to $3.00 till 6 P.M. |
| SPECIALS | Happy Hour Monday through Friday from 5 to 7 P.M. |

**Summertime**                               *Restaurant/Nightclub*
422 Wantagh Avenue, Bethpage (Nassau)
(516) 433-9604

A big nightclub with trees and flowers and couples as well as singles. Dancing Wednesday through Sunday with a d.j.

| | |
|---|---|
| AVERAGE DRINK | $1.75 |
| COVER OR MINIMUM | $2.00 |
| PLASTIC | None |
| CROWD | All types, all ages |
| DRESS | Proper attire |
| OPEN | Monday through Saturday 11 A.M. to 4 A.M.; Sunday noon to 7 P.M. |
| FOOD | Continental/American—light or heavy meals; dinner prices range from $5.95 to $10.95; lunch available also   [cont'd] |

Divorced and Separated Club meets on
Sunday—call for details

### Top Rollers, Inc. *Roller Disco*
35-60 Long Beach Road, Oceanside (Nassau, in the
TSS Shopping Center)
(516) 536-6300

A big, lively atmosphere with dancing lights and special nights for
singles—call to find out when. Game room and separate dance
floor.

| | |
|---|---|
| AVERAGE DRINK | No liquor |
| COVER OR MINIMUM | $4.00 and $1.00 for skates |
| PLASTIC | None |
| CROWD | College students and others in their mid 20s |
| DRESS | Neat |
| OPEN | Call |
| FOOD | Restaurant-sized snackbar area |
| SPECIALS | Free wine and cheese nights—call for details |

### Tuey's *Rock Room*
Route 25A, Stony Brook (Suffolk)
(516) 751-3737

With over 200 feet of butcher block bar, a 30′ × 30′ dance floor,
live rock and roll, and plenty of singles, Tuey's is ready to party.
The bands are top Long Island names and play about five nights a
week. For a free monthly calendar of events, write to Tuey's, P.O.
Box 274, Stony Brook, NY 11790. There are tables and booths for
those who just want to listen.

| | |
|---|---|
| AVERAGE DRINK | $1.50 |
| COVER OR MINIMUM | $3.00 |
| PLASTIC | None |
| CROWD | All types, around 18 to 25 years old |
| DRESS | Neat and casual |
| OPEN | Wednesday through Monday, 9 P.M. to 4 A.M.; closed Tuesday |
| FOOD | None |

**Two-Morrow's Pub**                                    *Restaurant/Pub*
300 E. Main Street, Patchogue (Suffolk)
(516) 475-9723

Old world wood-and-stained-glass atmosphere with a twelve-foot fireplace and a seven-foot TV for sports fans. On the big, early American bar is a 25″ color TV. Couples and singles.

| | |
|---|---|
| AVERAGE DRINK | $1.25 |
| COVER OR MINIMUM | None |
| PLASTIC | None |
| CROWD | All types of people 23 and up |
| DRESS | Proper attire; casual after 8 |
| OPEN | Monday through Saturday 11:30 A.M. to 4 A.M.; closed Sunday |
| FOOD | Huge burgers and sandwiches till 1 A.M.; $2.65 to $4.95 |
| SPECIALS | Friday from 4 to 6 P.M.—"two-fers"; Thursday—Nurses' Night |

**Uncle Sam's**                                              *Disco*
2965 Hempstead Turnpike, Levittown (Nassau)
(516) 731-2458

A huge room with lots of singles, lights, mirror balls, seven bars, a lounge, game room, video system, and three-tiers (two for dancing, one for seating). Live music Wednesday, d.j. the rest of the week.

| | |
|---|---|
| AVERAGE DRINK | $2.00 |
| COVER OR MINIMUM | $5.00 |
| PLASTIC | None |
| CROWD | Mixed crowd in their 20s and early 30s |
| DRESS | Designer jeans are OK |
| OPEN | Tuesday through Saturday 9:30 P.M. to 4 A.M. |
| FOOD | None |
| SPECIALS | Call for details |

**United Skates of America**                    *Roller Skating*
1276 Hicksville Road, North Massapequa (Nassau)
(516) 795-5879

Roomy but comfortable, with friendly people. Call to find out when the singles' nights are. Live d.j.

| | |
|---|---|
| AVERAGE DRINK | No liquor |
| COVER OR MINIMUM | $3.50 |
| PLASTIC | MC, V with a minimum of $10.00 |
| CROWD | Neighborhood people and others from 19 to 25 |
| DRESS | Neat |
| OPEN | 18 years and over should stop by on Tuesday, Thursday, Friday and Saturday night; open daily as well |
| FOOD | Snacks |
| SPECIALS | Call to find out |

**U.S. Blues**                    *Restaurant/Dancing*
1353 Old Northern Boulevard, Roslyn (Nassau)
(516) 621-7904

Many singles, and live music Wednesday through Sunday. D.j. Monday and Tuesday. Casual but contemporary with a large bar and music area.

| | |
|---|---|
| AVERAGE DRINK | $2.50 |
| COVER OR MINIMUM | $3.00 at the door during entertainment |
| PLASTIC | AE, CB, DC, MC, V |
| CROWD | All types, many in their 20s |
| DRESS | Casual |
| OPEN | Seven days, 11 A.M. to 4 A.M. |
| FOOD | Lunch, dinner, late snacks; dinner is from $4.95 to $9.95 |
| SPECIALS | Happy Hour, 4 to 7 P.M. nightly |

**Westbury Music Fair**                    *Concerts/Theater-in-the-Round*
Brush Hollow Road, Westbury (Nassau)
(516) 333-7228

Some singles, many groups of friends, and many couples make up
the 3000 strong who flock to hear the likes of Paul Anka, Tom
Jones, Diana Ross, Mitzi Gaynor, Rick Springfield (from "General
Hospital"), and others. The main socializing area is The Wine and
Cheese Lounge, which holds 200 people. There's also a bar in the
lobby waiting area in case you need an emergency drink. Both are
open only during show hours. The place itself is well-kept, clean,
and contemporary despite its hugeness.

| | |
|---|---|
| AVERAGE DRINK | $2.50 |
| COVER OR MINIMUM | $8.75 to $15.00 |
| PLASTIC | MC, V |
| CROWD | All kinds, all ages, depending on the show |
| DRESS | Dressy |
| OPEN | Call or check the paper |
| FOOD | Cheese and crackers in The Wine and Cheese Lounge |

**Wheels Plus**                              *Roller Skating*
70 Veterans Memorial Highway, Commack (Suffolk)
(516) 499-4203

There's a good chance no one will notice you falling every few
minutes, with the disco lights, music, and live d.j. covering for you.
"Late Skate Sessions" are held Friday, Saturday, and Sunday, and
"Adult Night" happens on Wednesday, all with a fair share of
singles. The decor is a contemporary orange and blue, and they
boast a game room with the same disco floor as seen in "Saturday
Night Fever." Pro shop is right there, too.

| | |
|---|---|
| AVERAGE DRINK | No liquor |
| COVER OR MINIMUM | $3.50 plus $1.00 for skates |
| PLASTIC | None |

| | |
|---|---|
| CROWD | Neighborhood people and others; Wednesday night is 18 and over, Sunday is 16 and over |
| DRESS | Anything |
| OPEN | Call—it varies |
| FOOD | Snack bar |
| SPECIALS | Occasionally—call them |

### The Wine Gallery                                        *Bar/Restaurant*
2172 Hempstead Turnpike, East Meadow (Nassau)
(516) 794-8065

Stained glass, antique light fixtures, lots of plants, two dining rooms, and a seventy-five-person bar provide a good atmosphere for socializing.

| | |
|---|---|
| AVERAGE DRINK | $1.75 to $2.00 |
| COVER OR MINIMUM | None |
| PLASTIC | AE, DC, MC, V |
| CROWD | Business people and professionals from 21 to 50 |
| DRESS | Casual but neat |
| OPEN | Monday through Saturday 11 A.M. to 4 A.M.; Sunday 5 P.M. to 4 A.M. |
| FOOD | Continental—large or small meals till 3 A.M.; dinner is from $6.95 to $17.95 |
| SPECIALS | Hors d'oeuvres at the bar during cocktail time |

### Winner's Circle                                        *Disco/Nightclub*
39 Post Avenue, Westbury (Nassau)
(516) 997-4050

Dancing from Wednesday through Sunday in this cozy, comfortable room. Disco, Top 40 and oldies. Many singles.

| | |
|---|---|
| AVERAGE DRINK | $1.75 |
| COVER OR MINIMUM | $3.00 on Friday and Saturday |
| PLASTIC | None |

| | |
|---|---|
| CROWD | All types, from 25 to 35 |
| DRESS | Neat casual—dress jeans OK, but no crummy jeans |
| OPEN | Wednesday through Sunday 8 P.M. to 4 A.M. |
| FOOD | Sandwiches and snacks; $3.00 to $4.00 |
| SPECIALS | Dance Contest on Thursday; call for other specials |

**Aphrodite**                                    *Greek Restaurant/Bar*
610 W. Hartsdale Avenue, White Plains (Routes 100A and 100B)
(914) 428-6868

Is it possible to combine belly dancers, Greek songs, and disco music? Singles go mainly Wednesday and Friday to find out, and maybe dance a bit. No music Monday. The decor is contemporary Mediterranean.

| | |
|---|---|
| AVERAGE DRINK | $2.00 |
| COVER OR MINIMUM | None |
| PLASTIC | AE, DC, MC, V |
| CROWD | All types, ages 25 to 60; singles parties on Wednesday—call for exact dates and details |
| DRESS | Casual |
| OPEN | Seven days, noon to closing |
| FOOD | Lobsters and ribs, some Greek food; dinner is from $3.95 to $14.75; lunch available also |

**Bartholomew's**                                    *Restaurant/Bar*
2 Weaver Street, Scarsdale
(914) 725-3900

A big, old English-style bar and restaurant with a lounge upstairs. Easy listening rock and folk music from Wednesday through Saturday. Mixed couples and singles.

| | |
|---|---|
| AVERAGE DRINK | $2.50 |
| COVER OR MINIMUM | None |
| PLASTIC | AE, MC, V |
| CROWD | All types of people, mainly in their 20s |
| DRESS | Gentlemen must wear collars on their shirts |

| | |
|---|---|
| OPEN | Sunday through Thursday noon to 1 A.M.; Friday and Saturday noon to 2 A.M. |
| FOOD | Steak, seafood for lunch and dinner; dinner prices range from $8.95 to $15.95 |

## The Bijou
*Lounge/Disco/Restaurant*

Holiday Inn, Route 119, Tarrytown Road, Elmsford
(914) 592-5680

A big, large, friendly room filled with single people. It's a lounge and dining room, then at 10 P.M. it becomes a disco with a d.j., flashing lights, and recorded music.

| | |
|---|---|
| AVERAGE DRINK | $2.00 to $3.00 |
| COVER OR MINIMUM | None on weeknights, $2.00 on weekends |
| PLASTIC | AE, DC, MC, V |
| CROWD | Business people in the lounge at Happy Hour, and a disco crowd later and on weekends of about 22 to 35 years old |
| DRESS | Fashionable; no jeans |
| OPEN | The bar is open seven days from 11 A.M. to 2 A.M. (Friday and Saturday till 3 A.M.); the disco is open from 10 P.M. to closing |
| FOOD | Steak, seafood till 10 P.M.; dinner is $8.00 to $12.00 |
| SPECIALS | Happy Hour Monday through Friday, 4 to 9 P.M.—that's two drinks for the price of one, and hot hors d'oeuvres |

## Bumpers
*Bar*

628 North Avenue, New Rochelle
(914) 636-9697

A small, very friendly, dark wood bar with a good number of singles and occasional live music.

| | |
|---|---|
| AVERAGE DRINK | $1.25 |
| COVER OR MINIMUM | None |

| | |
|---|---|
| PLASTIC | None |
| CROWD | Many college people and others aged 18 to 25 |
| DRESS | Casual |
| OPEN | Seven days, 9:30 A.M. to 4 A.M. |
| FOOD | None; we're talking serious drink and socializing here |
| SPECIALS | Happy Hour Thursday 8 to 10 P.M.; Wednesday is Two-For-One Night; call for other specials |

**The Casbah**                                           *Nightclub/Restaurant*
384 North Avenue, New Rochelle
(914) 576-2392

You've seen it on TV talk shows. Now see it live. Male "burlesque" on Monday, Thursday, and Friday night—but it's just between the women and the performers until 11:30 P.M. when men are admitted. On Saturday night everyone is admitted to dance to the live music (often name groups) or just sit and talk. Wednesday a d.j. spins discs, takes requests, and plays a good deal of old rock and roll. The atmosphere is comfortable, cozy, and personal, with mixed couples and singles.

| | |
|---|---|
| AVERAGE DRINK | $2.00 |
| COVER OR MINIMUM | $5.00 |
| PLASTIC | None |
| CROWD | All types of people from 20 to 80 years old |
| DRESS | Casual but neat |
| OPEN | Monday, Thursday, Friday from 7:30 P.M. to 4 A.M.; Wednesday and Saturday from 9 P.M. to 4 A.M. |
| FOOD | Sandwiches available during shows for about $2.50 |
| SPECIALS | Chocolate pudding wrestling every other Wednesday |

**Characters** *Bar*
607 North Avenue, New Rochelle
(914) 636-9576

If you're in the mood for a party, here's your place. The crowd is
very friendly and very single. Thursday and Saturday the live bands
boost the mood even more with their party-rock sounds. Photographs of sports and movie celebrities are all over the walnut paneled walls.

| | |
|---|---|
| AVERAGE DRINK | $1.45 |
| COVER OR MINIMUM | $2.00 when there's music |
| PLASTIC | None |
| CROWD | Students and local young people from 21 to 25 |
| DRESS | Casual to anything |
| OPEN | Seven days, 10 A.M. to 4 A.M. |
| FOOD | None |
| SPECIALS | Call for details |

**The City (at the Sheraton Plaza)** *Restaurant/Disco*
1 Sheraton Plaza, New Rochelle
(914) 576-3700

The room is sophisticated but certainly not lacking in warmth.
Mixed couples and singles dance to the live disco band from 10 P.M.
to 4 A.M. Wednesday through Sunday and from 11 P.M. to 4 A.M.
Friday and Saturday.

| | |
|---|---|
| AVERAGE DRINK | $3.00 at the disco, $2.50 if you're having dinner |
| COVER OR MINIMUM | No cover, three drink minimum on weekends |
| PLASTIC | AE, DC, MC, V |
| CROWD | All types of people, many in their 20s |
| DRESS | No jeans, T-shirts, or sneakers |
| OPEN | Seven days, 7 A.M. to 4 A.M.; disco from 9 P.M. to 4 A.M. nightly |

| | |
|---|---|
| FOOD | Breakfast, lunch, and dinner; Continental menu at dinner, with prices ranging from $9.95 to $12.95 |
| SPECIALS | Happy Hour Monday through Thursday from 5:30 to 8 P.M. |

## Crazy Horse Café           *Club*
72 Centre Avenue, New Rochelle
(914) 576-2228

The singles scene goes country with old western decor, a small café area, and lots of games and amusements. Live music happens basically from Thursday through Sunday. Wednesday is often Talent Night. A d.j. holds down the fort on other nights and between sets.

| | |
|---|---|
| AVERAGE DRINK | $2.00 |
| COVER OR MINIMUM | $2.00 when there's a band |
| PLASTIC | None |
| CROWD | Single professionals from 25 to 30ish |
| DRESS | Casual |
| OPEN | Seven days, noon to 4 A.M. |
| FOOD | None |
| SPECIALS | Call for details |

## Dakota Rob Roy         *Restaurant/Lounge*
Old Route 22, Armonk
(914) 273-3071

An elegant atmosphere, plus red carpeting, a primarily singles crowd, and occasional live music.

| | |
|---|---|
| AVERAGE DRINK | Varies |
| COVER OR MINIMUM | $2.00 |
| PLASTIC | None |
| CROWD | Local people in their 20s |
| DRESS | Casual |
| OPEN | Call for days and hours; it varies |
| FOOD | None |

**Dudley's**                                                    *Lounge*
6 Rockledge Avenue, in the Sparta Section of Ossining
(914) 941-8674

The romantic mood suits both couples and singles with Victorian
decor, plants, and stained glass. Live piano/vocal Wednesday
through Saturday.

| | |
|---|---|
| AVERAGE DRINK | $2.00 |
| COVER OR MINIMUM | Two drink minimum during music |
| PLASTIC | AE, DC, MC, V |
| CROWD | Professionals from 24 up |
| DRESS | Jackets preferred |
| OPEN | Tuesday through Friday and Sunday from noon till closing; Saturday from 6 P.M. to closing; closed Monday |
| FOOD | American menu with dinner ranging from $8.95 to $14.95; lunch available also |
| SPECIALS | Happy Hour Tuesday through Friday from 5 to 6 P.M. |

**Encore**                                                      *Lounge*
9-11 Huguenot Street, New Rochelle
(914) 636-9409

Just redone, Encore has a contemporary but mellow decor, a
twenty-eight-stool bar, and a mainly single crowd. You can dance
to recorded music and occasional live bands. Stormy, the manager,
assures us of a good time.

| | |
|---|---|
| AVERAGE DRINK | $2.25 |
| COVER OR MINIMUM | None |
| PLASTIC | None |
| CROWD | Office people in the afternoons, joined by just about everyone else at night; age range, 21 to 35 |
| DRESS | No T-shirts or other grungy things |
| OPEN | Seven days, 11 A.M. to 4 A.M. |
| FOOD | Cheese boards, etc.  [cont'd] |

**Foley's**                                          *Bar*
479 Bedford Road, Pleasantville
(914) 769-9822

Lots of fun, lots of singles, and a great "down and dirty" atmosphere.

| | |
|---|---|
| AVERAGE DRINK | $1.00 |
| COVER OR MINIMUM | None |
| PLASTIC | None |
| CROWD | Neighborhood and college people in their 20s |
| DRESS | Anything |
| OPEN | Seven days from 10 A.M. to 3 A.M. |
| FOOD | Lunch, about $2.00 to $4.00; no dinner |

**Fore N Aft North**                               *Nightclub*
Route 6, Brewster
(914) 279-6822

If your ship is in dry dock, climb on board here instead. Lots of other singles do. Live rock music nightly for dancing or listening.

| | |
|---|---|
| AVERAGE DRINK | $1.75 |
| COVER OR MINIMUM | $2.00 |
| PLASTIC | None |
| CROWD | All types, from 18 to 22 |
| DRESS | No tatters |
| OPEN | Wednesday through Sunday from 8 P.M. to 2 A.M. |
| FOOD | Snacks |
| SPECIALS | There are nightly specials but they change, so call for details |

**Fore N Aft South**                                          *Nightclub*
Route 22, White Plains
(914) 761-2417

Singles from all over sail in here to enjoy the live rock music nightly.

|  |  |
|---|---|
| AVERAGE DRINK | $1.25 to $1.50 |
| COVER OR MINIMUM | $1.00 to $2.00 |
| PLASTIC | None |
| CROWD | Many college students from 18 to 25 |
| DRESS | Clean and neat |
| OPEN | Wednesday through Sunday from 8:30 P.M. to 3 A.M. |
| FOOD | Snacks |
| SPECIALS | Call to find out what's happening that night |

**Harlow's**                                                  *Supperclub*
566 Main Street, New Rochelle
(914) 632-4308

If you were really meant to live in the 1920's instead of the 1980's, join the other couples and singles in this large club. A five-piece band provides dance music and entertainment on Wednesday, Friday, Saturday and Sunday nights, and there's a piano bar from 5 P.M.

|  |  |
|---|---|
| AVERAGE DRINK | $2.50 |
| COVER OR MINIMUM | None |
| PLASTIC | AE |
| CROWD | Varied, but you must be over 25 to get in |
| DRESS | Jackets required |
| OPEN | Tuesday through Sunday from 11 A.M. to 4 A.M.; closed Monday |
| FOOD | Lunch, dinner, late snacks; dinner goes for $2.25 for a burger to $14.00 for filet mignon |

**Irish Eyes**                                            *Restaurant/Pub*
660 Saw Mill River Road, Ardsley (junction of Route 9A and
Ashford Ave.)
(914) 693-1222

Listen or sing along to the Irish country ballads and folk music
from 9 P.M. to 1 A.M. nightly. The decor is "pub" and the crowd is
perhaps 50 percent single.

| | |
|---|---|
| AVERAGE DRINK | $2.00 |
| COVER OR MINIMUM | None |
| PLASTIC | AE, V |
| CROWD | All types, all ages |
| DRESS | Casual but neat |
| OPEN | Tuesday through Sunday in the summer from 9:30 A.M. to 4 A.M.; open all seven days in the winter |
| FOOD | American and Irish food for lunch and dinner; brunch served on weekends; dinner prices range from $5.95 to $10.95 |

**Januaries**                                                    *Disco*
202 Westchester Avenue, White Plains
(914) 946-6681

Your basic modern, friendly disco with a d.j. from 9 P.M. nightly.

| | |
|---|---|
| AVERAGE DRINK | $2.00 |
| COVER OR MINIMUM | $3.00 |
| PLASTIC | AE |
| CROWD | Weekdays business people, weekends everyone; ages 21 and up, with an emphasis on the 20s |
| DRESS | Casual |
| OPEN | Monday through Friday noon to 4 A.M.; Saturday and Sunday 7:30 P.M. to 4 A.M. |
| FOOD | Lunch on weekdays averages about $3.00; no dinner |

Monday through Friday, Happy Hour from 5 to 7 P.M.; Thursday is Bar-B-Q Night; call for other specials

## Left Bank                                            *Nightclub*
20 East First Street, Mount Vernon
(914) 699-6618

The manager describes it as "a cross between decadent, posh, and rock and roll," with an 800 to 1000 person capacity, most of whom are single. Their PR department has described it as a "rock and roll fortress" with live, top name talent every night except Thursday. Thursday they have a live radio show and recorded music. The building itself was, in its youth, the original Bank of New York and is now converted—but the beautiful marble walls still remain.

| | |
|---|---|
| AVERAGE DRINK | $1.75 to $2.00 |
| COVER OR MINIMUM | $5.00 to $9.00 |
| PLASTIC | None |
| CROWD | All types of people from 18 to 30 |
| DRESS | Casual but neat |
| OPEN | Wednesday through Sunday from 9 P.M. to 4 A.M. |
| FOOD | Hot dogs |
| SPECIALS | Vary, so call for details |

## Marty and Lenny's                                    *Disco*
50 LeCount Place, New Rochelle
(914) 576-2244

A large, earth-colored room with three bars, mirrored walls, and green couches. Recorded music with disco lights, and a mixed couples/singles crowd.

| | |
|---|---|
| AVERAGE DRINK | $2.50 |
| COVER OR MINIMUM | $5.00 after 10 P.M. on weekends |
| PLASTIC | AE, DC, MC, V |
| CROWD | All types, from 25 to 50 |

|  |  |
|---|---|
| DRESS | Neat but casual; jackets required in the summer |
| OPEN | Wednesday through Sunday from 8 P.M. to 4 A.M. |
| FOOD | Outdoor grill in the summer |
| SPECIALS | Happy Hour is from 4 to 8 P.M. Thursday through Saturday in the summer; winter specials change, so call first |

## Maude's                                    *Country Tavern*
16 Depot Square, Tuckahoe
(914) 337-2590

An airy, bright mood with barn siding, green plants, and lots of light. Topping off the pleasant atmosphere on Wednesday, Thursday, Saturday, and Sunday is music for easy listening. Primarily singles.

|  |  |
|---|---|
| AVERAGE DRINK | $2.00 |
| COVER OR MINIMUM | None |
| PLASTIC | DC, V |
| CROWD | All types, from 25 up |
| DRESS | Men must have collars on their shirts |
| OPEN | Tuesday through Friday from 10:30 A.M. to 4 A.M.; Saturday and Sunday from 7 P.M. to 4 A.M.; Monday 5 P.M. to 4 A.M. |
| FOOD | Lunch and dinner; hamburgers and sandwiches; average $3.25 |
| SPECIALS | Vary, so call |

## Montage                                    *Lounge/Dancing*
Holiday Inn, 1 Holiday Inn Drive, Mt. Kisco
(914) 241-2600

There's something for everyone here. If you want to sit and talk, there are many other singles in the lounge to do that with. If you want to boogie, there's a dance room (with the disco lights) and live entertainment Wednesday, Friday, and Saturday and a d.j. the other nights.

| | |
|---|---|
| AVERAGE DRINK | $2.25 |
| COVER OR MINIMUM | $3.00 on Friday and Saturday |
| PLASTIC | AE, DC, MC, V |
| CROWD | Weeknights all types, weekends it's more local; age span is from 20 to 36 |
| DRESS | Casual but chic; no sloppy jeans or sneakers |
| OPEN | Seven days from 11:30 A.M. to about 3:30 A.M.; Sunday it closes around midnight |
| FOOD | Lunch; at night, hot and cold hors d'oeuvres with cheese at the bar, or you can go to "Teddy's" in the next room and have dinner for $6.75 to $15.95 |
| SPECIALS | Happy Hour 4:30 to 7 P.M., Monday through Friday |

**Moonlight Mile Again**                    *Bar/Restaurant*
533 Warburton Avenue, Hastings-on-Hudson
(914) 478-9648

An English pub with American rock and roll from Wednesday through Saturday. Mostly listening and socializing rather than dancing, and a mixed couples/singles crowd.

| | |
|---|---|
| AVERAGE DRINK | $1.50 to $1.75 |
| COVER OR MINIMUM | $2.00 |
| PLASTIC | None |
| CROWD | Mixed crowd, lots of college people and locals aged 20 and up |
| DRESS | Jeans and shirts with collars |
| OPEN | Monday through Saturday 10:30 A.M. till; Sunday 7 P.M. till |
| FOOD | Lunch, supper, late supper; quiches, burgers, soups; $2.75 to $4.75 |
| SPECIALS | Happy Hour 5 to 7 P.M., Monday through Friday |

**New Westchester Theatre**                    *Lounge and Concert Hall*
600 White Plains Road, Tarrytown
(914) 631-9100

You can go to the large concert hall to hear music (shownights vary—call or check paper for schedule), or you can join the other singles in the small "Celebrity Lounge" to socialize.

|  |  |
|---|---|
| AVERAGE DRINK | $1.75 |
| COVER OR MINIMUM | None in the lounge, $12.50 for the concerts |
| PLASTIC | MC, V |
| CROWD | All types, all ages |
| DRESS | Casual |
| OPEN | The lounge is open from 11 A.M. to 3 P.M. and from 4 P.M. to closing, Monday through Saturday |
| FOOD | Lunch only, runs about $3.00 |
| SPECIALS | Happy Hour Monday through Friday at 4 P.M. with free buffet on certain nights (varies) |

**Nunzio's**                                       *Restaurant*
5 Hunts Lane, Chappaqua
(914) 238-8807

This cozy restaurant with historical pictures on the walls hosts two of the Westchester singles organizations, Chances "R" (meets there on Wednesdays) and Sports Rites (Sundays). The rest of the week it's mostly couples. You can call either of these singles organizations for details (listed in Chapter 2) or you can just appear at Nunzio's door at about 8 P.M. on Wednesday or Sunday.

|  |  |
|---|---|
| AVERAGE DRINK | $1.50 |
| COVER OR MINIMUM | $5.00 usually includes everything but the drinks |
| PLASTIC | AE, MC, V |
| CROWD | All types, 30s and up |

| DRESS | Casual |
|---|---|
| OPEN | Monday through Friday noon to closing; Saturday and Sunday, from 5 P.M. |
| FOOD | Italian and seafood; dinner prices range from $5.95 to $12.95; weekday lunches available also |
| SPECIALS | Happy Hour Monday through Friday from 4 to 7 P.M. with complimentary hors d'oeuvres |

**Olliver's**                                  *Restaurant with Bar*
15 S. Broadway, White Plains
(914) 761-6111

Lush, Victorian decor with a late night hard-core singles crowd at the expansive bar. The mood is very "Maxwell's Plum" which means you can just walk in and strike up a conversation with someone who strikes your fancy.

| AVERAGE DRINK | $1.75 |
|---|---|
| COVER OR MINIMUM | None |
| PLASTIC | AE, DC, MC, V |
| CROWD | Professionals, students; age span is from 22 to 40 |
| DRESS | Casual but proper which means no T-shirts, sneakers, shorts, or sandals on men; men's shirts must have collars |
| OPEN | Seven days, 11 A.M. to 4 A.M. |
| FOOD | American cuisine till 11 P.M., salads and sandwiches after that; dinner prices range from $6.95 to $14.95 |

**Pastor's Broadway**                      *Restaurant/Dance Room*
811 N. Broadway, North White Plains (on Rt. 22)
(914) 997-7373

Dance to the live band Wednesday, Friday and Saturday (rock and disco), or simply sit and talk to someone about the pictures of

Broadway shows that hang on the walls. Mixed couples and singles.

| | |
|---|---|
| AVERAGE DRINK | $2.00 |
| COVER OR MINIMUM | None |
| PLASTIC | AE, DC, MC |
| CROWD | All types, from 20 to about 38 |
| DRESS | Neat but casual |
| OPEN | Monday through Saturday from 9 P.M. to 2 A.M.; closed Sunday |
| FOOD | Dinner till 1 A.M.; salad bar, steak, seafood; $7.00 and up |
| SPECIALS | Happy Hour Monday through Friday from 5 P.M. to 7 |

**Peach Trees**                                    *Restaurant/Disco*
The Mall, New Rochelle
(914) 235-7900

An elegant but casual atmosphere with both couples and singles. Live jazz for Sunday brunch, and disco from 9 P.M. to 4 A.M. Wednesday through Sunday.

| | |
|---|---|
| AVERAGE DRINK | $2.50 |
| COVER OR MINIMUM | $5.00 to $7.00 |
| PLASTIC | AE, CB, DC, MC, V |
| CROWD | All types of people; women must be 21 and men 24 to get into the disco |
| DRESS | Proper attire |
| OPEN | Seven days from 10 A.M. |
| FOOD | Lunch, dinner; American food; dinner ranges from $3.50 to $7.95 |
| SPECIALS | Happy Hour happens Wednesday, Thursday and Friday; call for other specials |

**Peter Pastor's**                                   *Restaurant/Bar*
149 Mamaroneck Road, White Plains
(914) 761-5160

Casual atmosphere with live music and dancing Tuesday through
Saturday. The bar seats thirty-five with mixed couples and singles.

| | |
|---|---|
| AVERAGE DRINK | $2.00 |
| COVER OR MINIMUM | None |
| PLASTIC | AE, CB, DC, MC, V |
| CROWD | All kinds of people from about 30 up |
| DRESS | Casual |
| OPEN | Monday through Saturday from 11 A.M. to about 3 A.M.; closed Sunday |
| FOOD | American/Italian lunch and dinner; late night snacks; dinner prices range from $8.50 to $16.00 |


**Ralph (Hys)**                                   *Cocktail Lounge*
**(at the Yorktown Motor Inn)**
Route 202 off Taconic Parkway, Yorktown
(914) 962-4517

A big, friendly room with wood, carpeting, and lanterns. Live music and dancing Friday and Saturday nights. Mixed couples and
singles.

| | |
|---|---|
| AVERAGE DRINK | $2.00 |
| COVER OR MINIMUM | None |
| PLASTIC | V |
| CROWD | Professionals, neighborhood, from 25 to 45 |
| DRESS | Proper |
| OPEN | Monday through Saturday from 4 P.M. to whenever |
| FOOD | Steak and seafood, from about $7.00 to $13.00 |
| SPECIALS | Happy Hour Monday through Friday, 4 to 6 P.M. |

**Rising Sun**                                          *Rock Club*
767 Yonkers Avenue, Yonkers
(914) 476-4662

Everything you've always wanted to know about Rising Sun: two
bands nightly with some big names and some local talent, large
dance floor, brand new stage, earthy decor, a seventy-foot horseshoe bar, 300-person capacity, and almost all singles.

| | |
|---|---|
| AVERAGE DRINK | $2.00 |
| COVER OR MINIMUM | $3.00 |
| PLASTIC | None |
| CROWD | All types, from 18 to about 28 |
| DRESS | Decent |
| OPEN | Wednesday through Sunday 8 P.M. to 3 A.M. |
| FOOD | Peanuts, chips, etc. |

**Sadies**                                      *Restaurant/Lounge*
128 Bedford Road, Katonah
(914) 232-9784

Just a pleasant place to be. Rustic decor, with a copper bar and
stained glass. Soft Southern rock on Friday and Saturday, and a
piano bar on Tuesday. Mixed couples and singles.

| | |
|---|---|
| AVERAGE DRINK | $1.50 |
| COVER OR MINIMUM | $1.00 |
| PLASTIC | AE, MC, V |
| CROWD | Business people in the afternoons, all types at night; age span at night is from 18 to 30 |
| DRESS | Casual but neat |
| OPEN | Monday through Saturday 11:30 A.M. to 2:30 A.M.; Sunday 5 P.M. to 2:30 A.M. |
| FOOD | None |
| SPECIALS | Monday through Friday, Happy Hour from 4 P.M. to 7 |

**The Sandbar** *Café*
77 Pelham Road, New Rochelle
(914) 636-9587

The question is this: How can such a big bar fit in such a small room? The answer: Where there's a party, there's a way. Live rock, jazz, and country music Wednesday through Sunday. Mostly singles.

| | |
|---|---|
| AVERAGE DRINK | $1.75 |
| COVER OR MINIMUM | $2.00 |
| PLASTIC | None |
| CROWD | College students and others from 23 to 30 |
| DRESS | Not too outrageous, OK? |
| OPEN | Seven nights, 6 P.M. to 4 A.M. |
| FOOD | Snacks |
| SPECIALS | Vary, so call |

**Scotch 'N Sirloin** *Bar/Restaurant*
200 Hamilton Avenue, White Plains (in the White Plains Mall)
(914) 948-2070

Cozy, friendly pub atmosphere with live mellow jazz Friday and Saturday from 9 P.M. to 1 A.M. Mixed couples and singles. If there aren't enough singles (which is unlikely) there are electronic games to keep you busy.

| | |
|---|---|
| AVERAGE DRINK | $1.75 |
| COVER OR MINIMUM | None |
| PLASTIC | AE, DC, MC, V |
| CROWD | Professionals, business people, students, and locals from 25 to 55 |
| DRESS | Neat but casual |
| OPEN | Monday through Thursday 5 P.M. to 1-ish; Friday and Saturday to 2-ish; Sunday 4 P.M. to 9 |
| FOOD | Dinner till 11 P.M.; steak, ribs, seafood; prices range from $9.95 to $18.95 |

**The Single Wing**                                                    *Pub*
106 Westchester Avenue, White Plains
(914) 428-0109

There's a reason for the football decor—the owner is Bob Hylands
who played for the Green Bay Packers when they won the Super-
bowl and then joined the New York Giants. But whether you're a
sports fan or not, you'll find the atmosphere friendly and the mood
casual. There's a large bar with all the glasses hung upside down,
and a pleasant mixture of both couples and singles.

| | |
|---|---|
| AVERAGE DRINK | $1.75 to $2.00 |
| COVER OR MINIMUM | None |
| PLASTIC | MC, V |
| CROWD | Business people from 21 to 28 |
| DRESS | Men's shirts must have collars |
| OPEN | Monday through Saturday 11 A.M. to 4 A.M.; Sunday 6 P.M. to 4 A.M. |
| FOOD | Lunch Monday through Saturday; supper nightly from 8 P.M.; burgers and sandwiches are priced at around $3.50 |

**Tarantino's**                                          *Nightclub/Restaurant*
540 Palmer Road, Yonkers
(914) 969-1155

Don't think that the fancy, plush decor with the custom mirrored
walls isn't conducive to a friendly atmosphere and cozy conversation. After all, there's also a lounge with a fireplace and couches.
Wednesday through Sunday you can listen or dance to live music
from 9 P.M. to 4 A.M.—oldies, 1960's, Top 40, and Frank Sinatra-
type tunes, all done through a big new sound system. Mixed couples and singles.

| | |
|---|---|
| AVERAGE DRINK | $2.50 |
| COVER OR MINIMUM | None |
| PLASTIC | None |
| CROWD | Many executives, from 30 to 60 |
| DRESS | Proper attire |

| | |
|---|---|
| OPEN | Wednesday through Sunday 8 P.M. to 4 A.M. |
| FOOD | None |
| SPECIALS | Free breakfast at 3 A.M.! |

## Tuttles                                    *Lounge/Dance Room*
## (at the White Plains Hotel)
Lyon Place, White Plains (between S. Broadway and Waller Ave.)
(914) 761-8100

A very elegant room with live music Monday through Saturday—usually a big band sound. There's also a piano bar for you mellow couples and singles from 5 to 9 P.M. Monday through Friday.

| | |
|---|---|
| AVERAGE DRINK | $2.50 |
| COVER OR MINIMUM | $7.00 minimum Friday and Saturday |
| PLASTIC | AE, CB, DC, MC, V |
| CROWD | Executives during the week, all types on weekends; singles would feel more comfortable on weekends; the average age is about 40 |
| DRESS | Jackets required |
| OPEN | Seven nights: from 5 P.M. to 1:30 A.M. Monday through Thursday; Friday from 5 P.M. to 2:30 A.M.; Saturday and Sunday 4:30 P.M. to about 2:30 A.M. |
| FOOD | Continental menu with dinners ranging from $10.50 to $16.50; breakfast and lunch also available—call for times |
| SPECIALS | Happy Hour Monday through Friday, 5 to 7 P.M. |

## United Skates of America          *Roller Skating to Music*
645 N. MacQuesten Parkway, Mount Vernon
(914) 667-1118

Call to find out when the singles events are. There's a live d.j., and light shows—but best of all, there's a carpeted center area for resting.

| | |
|---|---|
| AVERAGE DRINK | No liquor |
| COVER OR MINIMUM | $2.50 to $3.00 |
| PLASTIC | Not for admission |
| CROWD | All types, all ages; when you call, they'll tell you when the best times for your age group are |
| DRESS | Neat; jeans are OK if they're decent |
| OPEN | Call |
| FOOD | Snack bar |

**Vinny's**                                                    *Restaurant/Bar*
468 Bedford Road, Pleasantville
(914) 769-5710

If you want "inventions" decor, have dinner in the antique, wood-and-brass room called "Patent Place." On weekends after dinner hour, the room turns into a cocktail lounge. If you want "comic" decor, and who doesn't at one time or another in their lives, sit in the room called "The Strip Joint." Live music occasionally, with both couples and singles.

| | |
|---|---|
| AVERAGE DRINK | $1.75 |
| COVER OR MINIMUM | None for the bar |
| PLASTIC | AE, MC, V |
| CROWD | All ages, all types; many students |
| DRESS | No jeans or sneakers in "Patent Place"; the rest of Vinny's is come-as-you-are |
| OPEN | Seven days, from lunchtime to midnight on weekdays and till whenever on weekends |
| FOOD | Italian; dinner prices range from $5.95 to $14.95 |

# Chapter 2

# *Organizations, Agencies, Clubs, and Services*

*Remember:* All of the organizations, agencies, clubs, and services listed here have been personally checked by a member of our staff, either in person or by phone. We've even checked with the Better Business Bureau for your safety. BUT. Ownership changes, management changes, personnel changes—and we can thus assume no responsibility for your experiences. With organizations requiring large membership fees, we suggest that you ask to attend first as a guest. Try to get references, and stay clear of anyone giving you a high pressure sales pitch. Never pay any money blindly in advance. And make sure you understand the terms of your contract.

**Able Travel Service, Inc.**
1750 Central Park Avenue, Yonkers, NY 10710 (Westchester)
(914) 793-6668

The owner and manager are both single and have both traveled a lot, so they know your particular needs. One of their specialties—camping in Europe for people under thirty-five. Also book Singleworld tours.

**Aerobics West Fitness Club**
131 W. 86th Street, New York, NY 10024 (between Columbus and Amsterdam Aves.)
(212) 734-8438

If you want to stay in shape and socialize at the same time, check out this lovely club—70 percent of the membership is single. Bask in the light from the huge windows by the pool, or sit comfortably in the California hot tub. There's a gym, sauna, games, and some exercise classes, too. Membership fees vary, so call them for details. Most of the bodies here belong to professional people, ages 28 to about 35.

235

**Air and Marine Travel**
10 Main Street, Brewster, NY 10509 (serving Westchester)
(914) 279-6124

Winter ski trips for singles and couples. Send for free ski brochure.

**Anytime Anywhere Travel**
35 King Street, Chappaqua, NY 10514 (Westchester)
(212) 295-7300, (914) 238-8800, (914) 769-3900

Ask for the owner, Hugh Aronson—he's single, too, and can make complete travel arrangements for you over the phone. Not bad if you're in a hurry. In business fifteen years. Books resorts, Club Med, Singleworld, and more.

**Briarcliff Racquet Club**
North State Road, Briarcliff Manor, NY 10510 (Westchester)
(914) 762-3444

Perhaps by now your drinking arm is doing just fine and what you need is work on your backhand. There are plenty of potential friends here who are working on their backhand, too. Meet them on any one of the four indoor or six outdoor courts. Or at the Sunday night parties that are held from September to May. There are also leagues, classes, and private lessons.

| | |
|---|---|
| COVER OR MINIMUM | $15.00 membership fee |
| PLASTIC | None |
| CROWD | Professionals and executives of all ages |
| OPEN | Year-round; usually 7 A.M. to 11:30 P.M. |
| FOOD | Beer, wine, and snacks are in the works |

**Cappy's Travel**
The Bazaar Mall, Mt. Kisco, NY 10549 (Westchester)
(914) 241-0383

Cappy Devlin, the owner, will not only book your trips but will spend as much time with you as needed to make sure you're getting exactly what you want. She'll counsel you on prices, tipping, ward-

*Organizations, Agencies,*

robe, what customs to expect where, and is especially good with single parents and their individual needs. Her main thing is to get you out there and doing things—whether it's a short weekend jaunt somewhere or a major vacation. Many of her clients are separated, divorced, or widowed—so call her. You're in good hands. Monday through Saturday 10 A.M. to 6 P.M. or evenings by appointment.

### Chances "R"
P.O. Box 313, Dobbs Ferry, NY 10522 (Westchester)
(914) 723-6205

A social organization catering to professionals and executives in the twenty-five to forty-nine age bracket with jackets required at cocktail parties. There's no membership fee—you pay according to the individual event which may be a party, tennis match, or other event. Call or write for their most recent schedule.

### Classical Music Lovers' Exchange
P.O. Box 31, Pelham, NY 10803

Classical music lovers of all ages get a list by mail of other music lovers. They then make calls or write to people of their choice. The price is fluctuating, so write for details.

### Compatibility Plus, Inc.
P.O. Box 3337, Wayne, NJ 07470 (serving Westchester, Long Island, and the boroughs)
(914) 997-1848, (203) 322-9612, (201) 256-0202, (212) 926-6275, (516) 222-1588

An introduction service that gears itself to professionals and business people of all ages. Call or write for their detailed forty-eight-question profile. You fill this out and send it back with your check. Further phone interviews are conducted if necessary, and you are matched by humans. For $175.00 you get a six-month membership and at least seven names. For $220.00 you'll keep busy for a year with at least fifteen guaranteed names.

**Crossroads**
321 E. 43rd Street, 101, New York, NY 10017
(212) 490-1250, (201) 592-6787

Crossroads sponsors parties and interest-related events in Manhattan, Westchester, and New Jersey. You can also join their "Networking Program" and receive names and numbers in the mail. The private membership includes people of all ages, and the price is $315.00 for six months, nonrefundable. To join, call Executive Director Cathleen Crawford between 10 A.M. and 6 P.M. for an interview appointment. MC and V accepted.

**Dateline**
316 Fifth Avenue, New York, NY 10001
(212) 889-3230, outside New York City
call (800) 451-3245

To join, call for their literature and read it over. If it sounds good to you, fill out the application, send it back with the fee, and check your mailbox from time to time over the next eight weeks. You are matched by people, not by computer (not that there's anything inherently wrong with a computer). It's $18.00 for three months (approximately three to twenty referrals), $28.00 for six months, $37.00 for nine months, and $45.00 for a year (approximately twelve to eighty referrals). Women under thirty-two and men over fifty get it all for half price, unless that becomes illegal in the near future. And because they're a national organization, an extra $10.00 will get you names of dates in other towns if you're traveling or moving.

**Directions Unlimited Travel**
344 Main Street, Mt. Kisco, NY 10549 (Westchester)
(914) 241-1700

Call them for bicycle tours to Europe, China, and throughout the USA. Or for cruises, ranch weekends or Club Med. Monday through Friday 9:30 A.M. to 5:30 P.M., Saturday 10 A.M. to 2 P.M.

### Esta Robinson's Art Tours
222 Park Avenue South, New York, NY 10003
(212) 475-2434

Esta hosts specialized New York City tours for singles and couples, including art tours. It costs about $15.00. Call for her schedule.

### For the Sports-Minded
575 Main Street, Suite 1511, Roosevelt Island, New York, NY 10044
(212) 758-1661

Sponsors cocktail parties, lectures, travel events, and sports. The membership fee is $35.00 a year which includes certain discounts for events, travel and merchandise plus a subscription to their publication, "Leisure Guide for Singles." If you want, you can simply subscribe to the "Leisure Guide" and go to the events as a nonmember.

### Glen Cove Racquetball and Health Club
4 Cedar Swamp Road, Glen Cove, NY 11542 (Nassau)
(516) 759-1700

Singles are welcome and are made to feel comfortable in this friendly, easygoing club. Try your skills at racquetball, wallyball (with a "w"), or join an exercise class.

| | |
|---|---|
| AVERAGE DRINK | A bar is in the process of being built |
| COVER OR MINIMUM | $2.00 to $10.00 |
| PLASTIC | AE, MC, V |
| CROWD | All kinds of people from 19 to 65 |
| DRESS | No cutoffs or black-soled sneakers |
| OPEN | Daily, call for times |
| FOOD | Snacks available |

## The Godmothers
25 Central Park West, New York, NY 10023
(212) 245-7175

Director Abby Hirsch calls her organization "a dating service for
the best and the brightest," and caters mainly to the bankers, brok-
ers, lawyers, and scientists among us. "This is not a marriage service," Ms. Hirsch explains. "It's really for adult, intelligent, successful people who are so absorbed in their careers that they
literally don't have time to meet new kinds of people." Your first
assignment after calling The Godmothers will be to write an auto-
biography describing in detail your last three relationships. You
must tell all—how they happened, why they fell apart, what you
want for next time. Then comes an in-depth, one-hour interview. If
you are accepted, you pay somewhere around $300.00 and are
guaranteed "the three best dates of your life." No credit cards
accepted.


## Gourmet Dinner Club
Westchester Date Book, P.O. Box 473, Pleasantville, NY 10570
(914) 949-6999

Lick your chops, call up an acquaintance you'd like to know better,
and announce that you can get two dinners for the price of one at
many fine Westchester and Manhattan restaurants. A season membership is about $16.00, credit cards accepted.


## Helena
400 Madison Avenue, New York, NY 10017
(212) 759-9009

An exclusive matching service catering to business and professional
people from twenty-seven to sixty. They interview you and analyze
you in a number of ways including a psych session and handwriting
analysis. The price varies with each individual situation, but they
do accept MC and V. Covers the whole East Coast including Canada.


*Organizations, Agencies,*

**Institute for Retired Professionals**
**(affiliated with The New School)**
66 W. 12th Street, New York, NY 10011
(212) 741-5682

A purely intellectual organization rather than a singles club, the Institute has many widowed and divorced members as well as some married couples. If you're sixty to seventy years old (average age is sixty-seven) and have knowledge in the arts and humanities, you'd have a lot in common with the friends you'd make here. There are 600 to 700 members. The $300.00 annual fee entitles you to take any of eighty courses given by these members, and two courses at The New School. Of course you must be able to teach something, too. Members receive a newsletter and a literary journal, and there are occasional trips and an outreach program.

**Interests Unlimited**
4450 Fieldston Road, Bronx, NY 10471
(212) 548-4445

Sponsored by Ethical Culture and catering to the specific needs of its members, you can call them Monday through Friday from 9 A.M. to 5 P.M. There is a possible $3.00 charge per meeting (not bad, you know?) but be sure to call—the group is more or less active depending on the needs of the community at any given time.

**Introlens**
127 E. 56th Street, New York, NY 10022 (between Park and Lexington)
(212) 750-9292

98 Cuttermill Road, Great Neck, Long Island, NY 11021
(516) 829-9595

1 N. Broadway, White Plains, NY 10601
(914) 428-6766

425 Broad Hollow Road, Melville, Long Island, NY 11747
(516) 752-9301

We are, after all, a part of the video generation. Why shouldn't we use it to our advantage? In any case, here's your chance to be on "television." Catering to professionals and nonprofessionals from eighteen to seventy-nine, they videotape you for prospective dates to see plus give you a two-hour personal interview. For starters, however, just go in for a free demonstration and screening. You can then fill out the application and if it's accepted, you pay from $150.00 to $500.00 depending on the plan you choose. Or you can send for their free audio cassette which explains the program in more detail. Your name is not given out to a potential date unless you both happen to select each other. Call Monday through Friday from noon to 9 P.M. and Saturday from noon to 6 P.M. AE, MC, and V accepted.

### JB's World
18 W. 55th Street, New York, NY 10019 (at Fifth Ave.)
(212) 582-6670

Call Joan Bernstein from 10 A.M. to 7:30 P.M. Monday through Friday for Club Med, skiing, Caribbean, Mexico, cruises, etc. "Customized vacations to fit your needs."

### Jerry Rubin Business Networking Salon
P.O. Box 497, New York, NY 10021
(212) 737-4841

Mr. Rubin has entered the public eye once again, this time with an organization that caters not only to singles, but to business people as well. "Business Networking" is described as "a high-level way for successful men and women to meet one another, make important connections, and expand their business and personal opportunities in the 1980's." This is done every Wednesday night at Studio 54. To get in you need an invitation and/or a business card, so call ahead to make arrangements. Admission is $6.00 and the cash bar, of course, is extra. "This is a deal making, contact creating situation," explains Mr. Rubin. "We introduce entrepreneurs to entrepreneurs, co-op sellers to co-op buyers. People develop mergers in the Salon more often than marriages." Nevertheless, there are mobs of single people who manage to connect, so don't pass this up! You'll meet people "from the worlds of finance, the arts, fashion, theater, law, medicine, film, politics, and business." AE accepted.

## Jewish Professional Singles Ltd.
P.O. Box 543, New York, NY 10028
(212) 734-5566

A clearinghouse catering to educated Jewish singles. More than half the subscribers have graduate degrees. After you join, your name and description is added to the bi-monthly newsletter. From there it's up to you to contact other people in the newsletter who sound interesting. Six months is $95.00, 1 year is $125.00, and a 2-year subscription is $175.00.

## Karlan's Travelmaster
1333 North Avenue, New Rochelle, NY 10804 (Westchester)
(914) 633-6700

Call Monday through Friday from 9 A.M. to 5:30 P.M. or Saturday from 10 A.M. to 2 P.M. for bookings to Club Med, Singleworld, Club Getaway, and Negril Beach in Jamaica.

## Le Trip
201 E. 25th Street, New York, NY 10010
(212) 683-3318

A "tour wholesaler" specializing in putting tours together for singles. Clients include professionals, artists, people in the sciences, and everyone else. The age range is from 22 to 45. They do not charge a room sharing fee.

## Long Island's Nightlife Club
4 Westgate Road, Farmingdale, NY 11735
(516) 242-7722

The only "disco discount club" we've come across so far. The $20.00 membership fee may well save you a lot of money during the year if you like to go out and boogie a lot. You get discount tickets to many of Long Island's hottest spots which usually entitle you to free admission and a free drink. Includes nightclubs, discos, cabarets, and many other places that glitter.

## Lotus Tours
444 Madison Avenue, New York, NY 10022
(212) 758-3662, (914) 664-7494, (516) 352-3103, (800) 221-4566

Call them for tours to Montego Bay and Negril Beach Village.

## Lucia's Singles of Westchester, Ltd.
Lucia Gentile, P.O. Box 188, Valhalla, NY 10595
(914) 997-8951

Lucia's is open to the public and sponsors ballroom and other dances several times a month with live music. Serving central and southern Westchester, it's about $5.50 and up per party plus drinks. They also organize singles weekends. Members ages range from 28 to mid-50s.

## Marion Smith Tennis and Social Parties
611 Prescott Place, North Woodmere, NY 11581
(516) 791-4852

Disco/buffets and tennis parties are held several times a month with outdoor tennis barbeques during the summer and weekend travel events. It's all centered on the lovely Sound Shore Indoor Tennis Club, 303 Boston Post Road, Port Chester, Westchester (call [914] 939-1300 for directions). Average price is from $7.00 to $16.00 per person per night and the parties are usually held on Friday and Saturday. Call Marion for her bimonthly newsletter or simply show up at the tennis club with your racket. They've been in business for two years and currently have 4800 members. The age span is from twenty-five to forty-five.

**The Matterhorn Club**
40 E. 49th Street, New York, NY 10017 (between Madison and
Park Aves.)
(212) 486-0500

A travel organization catering to both singles and couples, The
Matterhorn Club prides itself on the uniqueness of some of its trips.
When the 747 jet first came out, they chartered one for three hours
so members could have a cocktail party while flying over New
York. The President, Gil Zelman, says they were the first organization ever to charter a jet to Europe for skiing, and they also had the
first charter program to Egypt. He says they book top hotels, and
maintain a free "travel roommate service" for single members. For
$20.00 a year plus a one-time $10.00 initiation fee, you will get a
magazine every six weeks with various trip offerings, a Hertz discount card, a restaurant discount plan, and a buying service plan.
You also get reduced admission to their parties which are sponsored once or twice a month, often on the theme of recent trips, and
often with dancing. Party admission is $8.00 for members (which
includes the first drink) and $12.00 for guests.

**Meet Your Match**
P.O. Box 721, Woodside, NY 11377 (Queens)
(212) 424-8590

A small outfit, in business five years. You can arrange for a personal interview or do the whole thing by mail—whatever suits you
best. There are no computers, the matching is all done by hand—
and they like to stay in touch with you to see how everything turned
out. The fees range from $25.00 to $150.00 depending on your
needs, and you get a minimum of four first names, phone numbers,
and descriptions. Call daily from noon to 10:30 P.M.

**Mensa (American Mensa Limited)**
1701 W. 3rd Street, Brooklyn, NY 11223
(212) 376-1925

Everyone has to organize and geniuses are no exception. Mensa's goal is to provide contact between intelligent people all over the world. Although it is not specifically a singles organization, there are so many different types of people from almost every occupation that it would be a shame to pass this up. From doctors to business people to soldiers to students to prisoners to housewives to farm workers to scientists—Mensa members are about as diversified as you can get. (Imagine, if you will, what a Mensa party must be like!) The only thing these people have in common is their IQ which must be higher than 98 percent of the general population. Local meetings are held at various locations on a regular basis. To join, call or write for their application. They will provide the tests, you just sit back with your sharpened wit and breeze right on through. Annual membership is $30.00, with small additional fees for testing.

**Mimi's Travel Agency, Inc.**
600 Tuckahoe Road, Yonkers, NY 10710 (Westchester)
(914) 793-2240, (212) 863-3870

Call for Singleworld cruises, Club Med, or Le Trip.

**Mystical Horizons Ltd.**
(914) 221-0205, (914) 949-7014

This is an astrological dating organization that specializes in personal service. First you go in for an interview and a sixty-item questionnaire. Then they do a personality chart on you—it's not an in-depth astrological reading, but it does supposedly tell your moods and tastes. You sign a contract, pay them the money, and within two to three weeks they will have a compatible person for you. It's $65.00 for six months which includes one to three referrals, sometimes more.

**New Encounters for Singles**
Unitarian Church of Staten Island, 312 Fillmore Street at Clinton
Ave., Staten Island, NY 10301 (two blocks up from Richmond
Terrace, about 1.4 miles from the ferry terminal, near the Snug
Harbor Cultural Center in the New Brighton area of the North
Shore)
(212) 447-2204

The purpose here is to provide a supportive atmosphere for singles
aged twenty to fifty-ish who want to talk, grow, work things out.
From thirty to fifty people meet every Friday at 8 P.M. You pay
$3.00 at the door, there's no membership fee, and no mailing list.
Despite its name, it's not an encounter group, but a lively discussion
group covering contemporary issues of interest to divorced, widowed, and older singles. You can call or write for their literature, or
simply show up one Friday. It's nondenominational, and has been
in "business" (it's a nonprofit group) for two years.


**New Rochelle Travel Service, Inc.**
415 North Avenue, New Rochelle, NY 10801 (Westchester)
(914) 632-5900, (212) 933-3131

Bob Olson is your contact for ski trips to faraway places like Colo-
rado and Switzerland, Club Med trips, cruises, and bookings into
Caribbean hotels catering to singles.


**New York Health and Racquet Club**
20 E. 50th Street, New York, NY 10022 (near Fifth Ave.)
(212) 593-1500

132 E. 45th Street, New York, NY 10017 (at Lexington Ave.)
(212) 986-3100

24 E. 13th Street, New York, NY 10003 (near Fifth Ave.)
(212) 924-4600

1433 York Avenue, New York, NY 10021 (at 76th St.)
(212) 737-6666

110 W. 56th Street, New York, NY 10019 (at Ave. of the
Americas)
(212) 541-7200

What more could a body want? With swimming, racquet sports,
Nautilus Systems, whirlpools, sauna, steam rooms, classes, individual instruction, and many, many singles (50/50 men and women),
they've about covered it all! The mood is nothing short of luxurious. Call for prices.

|  |  |
|---|---|
| PLASTIC | AE, CB, DC, MC, V |
| CROWD | Lots of fitness-minded people with either beautiful bodies or beautiful-bodies-in-progress, including Bette Midler, Diane Keaton, Dustin Hoffman, and John Chancellor; age range, 25 to 55 |
| OPEN | 360 days a year: midtown clubs open 7:30 A.M. to 10 P.M. weekdays and 10 A.M. to 6 P.M. weekends; other clubs 10 A.M. to 10 P.M. weekdays and 10 to 6 weekends |
| FOOD | Four of the five locations have Natural Food Restaurants |

**New Trends Travel**
55½ Purchase Street, Rye, NY 10580 (Westchester)
(914) 967-8171

The owners are single and have traveled extensively. They're more
than happy to share their experiences with you, tell you how to rent
cars in strange countries, and how much to tip. Call during business
hours or on Saturday from 10:30 A.M. to 2 P.M. They're also willing
to see you evenings by appointment. Singleworld, Club Med, and
more.

**The Night Owl Dances**
115 E. 92nd Street, New York, NY 10028
(212) 289-7920

This social club has been in business ten years. Members enjoy
monthly cocktail parties with live dance music, various after-work

cocktail parties, buffet dinners, and some travel. It's all done in a very elegant way, with the parties held at posh restaurants throughout the city. The 300 members are between the ages of thirty-five and sixty. If you're interested in joining, speak to the gracious Beverly Paterno, founder, and arrange for an interview. If you meet the approval of the board members, the annual fee is $75.00. Parties are extra—about $35.00 to $40.00 per party, payable in advance, which includes an open bar. Guests may attend the parties for a slightly higher fee.

**N.I.S.F. (National Indoor Sports Facilities)**
30 Burt Drive, Deer Park, NY 11729 (Suffolk)
(516) 242-0707

The beauty of N.I.S.F. is that there's no membership fee. You simply pay as you go, whether it's volleyball, tennis, soccer, or any of the other sports available. Your fee also entitles you to the use of their lounge. Just call to find out what the schedule will be that week. It's easy, it's accessible, and it's more geared toward fun than serious competition. More and more singles are signing up for "Recreational Soccer," a term coined by N.I.S.F. Many couples, too. Indoor facilities, year round fun.

| | |
|---|---|
| AVERAGE DRINK | You can buy soda or juice for a modest price, or you can bring your own liquor |
| COVER OR MINIMUM | A volleyball game will cost about $4.00 for two hours of playing time; soccer is $3.00 an hour |
| PLASTIC | MC, V |
| CROWD | Professionals, doctors, lawyers from 20 to 40 |
| FOOD | Sometimes |

**The Outdoors Club**
P.O. Box 227, Lenox Hill Station, New York, NY 10021

Yes, Virginia, there is a world beyond the city. It's got trees and rivers and lakes and rocks and dirt and weather. And The Outdoors Club will show you all of it—through walking tours, hikes, canoe trips, conservation tours, backpacking expeditions, and other events like square dances. While it's not specifically a singles organization, most of the 400 members are unattached and many are in their 20s and 30s. Membership is $5.00 a year, slightly less for students and seniors, and includes a newsletter. Trip costs are extra, and may range from $10.00 to $100.00. In business three years.

**Parents Without Partners**

Brooklyn Chapter
(212) 232-9336, (212) 376-5515

Manhattan Chapter
(212) 523-1313

Nassau Chapter
(516) 931-2682

Queens Chapter
(212) 830-5042, (212) 591-7808

Staten Island Chapter
(212) 356-9349

Suffolk Chapter
(516) 732-2100

Westchester Chapter
(914) 667-7396

A social, educational, and cultural group with members aged eighteen to eighty. There are monthly orientations, weekend dances, child/parent activities, foreign language groups, and more. Twenty dollars will take you through a whole year.

**Party Vine**
202 E. 77th Street, New York, NY 10021 (between Second and Third Aves.)
(212) 988-6052

A generous monthly calendar of social events for singles aged twenty-one to forty-five, with open bar parties Friday and Saturday (jackets required). Members pay about $6.00, guests may pay $9.00. To get on the mailing list you must attend one of the parties and sign up in person—not a huge sacrifice, since there's plenty of dancing and socializing. Party Vine usually draws a nice large crowd. Call for recorded details.

**Paula's Society of Singles**
RD 2, Lake Woods Drive, Katonah, NY 10536 (Westchester)
(914) 232-4291

An all around social club sponsoring ten to twenty parties a month, mostly in the Westchester area. There are weekend dance parties, travel and sports events for people in the thirty-five to fifty age range. Jackets required. To join, simply call to find out when and where the next party will be. Then go. That's all there is to it. Or you can subscribe to the newsletter for $2.00. It's a pay as you go situation with events running from $4.50 to $20.00 depending. Paula runs a personalized organization and has been in business eight years. She's also got a separate group for younger people—call for details on that.

**Peak Tours, Inc.**
134 N. Franklin Street, Hempstead, Long Island, NY 11550
(516) 481-4800, (212) 445-7100, (914) 997-7020

Singleworld, Senior Citizen Tours, cruises, and Club Med. They can also arrange room sharing.

**People Resources**
30 W. 57th Street, New York, NY 10019, with branches in
Nassau and Westchester
(212) 765-7770

President Joe O'Connell refers to his organization as a "life-style resource center for single people." That means you can pretty well write your own ticket. Video introductions are available, or you can forgo the TV camera for a biography listing, or you can do both. Prices vary according to the program you choose. He also runs a "professional reference library"—that means that through his videotapes and biographies you can find that great looking lawyer you were hoping for, to get you out of whatever trouble you've gotten into; you can find the interior decorator of your dreams to redo your apartment; a caterer for your next extravaganza; the shrink you've always wanted to fall in love with, and more. All single. In addition to providing introductions for dates or professional services, People Resources sponsors seminars, rap groups, and lectures on subjects of special interest to singles, plus a wide array of social events. To join, call or write for their brochure, then make an appointment for an interview. If you choose video, a counselor will help you prepare. You are filed by your first name only to insure privacy. Both you and your potential "match" must approve of each other before phone numbers are given. The age range is twenty-one to eighty-one and they cater to all types of professional people.

### Professional Dating Service
P.O. Box 181, Brooklyn, NY 11236
(212) 649-6624

A do-it-by-mail dating service catering to well-educated and professional people in their 20s, 30s, and 40s. Just call them, fill out the application, mail it back, and wait for the counselors to process it and write to you with first names and phone numbers. Call from 11 A.M. to 4 P.M. and from 10 P.M. to 11 P.M. Monday through Friday. In business since 1977.

### Rae Metzger's Concert Socials
110 W. 96th Street, Suite 9D, New York, NY 10025
(212) 749-5464

Weekly concerts for all age groups and all tastes—classical, folk, Broadway musical, ballet—plus socializing before and after. It's nondenominational, meets at various locations around New York City, and you don't have to be a member or pay membership fees. Admission to the concerts are around the $7.00 range. Call for their schedule.

### Richnik's Ltd.
951 Second Avenue, New York, NY 10022
(212) 688-2797

Annual membership fee for this singles travel organization is around $15.00. They sponsor long-term group travel, runs to the Catskills, tennis parties and other get-togethers for professionals and business people from 24 to 40ish.

**St. Bartholomew's Community Club**
109 E. 50th Street, New York, NY 10022 (at Park Ave.)
(212) 751-1616 and ask for Bill Roberts, Club Director

No matter what your interests are, you'll probably find them here. St. Bartholomew's is an interdenominational/nondenominational organization made up primarily of singles, which opts for action and activity rather than the Lonely Search for a companion. The organization revolves around committees—each committee sponsors a different activity, and each of the 1600 members can join several committees. To join, you must live and work in Manhattan and be eighteen to thirty-four years old at the time of your application. You are then interviewed and if accepted you can arrange to pay on a sliding scale basis. Including athletic fee, you might pay $200.00 to $300.00 a year. Here are some of the functions:

- Video Committee
- Sports Committee for activities outside the club
- Full athletic facilities at the club, including swimming, aerobic dancing, and much more
- Neighborhood Committee for small functions
- Entertainment Committee for large functions
- St. Bart's Players—a drama group
- Sailing Committee
- Leasing yachts
- Women's Network—really coed, to meet members' professional needs
- Communications Committee for brochures, a newspaper, and a literary magazine
- An outreach program
- Course Committees, with courses in finance, pottery, darkroom, etc.

### Scientific Dating Service
147 W. 42nd Street or 1472 Broadway, New York, NY 10036
(212) 921-1124

All types, all ages. Come in for an interview and fill out an application. Then the gentlemen contact the ladies. In business twenty-three years. Prices vary.

### Selectra-Date, Inc.
P.O. Box 407, Fort Lee, NJ 07024 (serving the New York area)
(201) 461-8400

A quick, easy way to fill up your calendar with dates and impress friends and relatives. Ask for their forty-five-item questionnaire and mail it back along with $25.00. A computer then finds you five compatible people and sends you their names and numbers. The rest is up to you. In business since 1966.

### Seminars for Singles
114-41 Queens Boulevard, Suite 100, Forest Hills, NY 11375 (Queens)
(212) 268-2932

If you're boring yourself to tears with your same old "bar rap" night after night, give Heather Edelman a call for help. Her unusual organization sponsors discussions and seminars dealing with topics relevant to singles. There are four locations available, and $40.00 buys entry into four weekly meetings. The age range is eighteen to sixty-five, with anywhere from six to thirty people attending each meeting. Heather is a trained psychotherapist, and you can ask her about additional group or individual therapy if you're interested.

### Separated, Divorced, and Remarried Catholics
St. Patrick's Church, 180 Church Place, Yorktown Heights, NY 10598 (Westchester)
(914) 962-5050

A support and social group meeting the first Tuesday of every month. Call for details.

**Separated, Divorced, and Remarried Catholics of Westchester**
59 E. Main, Elmsford, NY 10523 (Westchester)
(914) 592-6789

A spiritual group, not just a social gathering, with lectures, raps, parent/child activities. Call for details.

**The Singing Experience**
929 Park Avenue, Suite 5B, New York, NY 10028
(212) 472-2207

If you've been singing in the shower and are now aching for the exposure of singing in the elevator, why not call Linda Amiel Burns and do it right? By the end of her five-session, twenty-hour workshop you may well be singing in a New York City nightclub! Past participants have performed at places like The Fives, The Grand Finale, Dangerfield's, and Ted Hook's Onstage. Linda provides the instruction and the accompanist and handles all the details, all you have to do is express yourself in song. The group is about 90 percent singles, and the cost of the workshop is $200.00.

**Single-Friends of Long Island**
P.O. Box 847, Amityville, NY 11701
(516) 454-6735

A social and travel organization for singles in their 30s, 40s, and 50s, with an emphasis on the 40s age group. In business two years, you don't have to join or pay a membership fee—instead you can pay as you go. The dances are about $3.00 and are usually held twice a week in the Farmingdale, Massapequa, Plainview, and Syosset areas. President Ted Karras also puts out a very informative newsletter covering the Long Island singles social and support group scene—it's worth the $5.00 fee for an eight-month subscription. For a sample, send a self-addressed stamped envelope to Ted at the above address.

### Single Parent Family Project
Single Parent Support Center, 16 W. 23rd Street, NY 10010
(212) 620-0755—ask for Sue Jones

Currently 250 members, but they're open for more. Director Sue Jones organizes many many activities, including monthly "Spotlight Meetings" which tackle subjects specifically relevant to single parents—like housing problems, work space arrangements, and dating problems. Sue arranges for counseling, plans parties, rap groups, and even a special "Fathers' Group." Another plus here—the Project acts as a clearing house for information on other groups throughout Long Island and the city. Through Sue, you have access to about twenty other groups, some of which may be closer to your home. "Long Island people have a phobia about coming into the city," she says, "so we have many groups out there." All this for only $10.00 a year? And your $10.00 also includes a monthly bulletin of events.

### Singles Communications Network
323 Main Street, Beacon, NY 12508 with interviews available in Westchester and Manhattan
(914) 831-2996

A dating service that caters to professionals, teachers, nurses, etc., and screens applicants in person. They guarantee at least one referral a month for the duration of your membership, sent to you by mail. If, however, you only get one a month, you get an extra six months of membership fee. The cost is $95.00 to $140.00 for six months to a year. In business three years.

### Singles Lifestyle International
25 Canterbury Road, Suite 3J, Great Neck, NY 11021
(516) 829-5222 from 11 A.M. to 5 P.M. weekdays

Founded by marketing consultant Allen Dorfman after his own divorce, S.L.I. has become one of the largest social organizations in the area, catering to business and professional women in the twenty-five to forty age range and men from twenty-seven to forty-five-ish. There's no annual membership fee or dues—you just pay from $4.00 to $7.00 per party plus cash at the bar. They average about twenty parties a month, located throughout the tri-state area. One is bound to be near you! Here's what you do: Call Allen for a courtesy copy of his current "Monthly Social Calendar of Events." Then just pick yourself up and go to one of the parties. From there you can decide if you want to be on their mailing list—without charge. (By the way, you can also call Allen if you're planning a trip—he specializes in singles travel as well.)

### Singles Playground Ltd.
Functions held at Fox Hollow Inn, 7725 Jericho Turnpike, Woodbury, NY 11797 (Nassau) (phone 516-921-1415). Other Long Island locations are being planned.
(516) 549-1099—ask for Arlene or Bill

Run by "Arlene and Bill of Dix Hills" and their partner, Singles Playground Ltd. sponsors large parties in a luxurious and sophisticated atmosphere. (Arlene met Bill at one of her own parties.) The live band plays all types of music, from disco to rock to pop, and the dance floor is big enough to accommodate the vast number of people who attend. Going to Fox Hollow Inn's "TreeHouse" is more like attending a posh private party than a public singles event—and why not? A bit of class never hurt anyone. Other functions are available, too, from time to time—call for details.

| | |
|---|---|
| AVERAGE DRINK | $2.50 |
| COVER OR MINIMUM | $8.00 at the door; no membership fee |
| CROWD | Well-to-do professional and business people from age 30 to 35 and up |
| DRESS | Gentlemen must wear jackets |
| OPEN | Every Tuesday at Fox Hollow Inn, from 8 to 11 P.M.; other dates, places and times are in the works |
| FOOD | Generous hot and cold buffet, no extra charge |

**Singles Unlimited**
Sacred Heart School, Central Avenue, Hartsdale, NY 10530
(Westchester)
(914) 949-0028

A nondenominational group sponsored by the Sacred Heart
Church and featuring Bible readings, cultural, sports, and social
events. Deacon Paul Harrington moderates the group every other
Thursday at 8 P.M. with wine and cheese following some meetings.
There may be a charge of $1.00.

**Singleworld**
444 Madison Avenue, New York, NY 10022
(212) 758-2433

Travel packages and cruises for singles. Call your travel agent or
any of the travel agents listed in *The Complete New York Guide for
Singles*. Share rates and escorts available.

**Ski-O-Rama Tours**
1301 Franklin Avenue, Garden City, Long Island, NY 11530
(212) 895-5310, (914) 428-4600, (516) 294-9800

Skiing tours of the Rockies and other areas; Hawaii, the Bahamas,
Tanglewood cultural tours. The groups are a mixture of singles and
couples.

**Solo Flights**
8 Washington Avenue, Westport, CN 06880 (serving the
New York area)
(203) 226-9993

As the name implies, this is a travel center exclusively for singles.
You get vacation advice, room sharing arrangements, and personal
service. Club Med, group trips, Singleworld, Le Trip, and more.
Many professionals and business people use Solo Flight's services.

**Sound Shore Tennis Club**
  See **Marion Smith Tennis and Social Parties**, page 244.

**Sport Rites Club**
P.O. Box 644, Rye, NY 10580 (Westchester)
(914) 946-7770

It's easy to fit into one of their many groups and activities. Here's a partial list:

- The Rap Room—small groups meeting in someone's home for discussions.
- Purple Toes—a wine tasting party for singles in their 30s and 40s, with about fifty to seventy people attending.
- The Single Grape—wine tasting/disco lovers in their 20s and 30s, with about 200 people attending.
- T.G.I.F.—young professionals in their 20s gather for a buffet and disco.
- Executive Suite Cocktail Parties—mellow gathering of people in their 30s and 40s.
- Gourmet Adventures—monthly dinner parties at various restaurants.
- Sports Activities—hiking, skiing, tennis, sailing, scuba diving, canoeing.

Annual membership fee is $22.00 which includes the monthly newsletter.

**Sunshine Travel Agency**
497 New Rochelle Road, Bronxville, NY 10708 (Westchester)
(914) 961-1800 (ask for Nancy)

Nancy, the owner, is single and can share her advice and experience with you. Club Med, Singleworld, Le Trip, and more.

**Team**
134 W. 32nd Street, New York, NY 10001 (between Ave. of the Americas and Seventh Ave.)
(212) 946-6333 or reach the service at (212) 244-4270

Established in 1966, Team claims to be the oldest established computer introduction service in New York City. Most of the work is done by mail, and their clientele includes all professions, all ages, and all backgrounds. The $25.00 membership fee will get you five names and various parties or meetings.

## Tiffany Select
210 Fifth Avenue, New York, NY 10010 (between 23rd and 24th Sts.)
(212) 757-6300

Written up in both *The Wall Street Journal* and *The National Enquirer*, this party club caters to men who are millionaires and women who are beautiful. If you fit into one of these hopeless categories, call and ask for an application. Men must verify their financial status, and women must make an appointment for a personal interview. If you are accepted, you will then be invited to the various parties and social events. The application fee is $20.00, and party costs are about $10.00 for the beautiful women and $25.00 for the wealthy men. You will often be invited to the club's private East Side penthouse and people apparently fly in for these fêtes from Boston, Philadelphia, and Florida. Chairman of the board Bill Sergio, himself a millionaire, explains that very rich men simply don't have time to take their chances at singles bars. Through Tiffany Select (not connected with the jeweler) they can meet people who have already been screened. *The Wall Street Journal* of February 26, 1982, quotes an architect and executive vice president of a construction company as saying, "This isn't as impersonal as bars."

## Together
Crescent Office Park, 3601 Hempstead Turnpike, Levittown, NY 11756
(212) 895-4636

If you'd like some personal attention rather than a computerized printout, go into one of their offices (call for the nearest office—they've got twenty-five locations scattered over six states) for an interview, from noon to 8 P.M. weekdays and from 11:30 A.M. to 4:30 P.M. Saturday. Prices vary according to the length of time you

*Organizations, Agencies,*

decide to enroll. They bridge all socioeconomic groups and all ages from eighteen up for women, and from twenty-one up for men. AE, MC, and V accepted.

**Travel Designs**
16 Squirrel Hill Road, West Hartford, CN 06107
(203) 521-4386

Run by Sydelle Baskind, a single traveler herself, the company specializes in putting together short- or long-term trips for singles. She also organizes groups and tours and tries to cut down on some of the extra expenses singles so often have to bear.

**Turning Point International Ltd.**
108-18 Queens Boulevard, Forest Hills, NY 11375 (Queens)
(212) 263-4747

Everything is personalized at this dating and party organization, from your beginning interview to many of your introductions. Other introductions may be sent to you by mail. There is travel, sports, and cultural events, and the members range in age from twenty to sixty-five. A fee of $295.00 a year guarantees you one to six referrals a month plus the monthly newsletter. Call Monday through Friday from noon to 8 P.M. for more details. MC and V accepted.

**Umbrella Singles**
Church Street, Woodbourne, NY 12788 (serving Westchester and the New York area)
(914) 434-6871

Leonard Moss, the owner, is perhaps one of the most knowledgeable "singles travel" people in the area. In business three years, he is basically a trip wholesaler matching groups with vacations. He will at times simply take over resorts and run singles weekends. Other times he'll organize weekends based on specific themes such as music or concerts. Most of his clients are groups—but if an individual wants to call, they'll be put on his mailing list or referred to a group. So if you're a single in search of a social vacation, why not call Leonard and let him worry about it?

## Unique Racquetball and Health Clubs, Inc.
2229 Nesconset Highway, Lake Grove 11755 (Suffolk)
(516) 981-8866

530 Hicksville Road, Bethpage 11714 (Nassau)
(516) 822-5511

1191 Portion Road, Farmingville 11738 (Suffolk)
(516) 698-3737

3098 Long Beach Road, Oceanside 11572 (Nassau)
(516) 766-4440

Couples and singles are welcome to join (you can go a few times as a guest to try it out) and enjoy the twelve courts and a cool drink afterwards at the bar. (The health facilities such as whirlpool, sauna, and Universal are not coed. The racquetball and of course the bar, are.)

| | |
|---|---|
| AVERAGE DRINK | Varies |
| COVER OR MINIMUM | Individual membership fees may be about $80.00 for a whole year |
| PLASTIC | For membership, major credit cards accepted |
| CROWD | All types, all ages |
| DRESS | No cutoff jeans |
| OPEN | Monday through Friday 8 A.M. to midnight, Saturday 7 A.M. to 11 P.M. |
| FOOD | Snack machines |

## Westchester Singles Council
c/o Westchester County Department of Parks, Recreation and Conservation, County Office Building, Room 612, 148 Martine Avenue, White Plains, NY 10601
(914) 682-2414

No matter what else you're into out there in Westchester, you should give these people a call. Basically a forum of singles organizations and support groups, they provide an excellent source of continuing information on what's happening. Singles in Westchester have their own specific problems and needs, and the Singles Council can help.

**Widows and Widowers**
St. Patricks Church, 180 Church Place, Yorktown Heights 10598 (Westchester)
(914) 962-5050

A support and social group for Catholics. Call for details.

**Widows and Widowers Club**
470 Mamaroneck Avenue, White Plains, NY 10605 (Westchester)
Plus eight other locations, so call for the spot nearest you.
(914) 948-8004

An affiliate of Family Services of Westchester, the group meets once a month with supportive and social activities. The age range is from about thirty-six to seventy-five and the annual fee is $7.00. The group also has access to counselors and other community services.

**Winterfun/Summerfun Unlimited**
3 Bayne St., Norwalk, CN 06851 (mornings) (serving the New York area)
(203) 846-2203

Empress Travel, 497 Connecticut Avenue, Norwalk, CN 06854 (afternoons)
(212) 581-7916, (203) 853-9404

Judy Nathanson, a writer and expert on the singles travel scene, runs this program year-round. It's more than a travel agency—Judy can arrange trips for you, including room sharing and tour escorts, so all you have to do is show up. There are short weekends or long vacations—call her to see where you fit in. Among other groups, she works closely with Umbrella Singles, Le Trip, Singleworld, For the Sports-Minded and Club Med.

**Young Adults of Temple Israel**
1000 Pinebrook Boulevard, New Rochelle, NY 10804
(Westchester)
(914) 375-0492

A social, cultural, and sports organization for singles twenty-one to about thirty-eight—and you don't necessarily have to be a member of the Temple. There are monthly dances, cocktail parties, brunches, baseball leagues in the summer, volleyball in the winter, and more. The membership fee is $20.00 plus a few dollars for certain specific activities.

**Young Jewish Singles**
30 Oakley Avenue, Mount Vernon, NY 10550 (Westchester)
(914) 664-0500, (212) 583-9833

Cosponsored by the YM-YWHA of Lower Westchester, the Yonkers Community Jewish Center, and the Mid-Westchester YMHA, the majority of members are in the twenty to thirty-five age range and have never been married. The group is open to everyone, and offers a variety of social, cultural, recreational, and educational programs year-round as well as special events centered around the Jewish holidays. If you want to be a member, there's a $20.00 annual fee. Their monthly calendar is available free upon request.

**Young Widows and Widowers of Westchester**
c/o Westchester Jewish Community Services, Attn: Mrs. Lilly Singer, 172 South Broadway, White Plains, NY 10605
(Westchester)
(914) 949-6761 (call for locations)

Sponsored by the Westchester Jewish Community Service, the group meets twice a month in the evenings for social, cultural, emotional, and moral support. They also maintain a hot line and have other services available such as therapy and help for children. Membership fee is $10.00.

*Organizations, Agencies,*

## "Y" Singles of Northern Westchester
344 Main Street, Mount Kisco, NY 10549 (Westchester)
(914) 241-2064

A nonsectarian rap, social, cultural, and family group for singles aged twenty to fifty-five. You don't have to be a member to attend their weekly meetings, but if you want to join it's $25.00. Single parents, $30.00.

# Chapter 3

# *Special Interest Index*

Find your interest—we've got the place for you!

Crossroads (New York City, New Jersey, and Westchester), 238
Dateline (New York City), 238
Godmothers, The (New York City), 240
Helena (New York City), 240
Introlens (New York City, Long Island, and Westchester), 241
Meet Your Match (Queens), 245
People Resources (New York City, Nassau, and Westchester), 251
Professional Dating Service (Brooklyn), 252
Scientific Dating Service (New York City), 254
Selectra-Date, Inc. (New York City), 254
Singles Communication Network (New York City and Westchester), 256
Team (New York City), 259
Together (Long Island), 260
Turning Point International Ltd. (Queens), 261

DISCO/DANCING

See also Rock/New Wave/Oldies
NOTE: Many places listed under "Low-Key Places for Singles" also have small dance bands.

Adam's Apple (Manhattan, Upper East Side), 17
Apple Orchard (Long Island), 166
Barbizon Plaza Library (Manhattan, Midtown West), 76
Bijou, The (Westchester), 213
Bond International Casino (Manhattan, Midtown West), 76
Café Society (Manhattan, East Side), 95
Camelot Inn (Long Island), 171
Camouflage (Queens), 150
Carnaby Street (Manhattan, Upper East Side), 20
Channel 80 (Long Island), 172
Cheers (Long Island), 172
City, The (Westchester), 215
Clark Smathers (Long Island), 174
Club 57 (Manhattan, Greenwich Village), 114
Colonie Hill Top o' the Hill Lounge (Long Island), 174

Copacabana (Manhattan, Upper East Side), 21
Copperfield's (Long Island), 175
Court Street (Manhattan, Upper East Side), 21
Cruiser Club (Long Island), 175
Danceteria (Manhattan, Chelsea), 105
Decameron (Long Island), 177
D.L. Sutton's (Manhattan, Upper East Side), 23
Dublin Pub (Long Island), 178
Encore (Westchester), 217
Feathers (Long Island), 180
Fun House, The (Manhattan, Chelsea), 107
Ground Round, The (Staten Island), 157
Goodtimes (Long Island), 181
Hammerheads (Long Island), 183
Heckle and Jeckle's (Long Island), 184
Hurrah (Manhattan, Upper West Side), 51
Januaries (Westchester), 220
King of Hearts (Long Island), 188
Lancaster Cocktail Lounge (Staten Island), 158
La Ronde (Manhattan, Midtown West), 83
Lemon Tree (Queens), 151
Les Mouches (Manhattan, Chelsea), 108
Lime Tree Lounge (Long Island), 190
Long Island's Nightlife Club, 243
Magique (Manhattan, Upper East Side), 34
Malibu (Long Island), 192
Marty and Lenny's (Westchester), 221
Millennium (Long Island), 193
Montage (Westchester), 222
Mudd Club (Manhattan, Tribeca), 136
October's (Long Island), 196
Office, The (Staten Island), 158
Ones (Manhattan, Tribeca), 137
Pastor's Broadway (Westchester), 225
Peach Trees (Westchester), 226
Peppermint Lounge (Manhattan, Chelsea), 109
Quarterdeck Pub (Long Island), 198
Red Parrot (Manhattan, Midtown West), 89
Reggae Lounge, The (Manhattan, Greenwich Village), 127
Riddles (Long Island), 201

Roseland (Manhattan, Midtown West), 89
Rumrunner of Oyster Bay (Long Island), 202
Sally's (Manhattan, Midtown West), 90
Salty Dog, The (Manhattan, Upper East Side), 42
Sport Rites Club's Single Grape (Westchester), 259
Sport Rites Club's T.G.I.F. (Westchester), 259
Squat (Manhattan, Chelsea), 111
Starbuck's (Manhattan, Midtown East), 73
Stardust Room (Bronx), 164
Stilwende (Manhattan, Tribeca), 140
Studio, The (Manhattan, Upper East Side), 44
Studio 54 (Manhattan, Midtown West), 91
Sybil's (Manhattan, Midtown West), 92
Thursday's 24 (Manhattan, Midtown West), 92
Tramps (Manhattan, East Side), 99
Trax (Manhattan, Upper West Side), 58
Uncle Sam's (Long Island), 207
U.S. Blues (Long Island), 208
Wednesday's (Manhattan, Upper East Side), 45
Winner's Circle (Long Island), 210

DIVORCED

*See* Widows, Widowers, and Divorced

FITNESS

*See* Sports and Fitness

FOLK MUSIC

Eagle Tavern, The (Manhattan, Chelsea), 105
Folk City (Manhattan, Greenwich Village), 117
Other End, The (Manhattan, Greenwich Village), 126
Rae Metzger's Concert Socials (New York City), 252

Singing Experience, The (Manhattan), 255

FOOD

Gourmet Dinner Club (Manhattan and Westchester), 240
Sport Rites Club's Gourmet Adventures (Westchester), 259

INTELLECTUAL AND LITERARY

Institute for Retired Professionals (New York City), 241
Mensa (Brooklyn), 246
92nd Street Y (Manhattan, Upper East Side), 37
St. Bartholomew's Community Club (Manhattan, Midtown East), 253

JAZZ/BLUES/AVANT-GARDE

Angry Squire (Manhattan, Chelsea), 101
Arthur's Tavern (Manhattan, Greenwich Village), 111
Black Beans Music Studio (Manhattan, Chelsea), 102
Bradley's (Manhattan, Greenwich Village), 112
Chilie's (Manhattan, Midtown West), 80
Cookery, The (Manhattan, Greenwich Village), 115
Dan Lynch (Manhattan, Greenwich Village), 116
Fat Tuesday's (Manhattan, East Side), 96
Folk City (Manhattan, Greenwich Village), 117
Horn of Plenty (Manhattan, Greenwich Village), 120
Jazz Forum (Manhattan, Greenwich Village), 121
Jazz Gallery (Manhattan, Chelsea), 107
Jazzmania (Manhattan, Chelsea), 107
Lush Life (Manhattan, Greenwich Village), 124
Public Access Synthesizer Studio (Manhattan, Chelsea), 109
Rae Metzger's Concert Socials (New York City), 252

*Special Interest Index*

Seventh Avenue South (Manhattan, Greenwich Village), 128
Singing Experience, The (New York City), 255
South Street Seaport Museum District (Manhattan, Lower Manhattan), 139
Star and Garter (Manhattan, Greenwich Village), 128
Sweet Basil (Manhattan, Greenwich Village), 129
Village Vanguard (Manhattan, Greenwich Village), 130
West End Café, The (Manhattan, Upper West Side), 59


LOW-KEY PLACES FOR SINGLES

Algonquin lounges, The (Manhattan, Midtown West), 75
Amber Lantern (Queens), 149
Angry Squire (Manhattan, Chelsea), 101
Apartment, The (Long Island), 165
Aphrodite (Westchester), 212
Applause (Manhattan, Midtown East), 59
Astor's (Manhattan, Midtown East), 60
Barrymore's (Manhattan, Upper East Side), 18
Bartholomew's (Manhattan, Upper East Side), 18
Bartholomew's (Westchester), 212
Billymunk (Manhattan, Midtown East), 60
Blueprint, The (Manhattan, Midtown East), 61
Bobby Van's (Long Island), 169
Bombay Bicycle Club (Long Island), 169
Botany Rocks (Manhattan, Chelsea), 102
Brass Moon Café (Manhattan, Tribeca), 131
Brown Derby (Brooklyn), 144
Bunnery Pub, The (Long Island), 170
Cachaca (Manhattan, Upper East Side), 20
Café Galleria (Brooklyn), 144
Caffé Fontana (Manhattan, Midtown West), 78

Callback, The (Manhattan, Midtown West), 78
Cantina Caffé de Medici (Manhattan, Soho), 132
Carnegie Tavern (Manhattan, Midtown West), 79
Casbah, The (Westchester), 214
Cellar, The (Manhattan, Upper West Side), 49
Central Falls (Manhattan, Soho), 133
Central Parc (Manhattan, Midtown East), 62
Chandler's (Long Island), 171
Charlie Brown (Manhattan, Midtown East), 63
Charlie's Inn (Bronx), 162
Chelsea Commons (Manhattan, Chelsea), 103
Chelsea Park (Manhattan, East Side), 96
Chip's Pub (Manhattan, Upper West Side), 49
Cinnamon (Long Island), 173
C.J.'s (Long Island), 173
Colbeh Club 56 (Manhattan, Midtown West), 80
Conservatory, The (Manhattan, Upper West Side), 50
Cotton Club, The (Manhattan, Upper West Side), 50
Cronie's (Manhattan, Upper East Side), 22
Dering Harbor Inn (Long Island), 177
Dudley's (Westchester), 217
Dustins (Manhattan, Midtown East), 63
Ear Inn (Manhattan, Soho), 133
East Side Comedy Club (Long Island), 178
El Coyote (Manhattan, Greenwich Village), 116
Empire Diner, The (Manhattan, Chelsea), 106
Eric (Manhattan, Upper East Side), 24
Farkas (Manhattan, Greenwich Village), 117
Fearn's (Long Island), 179
Ferdi's Sidewalk Café (Manhattan, Midtown East), 64
Fifth Amendment, The (Long Island), 180
Fives, The (Manhattan, Midtown West), 81

14 Christopher Street (Manhattan, Greenwich Village), 118
Freddy's (Manhattan, Midtown East), 64
Front, The (Manhattan, Greenwich Village), 118
Garvin's (Manhattan, Greenwich Village), 119
Gazebo, The (Long Island), 181
Geppeto's Restaurant (Bronx), 162
Gleason's (Manhattan, Upper East Side), 26
Googies (Manhattan, Greenwich Village), 119
Goose and Gherkin (Manhattan, Midtown East), 65
Greenery, The (Manhattan, Upper East Side), 27
Greene Street (Manhattan, Soho), 134
Ground Round, The (Staten Island), 157
Gurney's Inn (Long Island), 182
Harlequin (Long Island), 183
Harley Street (Manhattan, East Side), 97
Harlow's (Westchester), 219
Harper (Manhattan, Upper East Side), 27
Heads and Tails (Long Island), 184
Home (Manhattan, Upper East Side), 29
Horn of Plenty (Manhattan, Greenwich Village), 120
Hudson Bay Inn (Manhattan, Upper East Side), 30
Irish Eyes (Westchester), 220
Janus (Manhattan, Upper East Side), 31
Jason's Park Royal (Manhattan, Upper West Side), 51
J.B. Tipton (Manhattan, Midtown East), 66
Jewel Restaurant (Manhattan, Upper East Side), 32
John Peele Room (Long Island), 187
Kelly's Village West (Manhattan, Greenwich Village), 122
Kenny's Castaways (Manhattan, Greenwich Village), 122
Kenny's Steak Pub (Manhattan, Midtown West), 83
King Cole Room, The (Manhattan, Midtown East), 66

Kitchen Center (Manhattan, Soho), 135
Lancaster Cocktail Lounge (Staten Island), 158
La Ronde (Manhattan, Midtown West), 83
La Rousse (Manhattan, Midtown West), 84
La Tertulia (Manhattan, Greenwich Village), 123
Laughing Mountain Bar and Grill (Manhattan, Tribeca), 135
McFeely's (Manhattan, Chelsea), 108
Mad Hatter East, The (Long Island), 192
Martell's (Manhattan, Upper East Side), 34
Michael Phillips (Manhattan, Midtown East), 67
Micky's (Manhattan, Midtown West), 84
Monkey Bar (Manhattan, Midtown East), 68
Moonlight Mile Again (Westchester), 223
Moonraker (Long Island), 194
Mr. O's Pub (Manhattan, Upper East Side), 36
My Father's Place (Long Island), 195
Nanny Rose (Manhattan, Upper West Side), 53
Northstage Theatre/Restaurant (Long Island), 195
Oak Bar, The (Manhattan, Midtown West), 85
Office, The (Staten Island), 158
O'Lunney's (Manhattan, Midtown East), 69
O'Lunney's (Manhattan, Midtown West), 85
On Broadway (Long Island), 196
Onde's (Manhattan, Midtown East), 69
O'Neals' (Manhattan, Midtown West), 86
O'Neals' Times Square (Manhattan, Midtown West), 86
One Fifth Avenue (Manhattan, Greenwich Village), 125
O'Neill's (Queens), 152
One Station Plaza (Queens), 152
Orchid, The (Manhattan, East Side), 97

*Special Interest Index*

## PARTY CLUBS

## PROFESSIONAL NETWORKING

NOTE: We only include organizations with both male and female members.

The vast number of women's networks not listed here are easily accessible through other sources.

## RELIGIOUS

## ROCK/NEW WAVE/OLDIES

*Special Interest Index*

Café Un Deux Trois (Manhattan, Midtown West), 77
Capulet's on Montague (Brooklyn), 145
Cattleman, The (Manhattan, Midtown East), 61
Characters (Westchester), 215
Charlies' (Manhattan, Midtown West), 79
Colonie Hill Top o' the Hill Lounge (Long Island), 174
Copperfield's (Long Island), 175
Court Street (Manhattan, Upper East Side), 21
Crazy Horse Café (Westchester), 216
Cruiser Club, The (Long Island), 175
Dakota Rob Roy (Westchester), 216
Davy Jones (Long Island), 176
Demarchelier (Manhattan, Upper East Side), 22
Drake's Drum (Manhattan, Upper East Side), 23
Emanon (Long Island), 179
Encore (Westchester), 217
Finnegan's Wake (Manhattan, Upper East Side), 24
Flanagan's (Manhattan, Upper East Side), 25
Foley's (Westchester), 218
Fore N Aft North (Westchester), 218
Fore N Aft South (Westchester), 219
George Martin (Manhattan, Upper East Side), 25
Grand Street Bar (Manhattan, Soho), 134
Grass (Manhattan, Upper East Side), 26
Henry Afrika Café (Long Island), 185
Herlihy's (Manhattan, Upper East Side), 27
Hobeau's (Manhattan, Midtown East), 65
Hoexter's Market (Manhattan, Upper East Side), 28
Holbrook's (Manhattan, Upper East Side), 29
Hoolihan's Old Place (Long Island), 185
Ichabod's (Manhattan, Upper East Side), 31
Iron Horse, The (Long Island), 186
J.G. Melon (Manhattan, Upper East Side), 32
Jimmy Days (Manhattan, Greenwich Village), 121

Joe Allen (Manhattan, Midtown West), 82
Jolly Bull Pub (Brooklyn), 145
J.P.'s (Manhattan, Upper East Side), 33
J.T. Bullitt (Long Island), 187
Kitty Hawk (Manhattan, Midtown East), 67
Library, The (Long Island), 189
Lion's Head, The (Manhattan, Greenwich Village), 123
Lone Piper, The (Long Island), 190
Mad Hatter, The (Long Island), 191
Mad Hatter, The (Manhattan, Upper East Side), 33
Marvin Gardens (Manhattan, Upper West Side), 52
Maude's (Westchester), 222
Maxwell's Plum (Manhattan, Upper East Side), 35
Mikell's (Manhattan, Upper West Side), 52
Millie's (Long Island), 193
Mimi's (Manhattan, Midtown East), 68
Molly Maguire's II (Manhattan, Upper East Side), 35
Montage (Westchester), 222
Montana Eve (Manhattan, Greenwich Village), 125
Mushrooms Pub (Long Island), 194
Nanny Rose (Manhattan, Upper West Side), 53
Nicola's (Manhattan, Upper East Side), 36
92nd Street Y (Manhattan, Upper East Side), 37
Nunzio's (Westchester), 224
Odeon, The (Manhattan, Tribeca), 136
Olliver's (Westchester), 225
O'Neals' Baloon (Manhattan, Upper West Side), 53
162 Spring Street (Manhattan, Soho), 137
Oren and Aretsky (Manhattan, Upper East Side), 37
P.J. Clarke's (Manhattan, Midtown East), 70
Quarterdeck Pub (Long Island), 198
Raffles (Long Island), 199
Rascals (Manhattan, Upper East Side), 39
Red Blazer, The (Manhattan, Upper East Side), 40

SUPPORT GROUPS AND

RAP SESSIONS

SPORTS AND FITNESS

TRAVEL

WIDOWS, WIDOWERS,

AND DIVORCED